The Culture of
Surveillance

The Culture of Surveillance

Watching as a Way of Life

David Lyon

polity

First published in 2018 by Polity Press

Reprinted 2018, 2019

Polity Press
65 Bridge Street
Cambridge CB2 1UR, UK

Polity Press
101 Station Landing
Suite 300
Medford, MA 02155, USA

ISBN-13: 978-0-7456-7172-7
ISBN-13: 978-0-7456-7173-4(pb)

A catalogue record for this book is available from the British Library.

Typeset in 10.5 on 12 pt Sabon
by Fakenham Prepress Solutions, Fakenham, Norfolk NR21 8NN
Printed and bound in by the UK by CPI Group (UK) Ltd, Croydon, CR0 4YY

For further information on Polity, visit our website:
politybooks.com

Contents

Acknowledgements

The more I got into this piece of writing, the more I realized that such an ambitious project is rife with risks. I set out to pull together in one place much marvellous scholarship on the everyday experience of surveillance, that I think adds up to a culture of surveillance. I also wanted to wean people away from George Orwell – I'm a believer in breastfeeding and its wholesome benefits, so read this rightly! – and to invite readers to consider other fictional accounts suited to the present, in particular, Dave Eggers' *The Circle*. And on top of that, I hoped to show that however enjoyable or innocent some aspects of surveillance might appear, they cannot safely be seen separately from the powerful forces of consumer, or now, 'surveillance' capitalism, or of administrative, national security and policing surveillance.

So it is with a great sense of gratitude to many people that I acknowledge help from many quarters, starting at home. My life-partner, Sue, has not only survived another book but has done so with patience and grace even though my distractions did wear these thin at times. What she demonstrates is captured in an ancient Hebrew word *hesed*, meaning 'steadfast love'. Other family members, in turn, both children and grandchildren, have borne with this project, with only occasional eye-rolling. They recognize my desire to make a difference, to offer to their generations ways of understanding and responding to the accelerating changes occurring each day; to help them live with hope.

My students and colleagues, especially those at Queen's University, have encouraged and challenged me with their comments and stories. Graduate students, in particular, have helped me see surveillance culture in broader ways than I originally envisioned. And what can I say to those who actually read drafts of the book – sometimes returning to reread a new version? My thanks are heartfelt, to Kiyoshi Abe, Kirstie Ball, Maggie Berg, Amos Cohoe, Pablo Esteban Rodríguez, Kevin Haggerty, Gary Marx, Lucas Melgaço, Torin Monahan, Mike Nellis, Midori Ogasawara, Brittany Shales, Emily Smith, Val Steeves, John Thompson and Daniel Trottier. Mary Savigar and Ellen MacDonald-Kramer at Polity, plus two anonymous readers, also directed me to rethink some aspects of the book. All their insights were invaluable to me; how I used them is entirely my responsibility, of course. The steady background work of Emily Smith and Joan Sharpe at the Surveillance Studies Centre also enables such endeavours as this to flourish. I am grateful too to Ann Bone for copy-editing and to Jean Whitaker, who kindly made the index.

Over the past few years several kind people have invited me to speak on surveillance culture and this has led to worthwhile conversations, critical comments and encouragement to persist with the project. As far back as 2010, Tom Lauer and Albert Meehan brought me to speak in their SurPriSe programme at Oakland University. I discussed 'Facebook and Homeland Security'. In 2012, Gavin Smith, now at Australian National University, invited me to lecture for 'Sydney Ideas', recorded for ABC and online. A variant, 'The emerging surveillance culture', appears in André Jansson and Miyase Christensen, eds, *Media, Surveillance, Identity* (New York: Peter Lang, 2014). Parts of chapter 3 began life when Jack Qiu invited me to address a conference at the Chinese University of Hong Kong, which appears in Francis L. F. Lee, Louis Leung, Jack Linchuan Qiu and Donna S. C. Chu, eds, *Frontiers in New Media Research* (London: Routledge, 2012). I gave a TEDx Queen's talk on 'Social media surveillance' in 2013, and in 2014 spoke at the Wolfe Institute, Brooklyn College, New York on '*The Circle* and surveillance culture', which later morphed into chapter 5. Pablo Esteban Rodríguez invited me to speak at LAVITS, the Latin American Surveillance Studies Network, in Buenos Aires, Argentina in 2016, where my topic resembled 'Surveillance culture: engagement, exposure, and ethics in digital modernity', which appeared in the *International Journal of Communication* 11 (2017).

Kingston, Ontario

Introduction: Surveillance Culture Takes Shape

Beyond Big Brother

Pick up any book on surveillance and most make reference to Big Brother or an Orwellian future. George Orwell's classic dystopian novel, *Nineteen Eighty-Four*, written in 1948, has informed and infused a popular sense of what surveillance entails for over half a century. 'There was', writes Orwell, 'no way of knowing whether you were being watched at any given moment.' Thus, he went on, the inhabitants of Oceania lived their daily lives 'from habit that became instinct – in the assumption that every sound you made was overheard, and, except in darkness, every moment scrutinized'.[1] It is those 'habits that become instinct' that speak of surveillance culture where, in the case of Oceania, the citizens' vision of the world was dominated by the screen warning that 'Big Brother is watching you' and their everyday practices mirrored that menacing reality.

But this book proposes that to understand surveillance culture, *Nineteen Eighty-Four* must be put on one side. Not that Orwell had nothing to say – far from it; his work is still deeply relevant, depicting some features distressingly familiar to many who lived through the twentieth century's dictatorships, warning against a subtle slide into state control within supposed liberal democracies and urging readers to seek a world of decency, tolerance and humanity. Rather, my message is that Big Brother is the wrong metaphor for surveillance today. To persist with the language of a totalitarian tyrant who threatens his victims with ravenous rats and kicking jackboots simply deflects attention from what is actually going on in the world of surveillance. Some surveillance situations are indeed sinister and sadistic and are rightly deplored as such. But most people's experience of surveillance today is not like that, which is why going beyond Big Brother is necessary now more than ever.

In the early 1990s, in my book *The Electronic Eye*, I observed that for all that may be learned from Orwell, he could not have guessed at the role that new, computer technologies on the one hand, and consumerism on the other, would play in creating surveillance as it was evolving in the late twentieth century. But I have since been obliged to recognize that surveillance has moved on again. What is experienced in the twenty-first century now depends deeply on the participation of those being surveilled. Indeed, as I suggest in this book's subtitle, not only being watched but watching itself has become a way of life. Orwell's characters lived in gnawingly fearful uncertainty about when and why they were watched. Today's surveillance is made possible by our own clicks on websites, our texting messages and exchanging photos. Ordinary people contribute to surveillance as never before. User-generated content engenders the data by which daily doings are monitored. This is how surveillance culture takes shape.

By the culture of surveillance[2] I refer to the sorts of things that an anthropologist might study – customs, habits and ways of looking at and interpreting the world. The focus is on surveillance in everyday life rather than, primarily, in the octopus tentacles of global intelligence and policing networks or the subtle and seductive sirens of corporate marketing. Understood here, the culture of surveillance is about how surveillance is imagined and experienced, and about how mundane activities of walking down a street, driving a car, checking for messages, buying in stores or listening to music are affected by and affect surveillance. And about how surveillance is also initiated and engaged by those who have become familiar with and even inured to surveillance.

So this book is not primarily about the culture of surveillance thought of in a literary or artistic sense. It spends little time exploring surveillance worlds that spring from creative imagination – in films, songs, novels, TV series or art. But it does pay attention to these insofar as they illuminate the more 'anthropological' worlds of surveillance in everyday life. Works of popular culture retain a vital importance. Many of them are wonderfully wise and offer penetrating perceptions of surveillance culture. Moreover, much has been written about the intriguing insights available in such literary, musical, video and artistic productions, that also help to throw light on culture in the 'way of life' sense.[3] That said, having noted that one has to go beyond Orwell to grasp the realities of surveillance today, I feel obliged to suggest some sites where the 'beyond' lies. They are scattered through this book but, for me, one in particular stands out.

The world of today's surveillance has everything to do with California's famous Silicon Valley, the incubator par excellence of the digital world that has so rapidly become familiar to so much of the world's population. It comes as little surprise, then, that one of the most telling inheritors of Orwell's mantle set his scene in Silicon Valley. In the title of a 2013 novel, *The Circle* is not only the name of the high-tech corporation where the protagonist, Mae, goes to work. It is also a metaphor for the way that all of life is increasingly subsumed into a digital world, encircled by cyberspace. Mae is ranked by her 'zings' at the keyboard and wears her 'TruYou' ID and 'SeeChange' camera at all times as she integrates herself into life at the hip and happy environment of glass-walled transparency. Despite momentary doubts, she rises rapidly to become an icon and a celebrity at the centre of The Circle's influence. She went fully transparent.

Dave Eggers, inspired author of *The Circle*, deliberately references Orwell through devices such as updated slogans. The latter's Freedom is Slavery gives way to Sharing is Caring in this soft surveillance world of consumer comforts and casual workwear. And as Peter Marks drily remarks, *The Circle* is a child of Big Data rather than Big Brother.[4] This is the point. Today's cultures of surveillance, those crucial ways of seeing and being in the digital milieu, are inseparable from the so-called data exhaust pouring from millions of machines every moment of every day and the greedy global effort to create value from them. What people perceive, by and large, is the amazing power of the internet to keep them connected, amused, entertained, supplied, updated, reassured and informed. As they engage with the online world, however, they not only improvise responses to the subtle ways that they are watched but also use those surveillance technologies for their own ends. Thus are new surveillance cultures born.

In short, then, this book brings together two different kinds of issues concerning surveillance in the twenty-first century. On the one hand is the truism that surveillance is an everyday fact of life that we not only encounter from outside, as it were, but also in which we engage, from within, in many contexts. It is sometimes welcomed as a means to greater security or convenience, sometimes queried or resisted as being inappropriate or excessive, and sometimes engaged as an enjoyable or reassuring possibility offered by systems or devices – there is a potential to observe or monitor others and ourselves as never before. Things like social media surveillance often seem like a soft set of activities, seemingly inconsequential, but as I shall insist, they actually contribute to social-cultural transformation. Watching has become a way of life.

On the other hand, the kinds of data now circulating in greater volume, velocity and variety – to use the words often applied to Big Data – than ever are of tremendous interest to a growing range of actors, not just government departments, security agencies and police, but also internet companies, healthcare providers, traffic engineers, city planners and many more. The data are very valuable, both financially, as commodities to be exploited and traded in billion dollar markets and related contexts, and also as the means of governing or even controlling others. Watching as a way of life is inextricably bound up with these other realities, which means that our theme is far from marginal or minimal in relation to the major ethical and political challenges of our times.

There is thus a tension between the digital lives of people routinely and innocently immersed in social media, game-like – or 'gamified' – online contexts and self-tracking, and those whose opportunities, life-chances and choices are affected, sometimes negatively, by how others collect, store, classify and analyse those data. One group of commentators points out that surveillance is clearly enjoyable, empowering and playful for some, and that this should be appreciated for the meaningful cultural phenomenon that it is. Others observe that those very activities may play into the hands of much more threatening forces and that therefore the focus of surveillance studies should be on the dehumanizing and freedom-denying aspects of today's monitoring and tracking. The characteristics of surveillance as a way of life are in many respects different from earlier surveillance cultures, for instance those in close-knit and geographically localized communities. Common features of today's surveillance include the data being easily quantified, highly traceable, likely to have an economic – monetized – dimension, and to be garnered at a distance – they are deterritorialized. They are less 'solid', more 'liquid', but still share patterns of connection and activity. And they are marked by deep ambivalence. Online consumers, for example, believe that they are free to choose what they buy, despite the ever more palpable fact of consumer surveillance. Yet they often try to present themselves in a highly favourable light that plays into the social surveillance in which they also engage.

I stress that the imaginaries and practices of surveillance culture today should be taken very seriously, and argue, simultaneously, that they cannot but be directly linked with our understanding of the kinds of surveillance carried out by internet companies, national security agencies and others. The same data often flow not only between us and other users but also between the public and private sectors. The same methods are used to make sense of and act on those data. And those participating in social media surveillance learn from the strategies of large organizations and vice versa. Also, becoming familiar with objects and technologies in one domain may normalize those in the other. Different cultural contexts help shape how people interpret their experiences of surveillance.[5]

Towards user-generated surveillance

Watching others, surveillantly, is an ancient practice. Throughout most of human history, surveillance has been a minority activity, something done by specific persons or organizations. Today, much surveillance is still a specialized activity, carried out by police and intelligence agencies and, of course, by corporations. But it is also something that is done domestically, in everyday life. Parents use surveillance devices to check children, friends observe others on social media, and it is increasingly common to use gadgets to monitor ourselves for health and fitness. The same kinds of watching occur, now using different tools, that offer the novel characteristics mentioned above. Thus watching becomes a way of life.

'Surveillance' is a tricky word. Its French origin in the word *surveiller* – literally, to 'watch over' – is clear enough. The problem is, what might a tight definition include and exclude? In what follows, surveillance means the operations and experiences of gathering and analysing personal data for influence, entitlement and management. As Gary Marx says, sagely, 'Surveillance technology is not simply applied; it is also *experienced* by subjects, agents and audiences who define, judge and have feelings about being watched or a watcher.'[6]

My definition still begs further questions, such as what counts as 'personal data'? These will be considered later. For now, note the breadth of coverage. Surveillance may be done, for example, by corporations that exert *influence* by looking at your social media profile to decide how to persuade you to buy their product, by government departments that judge your *entitlement* by looking at your bank records to determine if you qualify for social assistance, or agencies such as police making *management* decisions about the best route for a parade. But it may also be carried out by people in everyday life, on others, in checking profiles of interest or on ourselves, otherwise known as self-tracking.

Today's emerging 'surveillance culture' is unprecedented. A key feature is that people actively participate in and attempt to regulate their own surveillance and the surveillance of others. There is growing evidence of patterns of perspectives, outlooks or mentalités on surveillance, along with some closely related modes of initiating, negotiating or resisting surveillance. Who has not heard the popular mantras, trotted out by politicians and people in everyday life, 'If you have nothing to hide, you have nothing to fear'? Or, 'we need surveillance to keep us safe and secure'. Common enough, but controversial, as we shall see.

Surveillance culture has appeared as people engage more and more with the means of monitoring. Many check on others' lives using social media, for instance. At the same time, the 'others' make this possible by allowing themselves to be exposed to public view in texts and tweets, posts and pics. Some people also engage with surveillance when they worry about how much others, especially large, opaque organizations such as airlines or security agencies, know about them.

Lest the impression is given that the appearance of surveillance culture is somehow random, unanticipated or unavoidable, however, this book also stresses that the commercially available systems are designed to permit and enable such cultural developments to occur. The more you search on social media for the same kinds of people, checking them for similar interests and lifestyles, the more the companies can customize their advertising and personalize their profiles. This does not make those users into mere dupes of the system, of course. Some may use the systems in ways not intended by designers, ways that may even be more humane, just or democratic.[7] But the point is that significant aspects of surveillance culture reflect possibilities that are built into the commercial platforms.

People may respond in a variety of ways to emerging surveillance culture. For instance, they may take steps to block the surveillance of some, to limit who may view their lives. But many just get on with those lives, even if they know about some aspects of surveillance. In other words, like it or not, everyone has more of a stake in surveillance than when it was thought of as the 'surveillance state' or even the 'surveillance society'. Those words describe how surveillance is done to individuals and groups. The surveillance culture goes beyond these. While acknowledging what goes on in organizational surveillance, it turns the spotlight on all our very varied roles in relation to surveillance.

Thus surveillance culture is characterized by user-generated surveillance. Riffing on Web 2.0's notion of user-generated content, we can observe that the same technological capacities

– or 'affordances' as they are called, technically – allow users to contribute content and, at the same time, to generate forms of surveillance. On one hand, user involvement with devices and platforms such as smartphones and Twitter creates data used in organizational surveillance. And on the other, users themselves act surveillantly as they check up on, follow and score others with 'likes', 'recommendations' and other evaluative criteria. As they do so, they not only interact with their online connections, but also with the subtle ways in which the platforms are created to foster particular kinds of interchange.

So this book is also a kind of real-life map of today's surveillance world – though like Google's StreetView it does not cover *everything*! – focusing particularly on those who are willingly or unwillingly, wittingly or unwittingly, engaged with it in ordinary everyday life, producing user-generated surveillance. For instance, it considers what emotions are aroused by surveillance and devotes one chapter to an appraisal of Dave Eggers' *The Circle*.[8] This is one way of getting the feel for surveillance culture today, just as listening to The Police singing 'Every breath you take' or watching Florian Henckel von Donnersmarck's movie *The Lives of Others* or an episode of the TV series *Black Mirror* might.

Snowden and surveillance culture

A recent and ongoing example shows how surveillance culture relates to some pressing issues concerning surveillance in general. The kind of 'suspicionless surveillance' carried out by intelligence agencies such as the American National Security Agency (NSA), to which disillusioned subcontractor turned whistleblower Edward Snowden's disclosure of documents in 2013 drew attention, cannot be understood simply in terms of older – though still relevantly current – concepts such as 'surveillance state' or 'surveillance society'.[9] They are inadequate, not incorrect.

They now have to be supplemented with a concept that focuses more on the active roles played by surveillance subjects, not least because those roles make a difference both to our own lives and to the surveillance outcomes. Attending to what occurs within various aspects of surveillance culture helps to explain why the responses to Snowden – and to surveillance in general – have been so diverse. Some express outrage and mobilize politically. Some are grateful that governments are doing something about crime and terrorism. Others are just getting on with their lives as consumers, content with the convenience, unconcerned. But as we shall see, a critical issue is how far any consumers and citizens examine their own roles within the mushrooming surveillance systems of today.

The culture of surveillance was becoming visible from the turn of the twenty-first century, especially after the 9/11 attacks on America in 2001 and the advent of social media. Military, state and corporate collusion in organizational surveillance was evident in responses to 9/11. But soon after, the explosion of social media helped to create surveillance culture as a shadow of what might be termed managerial or entrepreneurial surveillance in which growing efforts were made to extract value from personal data. And surveillance culture became even clearer after Edward Snowden copied and released incriminating documents from the NSA in 2013. Historians may discern the first signs of surveillance culture in the later twentieth century, but now they are present on a broad scale and their contours are becoming clear.

What else is meant by surveillance culture? Raymond Williams defined culture as a 'whole way of life'.[10] This book investigates the notion that surveillance is becoming part of a whole way of life. Hence my use of the word 'culture'. Surveillance is no longer merely something external that impinges on 'our lives'. It is also something that everyday citizens comply with – willingly and wittingly or not – negotiate, resist, engage with and, in novel ways, even initiate and desire. From being an institutional aspect of modernity or a technologically enhanced mode of social discipline or control, surveillance is now internalized in new ways. It informs everyday reflections on how things are, and the repertoire of everyday practices.

But the idea of surveillance culture as a way of life could sound as if everyone is involved or implicated in the same way. As we shall see, nothing could be further from the truth. Surveillance culture is multifaceted, complicated, fluid and rather unpredictable. Williams's notion of culture took such complexity into account by suggesting that while there are dominant elements of any discernible culture – thus warranting the description of 'culture' – other elements may be identified as well. He spoke of 'residual' ones that represent older, fading aspects of culture, but which still play a cultural role. And of newer, 'emergent' ones, that might also be a part of dominant culture, but could also be oppositional or at least alternative to it.[11]

The surveillance culture discussed here accents the everyday dimensions of dominant political-economic surveillance systems. Interestingly, the document disclosures of Edward Snowden may be seen as residual and emergent at the same time. Residual in that he blew the whistle as a loyal and patriotic government worker, but emergent in that he initiated a new way of drawing attention to surveillance overreach – cooperating with journalists rather than simply exposing the facts on his own, to ensure maximum publicity. He certainly brings some important debates into the foreground – questions of digital rights in relation to both corporations and government departments and agencies, and of who has responsibility for flows of data across borders, flows that have clear consequences for life-chances and freedoms.[12] But also, crucially, his intervention shows clearly that the data in question were primarily generated by ordinary users, us, using the internet, phones and other everyday devices.

The Snowden disclosures also served – even if only briefly – to revitalize controversies over the role of online political activity that had surfaced widely from 2011 after the so-called Arab Spring, contested democratic movements in several Middle Eastern and North African countries,[13] and that were to flower again between September and December 2014 with the Umbrella Movement that protested Chinese limits on democracy in Hong Kong.[14] To what extent were the new media the means of fomenting popular and radical change and to what extent were they the tools of repression and the denial of democratic aspirations? This may also be read as a larger question for the whole book. If surveillance is constantly extended and intensified by digital means, how far can the same kinds of technology be used to limit, redirect or refashion surveillance for different ends?

Digital life: surveillance culture

Surveillance culture is best seen in relation to the astonishing growth of what may fairly be called 'digital modernity', from the twentieth but especially in the twenty-first century. By 'modernity' is meant the social, political, economic and cultural arrangements that have become globally dominant in the past 250 years or so. Western forms of modernity include industrial capitalism and liberal democracy. The media of communication are always vital to cultural developments and in many ways the television culture of the twentieth century made way for the internet culture – especially surveillance – in the twenty-first.[15] Exploring the origins, carriers and consequences of surveillance culture is a way of contextualizing more effectively the 'post-Snowden' world.

But 'digital modernity' does not exist on its own. It is wrapped up with another significant cultural shift, which plays down 'discipline'[16] or 'control' and foregrounds 'performance'.[17] This was not caused by the digital. It relates more to shifting identity sources from the world of work, producing, to the world of consuming. With weakening ties to obedience, law and obligation, a strong cultural current today supports liberty and desires and leans towards their satisfaction. The new imperative is to perform. It is individualistic and, among other things, fosters a fear of inadequacy. Accumulate those Facebook likes! Find out how many followers you have! Performance orientation is precarious, fragmented and in real-time – a situation exploited, as we shall see, by both government and corporation.[18] Expectations morph rapidly; lead times shrink. Relationships are fleeting. Under such circumstances, the very idea of regulating surveillance, for instance, is queried.

The presence of surveillance culture raises fresh questions for everyday involvement with digital media, questions with ethical and political aspects that, I shall argue, point to possibilities and challenges for 'digital citizenship'. Both surveillance and citizenship are now mediated by the digital and by the penchant for performance. What is the setting for this?

Surveillance culture is a product of contemporary late modern conditions or, simply, of 'digital modernity'. From the later twentieth century especially, corporate and state modes of surveillance, mediated by increasingly fast and powerful new technologies, tilted towards everyday life. The expansion of information infrastructures and our increasing dependence on the digital in mundane relationships facilitated this. All cultural shifts relate in significant ways to social, economic and political conditions. So today's surveillance culture forms through organizational dependence, political-economic power, security linkages and social media engagement. All these depend on the assumption that you are online or that you have a phone in your pocket or purse.

First, contrast surveillance culture with previous terms in common currency. The 'surveillance state' worked well in the postwar 'Orwellian' period and of course can still capture significant aspects of surveillance today, such as the activities of intelligence agencies. But even there, the 'surveillance state' is heavily dependent on commercial entities – internet and telephone companies – to provide the desired data.[19] While such data have been used, via warrants, by police and security agencies for decades, the mass scale on which this now happens alters the dynamic.

Not only the mass scale, either. The enthusiasm for Big Data 'solutions', for instance, is strongly correlated with the widespread and rapidly expanding volume of data from computers, phones, cameras, drones and sensors of all kinds, both fixed and mobile, and of course social media. Data are harvested constantly from devices and systems that are always on and stored for already existing surveillance needs or until some purpose is found for them. This mode of data gathering and analysis raises many questions for conventional understandings of surveillance and privacy.

Today, no one is unaffected by the very post-Orwellian collusion of governmental and corporate forces. As well, many of those data are themselves generated in the first place by the everyday online activities of millions of ordinary citizens. And this means that users collude as never before in their own surveillance by sharing – whether willingly or wittingly, or not – their personal information in the online public domain. 'Surveillance culture' helps to situate this collusion, this sharing. If this is 'state surveillance', it has a deeply different character from that which in popular terms is 'Orwellian'.

If the 'surveillance state' is an inadequate concept, what about 'surveillance society'? Well, while this notion helps to indicate the broader context within which the unsettling discoveries about the 'mass surveillance' engaged in by the NSA and its 'Five Eyes'[20] partners occur, it also falls short of explaining today's situation. 'Surveillance society' was originally used to indicate ways in which surveillance was spilling over the rims of its previous containers – government departments, policing agencies, workplaces – to affect many aspects of daily life. But the emphasis was still on how surveillance was carried out in ways that increasingly touched the routines of social life, from outside, as it were.[21] 'Surveillance society' was often used in ways that paid scant attention to citizens', consumers', travellers' or employees' experience of and engagement with surveillance.

From the later twentieth century onwards, surveillance became a central organizing feature of societies that had developed information infrastructures. The only way to manage the increasing complexity was to develop new categories to sort through differences.[22] Who is credit-worthy?[23] Everyone is rated and placed in some calculated category. Who should be on a no-fly list? There are criteria for deciding which groups are more likely than others. Organizations of all kinds sort data about people into groups, so that the persons themselves can be treated differently, depending on the group.

By the early twenty-first century, evidence was emerging of a third phase of computing, after the mainframe and personal computer phases, where computing machinery is embedded, more or less invisibly, in the environments of everyday life. This is the so-called and much hyped internet of things where the iconic smartphone, along with other devices and objects, communicates with users and with other everyday devices and where now Big Data is the buzzword. This extends in specific ways the reliance on surveillance as a mode of organization. Today's surveillance culture is informed by these developments.

Surveillance is also a major industry. Global corporations are involved, often with close links to government. The Snowden disclosures made this abundantly clear, if there was any doubt previously. The initial shock was discovering that the NSA has access to customer data from telephone companies – Verizon featured prominently in the June 2013 news – and also mines the customer databases of internet corporations such as Apple, Google, Microsoft, Amazon and Facebook, often referred to as the 'big five'.[24] On the one hand, such corporations engage in large-scale surveillance of their customers. And on the other, they share these data with government agencies.

Moreover, the character of the corporation connects the political economy and the culture of surveillance. The 'big five' corporations now dominate not only the internet but also, argues Shoshana Zuboff, the economic mode of operation. Their business model is increasingly geared to trying to predict and shape human behaviour, for revenue and market control, using Big Data techniques that frequently reduce customers to credit scores or their 'lifetime value'. Google's approach illustrates this objectification of persons most clearly. Explains Zuboff, this business model exhibits a 'formal indifference' towards both users and employees.[25] Their personal situations of power or plight mean nothing. They are disposable, replaceable. At the same time, as I shall show, in a surveillance culture users' responses to such attempted prediction and modification affect their success.

Clearly, there was already a 'culture of control'[26] evident in the later twentieth century, that morphed into the intensified security surveillance appearing after 9/11. The expansion relied heavily on recently ailing technology companies to create a new industry of 'homeland security'.[27] Securitization demands greater amounts of information about risk and how to handle it, which both weakens traditional privacy requirements and increases surveillance of what are deemed risky behaviours. In terms of surveillance culture, this reinforces the sense that surveillance is warranted, 'for our own good'. In practice, of course, this is also understood ambivalently.

This sense of risk, and the need to take steps to reduce it, is not only evident on the grand scale of national and international policy but also penetrates daily life at home, where self-tracking for health, income, and time management is an increasing phenomenon. Only a few years ago, the *New York Times* still thought of this as something for 'geeks and keep-fit addicts'.[28] Today, such self-monitoring is less unusual, often taken for granted, although geeks and jocks probably still dominate the field. Wearable devices have become increasingly popular, and now talk of the 'quantified self' is much more commonplace.[29] In this world, people seek a digitized form of 'self-knowledge' so that they can lead 'better lives' even though only a small fragment of the data is seen by them, the vast majority of the data ending up in the databases of the wearable device corporations.

Lastly, and perhaps best known, is the relation between social media and surveillance culture. Perhaps most striking among the Snowden revelations was the realization by broad swathes of the public that what happens on social media is open to both corporation and government. Jose van Dijck points out how this connects with 'dataism', the secular belief that users can safely entrust their data to large corporations.[30] Snowden put serious dents into dataism. A recent study of Americans' main fears shows that being tracked by corporations or government is close to the top of the list.[31] It would hardly be surprising if such findings have an impact in everyday uses of social media.

Snowden's disclosures did indeed disturb social media use.[32] For example, in the United States, 34 per cent of those aware of the government surveillance programmes (or 30 per cent of all adults) have taken at least one step to hide or shield their information from the government – changing privacy settings, using other communication media than social media or avoiding certain applications. A slightly smaller proportion (25 per cent) have changed their use of phones, email or search engines following Snowden. Knowing more about government surveillance produces more evidence of changed behaviour.

Let me say one more thing about the contexts of the surveillance culture. Having commented on its relation to organizational dependence, political-economic power, security linkages and social media engagement, note that surveillance culture has many facets and varies according to region. The point of using the concept of surveillance culture is to distinguish it from notions such as surveillance state or surveillance society by focusing on the participation and engagement of surveilled and surveilling subjects.

But surveillance culture will, like any culture, develop differently and often morph unpredictably, especially in contexts of increasing social liquidity.[33] It will, moreover, bud and blossom differently depending on historical and political circumstance. Here I refer primarily to North America and Western Europe, although readers in Asia, Latin America, Africa or the Middle East will recognize many features of surveillance culture, necessarily inflected by local circumstances. And surveillance culture is also expressed differently depending on gender, class, race and other such variables.

Distinctive directions

Before offering a guide to the rest of the book, let me indicate the gap that it fills. Today, many people write, talk and make films about surveillance, a situation quite different from what I experienced when I was first writing about surveillance thirty years ago. Indeed, today, many concern themselves with the cultural dimensions of surveillance. However, some who do so – including those who do so brilliantly, producing fascinating and important insights, such as Christena Nippert-Eng in the highly insightful *Islands of Privacy* – do not directly connect these with the larger sociological questions about surveillance.

In my work, I have always tried to comment on the cultural. But I have usually felt such a strong sense of urgency that my readers should understand the potential and actual negative impacts of surveillance that I have not lingered on the cultural aspects, even though they share in and help to mould and fashion those negative impacts. These effects of surveillance include privacy violations, the ways that surveillance undermines democratic participation and, especially, how it depends on social sorting.[34] This last term highlights how surveillance works by sorting the population into categories so that different groups may be treated differently. Social sorting contributes profoundly to the distribution of life-chances and choices, to fairness or injustice. Of course, I am not saying that surveillance is intrinsically sinister or malevolent. It is not in itself good or bad, but it is never neutral either. It is ever amenable to ethical assessment. Power relations are always present, for better or for worse.

However, particularly in the past decade, with the rise of Web 2.0, the cultural has forced its way into the foreground, above all in the rise and growing ubiquity of social media and of smartphone use. It is these dimensions of social life that now underlie much common understanding of surveillance, including its more conventional kinds, such as public space surveillance cameras. These factors embed surveillance in everyday life as never before, using telltale data given off under the innocent-sounding banners of 'user-generated content' or 'mobile communications'. And what is visible today is just the tip of the iceberg.

The Culture of Surveillance brings together the cultural and the political-economic, showing both how the cultural is a deeply important way of understanding surveillance *and* how the cultural cannot safely be seen on its own. The latter is not a separate dimension of surveillance. Today, it needs to be recognized for the increasingly important role its imaginaries and practices play in facilitating – but maybe also, in time, modifying – the structural, political-economic aspects of surveillance. Those latter aspects all too often violate privacy rights and may be unequal, unfair and unjust.

Playing Angry Birds, for example, is seen as a stress reliever and became wildly popular due to its simplicity, rewards, humour and predictability. Interacting with such a game on a mobile device while, say, commuting by bus or streetcar may be culturally represented as innocent fun. However, the game is geared by its designers to identifying and grooming those players most likely to buy-in, rather than to play for free. And that is only the consumer surveillance side. Early among the Snowden releases was a document showing how the United Kingdom's communications security agency, GCHQ (Government Communications Headquarters), taps into 'leaky apps' such as Angry Birds for sensitive data on the age, gender, location and even sexual orientation of players.[35] In this case, the cultural logic of a 'stress-relieving game' plays into both consumer and citizen surveillance, aspects of which are anything but.

Focusing on surveillance culture reveals the sheer complexity of surveillance today, warning against simplistic assumptions sometimes imputed to *Nineteen Eighty-Four*'s hapless Winston Smith versus Big Brother. The cultural dimensions of surveillance depend upon the technologies that help to sustain them, while at the same time offering the chance to challenge and shape those technologies. It is assumed that everyday life has a digital dimension; people rely on the smartphone and internet more completely than earlier generations relied on radio, TV or the telephone. By taking note of how the culture of surveillance is emerging, we may see not only how it normalizes and domesticates surveillance but also how it may contribute to the critique of surveillance and to the development of its constituent technologies for the common good. Finding technical limits and regulating through policy are essential, but at an everyday level the struggle is for hearts and minds in the mundane routines of daily, digital, life.

Mapping the culture of surveillance

Here is a guide through the rest of this book, chapter by chapter. The first part of the book, chapter 1, is 'Crucibles of culture' and offers the conceptual clues on which the rest of the book depends. The reader may wish to skip it to get to the descriptions of surveillance culture, although you may return here to see how things hang together. I stand on others' shoulders, and which ones will quickly become clear.

Zygmunt Bauman's 'liquidity', for example, is a reminder of the broad context of shifts within capitalist modernity, while those representing culture-as-everyday-life demonstrate the need to work within an interpretive tradition to grasp our own roles within the wider society. The Snowden disclosures illustrate the link. The shock of discovering how far government agencies monitor citizens' lives is matched by seeing how businesses are involved and by realizing that it is our own metadata[36] that fuel such surveillance.

Unfortunately, like many such 'shocks', people seem to recover from them without recognizing their deeper consequences. The very name, Edward Snowden, became a blur for many, a vague and fading memory of how overreaching security agencies were embarrassingly exposed. But if memories could be jolted it would be clearer that responding to surveillance and even initiating surveillance affects outcomes on a macro-scale within the milieu of the digital and the pressures to perform. Visibility always exhibits more than one face. The same person dearly desires and simultaneously shrinks from visibility. In the end, though I foreground visibility, I shall also ask if 'recognition' is in some ways more significant.

The second part of the book comprises three chapters exploring the main cultural currents of surveillance. It starts with the big picture of attitudes towards more conventional surveillance, moves through the growing taken-for-grantedness of surveillance in our lives and on to the everyday world of immersion in the offline-online world in which our feelings about surveillance have turned from doubt to desire. This part thus has a historical ring to it, but these cultures of surveillance are all also contemporary. As well, they may sound as if they offer explanations of why we comply so readily with surveillance, but I also stress the ways in which each may cause us to complain or to comport ourselves differently.

Chapter 2, 'From convenience to compliance', may sound like something from Aldous Huxley's *Brave New World* rather than from Orwell. After all, his dystopia was one of soft surveillance in which consuming was paramount and taking 'soma' helped one to escape reality. But whichever account is read, there is a tension between what might be thought of as the surveillance system and popular responses to it. The 'system' prompts performances that vary considerably depending on many factors. Whatever the new configurations of surveillance, now integrated with the internet, personal information is a much sought-after commodity. These ubiquitous data are desired for both control and commerce and in many cases those categories are not entirely separate. Patterns of power exist in the world of surveillance but the outcomes are very varied depending on cultural and historical differences. Cultures of surveillance develop differently depending on differing political economies and post-authoritarian – such as in the former German Democratic Republic – or colonial pasts.

What cultures of surveillance have in common is that surveillance simplifies social sorting and that the public's growing knowledge of this creates feedback loops and makes a practical difference. Among other responses, surveillance generates caution, if not fear, an insight found, for instance, in the psychoanalytic work of Jacques Lacan. For him, the 'gaze' creates anxieties from earliest childhood.[37] At the same time, others are reassured by surveillance, believing that it keeps them safe from crime, violence or terrorist attack. The longing to have 'someone to watch over me' may also spring from childhood experiences, even though in adult life it may be a prescription for a dangerous dependence.[38]

The emotional dimensions of surveillance are expressed in many different ways. As the growing reliance of contemporary economic growth on gathering and analysing personal data – pundits proclaim Big Data as the 'new oil' – becomes ever more apparent, so levels of concern and of compliance are likely to deepen. Especially since Snowden, those concerns are also bound up with security surveillance, which often has particularly negative implications for visible minorities. But the compliance is also likely to become more commonplace simply because of the convenience of using the internet and the devices from which data are drawn.

Chapter 3, 'From novelty to normalization', demonstrates how surveillance, because it is embedded in the routines of daily life, becomes, as it were, part of the furniture – sometimes literally. The latest smartphone or tablet will contain bells and whistles not previously encountered. But each one requires decisions about if or how it will be used. And those decisions depend in turn on what is thought to be beneficial, productive, risky or whatever. In other words, they must be assessed against the kinds of norms that have developed as the digital realm has expanded. Qualms may be expressed about the new potentials. Or maybe the new will seem like a logical next step in data-driven evolution, something quickly taken for granted.

A defining feature of surveillance cultures is the state of technology which enables new cultural forms to gestate. The use of interactive and 'smart' technologies shifts the focus from fixed to fluid surveillance, from hardware to software. The smart meter for domestic electricity can tell what TV programmes you are watching. This is a mundane aspect of the 'internet of things'. Your smartphone logs your location and your 'likes' as well as whom you contact. And if their use becomes widespread, self-driving cars will also transmit your data to numerous sites – 'for your safety'.

In 2017 a controversy arose over Roomba, the smart vacuum cleaner from iRobot. The machine maps the details of the home in order to enable a full cleaning routine to occur. A slightly inaccurate article gave the impression that such maps might be sold to technology companies such as Apple or Google. A minor media storm ensued as many worried that domestic privacy would be infringed, which evoked a response from iRobot, stating unequivocally that its customer data would never be sold.[39] Such disputes are now the stuff of daily tussles.

All this occurs within a wider cultural context in which gauging risk and opportunity is central, anticipating the future is a key goal, and of course where economic prosperity and state security are locked in a mutual embrace. The result? Smart surveillance and social sorting go hand in glove. Every mouse click, web search or text message gives off data exhaust that is used to create profiles which in turn score and rank users, placing them in consequential categories. Subtly, smart surveillance and social sorting inform and inspire surveil-lance imaginaries and practices, which in turn help to enable or constrain the further development of smart surveillance. Whether it is wearables in the workplace or appliances in the home, data are domesticated. How attitudes and actions develop in relation to this makes the difference between simply seeing surveillant environments as convenient and comfortable – or as challenging and contestable.

In chapter 4, the trilogy of angles on surveillance culture is completed by exploring 'From online to onlife'. Of all today's devices, smartphones are the most omnipresent, but many others, including wearable ones for fitness or health, are also in view here. The particular set of issues examined in this chapter concerns what it means to be immersed in life online and how this affects what is meant by being 'human'. It is about the subjective experiences that make up digitally dependent lives today. While the idea of being online is commonplace, it has become increasingly moot as more and more people do things, live their lives, online.

As the line between offline and online dissolves, software-driven devices have receded into the background. Socio-technical living spaces now feature devices – from fridges that remember to robot vacuums that 'know' the room they are cleaning – that are so integrated as to have a taken-for-grantedness that makes them a seemingly natural part of the lived environment. Because of this, the back end, where data are collected, disclosed and used by corporations, is really hard to see, let alone fully grasp in terms of consequences for people in those living spaces. The popular celebration of convenience, comfort and congeniality of social media appears to contribute to the apparent complacency.

The notion of 'onlife', coined by Luciano Floridi, was the subject of a European Community investigation discussed as the *Onlife Manifesto*.[40] It raises questions about how the sense of identity, relationships, reality and agency are mutating, and of course these have a strong bearing on surveillance, too. Now, surveillance often sparks responses relating to 'privacy'. This relates especially to state surveillance that makes being watched seem negative, undesirable. Some wish to escape, to hide, or just to be 'private'. But this seems myopic in a world of mass media and now social media, because the world of performance and celebrity makes being seen a matter of privilege, of desire. And if the chance for Warhol's fifteen minutes of fame was limited to TV, social media opens the floodgates.

The consequences for surveillance are far-reaching – from the unwanted eye to welcome watching. But in fact, these two belong together. In many cases, the welcome watching of performance is choreographed by what might otherwise be considered the unwanted eye. The link between personal performance, celebrity and surveillance is mediated by the corporate structure of the technology. Performances are not, after all, as spontaneous as they may seem. A subtle steering mechanism designed into the software by commercial imperatives prepares the way. The desire to be seen is no less real for all that and the performances may well be improvised, but one has to ask who built the set and encouraged the actors to take the stage.

The desire to be seen is thought by some to be narcissistic or even promiscuous – wanting to be visible to all and sundry. But it may equally be a deliberate practice of positioning oneself in a favourable light in order to achieve some basic and limited goals. Such intentional exposure – skilfully analysed by Erving Goffman in the 1950s[41] – is also seen in the desire to self-surveill using devices often dubbed the 'quantified self'. Here, self-tracking and life logging are central. Seen by some as a mode of self-reinvention, this may also be construed as capitulation to a sense of the self as commodity. At the same time, such desires may also help to naturalize and legitimate surveillance of all kinds, to encourage new modes of cooperation of the surveilled with their surveillors. Emerging surveillance imaginaries and practices evidence both kinds of possible outcomes.

Pulling threads together

In Part III, the final two chapters of the book consider what the culture of surveillance means for alternative futures, for ethics and for politics. We start with chapter 5, 'Total transparency', which uses Dave Eggers' *The Circle* as a springboard into further consideration of where the culture of surveillance may be leading. Change does often occur at dizzying speed, which prompts a turn to other sources for a larger sense of context. This novel, and to an extent the film[42] based on it, offers a contemporary fictional account of surveillance cultures, through the prism of an all-encompassing Silicon Valley corporation.

The novel follows the progress of Mae, a new employee at The Circle, as she enthusiastically embraces each technique of total transparency, persuaded that 'privacy is theft' and that wanting to be seen is natural; proof that she exists.

The novel's themes connect with various studies mentioned in this book, such as Nippert-Eng's *Islands of Privacy* and Marwick's 'social surveillance', and prompt debate over the true state of 'visibility' as a key question of the culture of surveillance. The question of visibility is in fact a basic issue in all surveillance, presented not only in photo images that have bloomed beyond the wildest dreams of their nineteenth-century inventors, but also in the metaphorical 'seeing' done with data. For example, performance-based ranking is also clearly in evidence in *The Circle* – as it also is in the 'Nosedive' episode of *Black Mirror* – now achieved not merely by the large impersonal organization but also by fellow workers, who score and rank each other. The biggest question is how far *The Circle* is utopian and how far dystopian?

Whatever the answer, surveillance culture not only helps us see how things *are*. It also opens a window on how things *could* be or *should* be. In chapter 6, 'Hidden hope', we see how surveillance imaginaries yield clues about the dynamics but also the duties of surveillance. Here we turn the lens from the one to the other. What might be some guides for considering the everyday ethics of surveillance – and might they also offer insights into surveillance on the very large scale? What actually occurs is always contextual, and thus our sought-for ethics requires a certain fluidity and flexibility.

Unfortunately, many matters technological are often treated as if they themselves are beyond ethics, in a world that ethics does not reach. They are treated as if they are exempt from ethical demands or insights. The pressure to perform online underscores the drive to get results, making it easy to forget that the results may as easily enhance or erase the common good. So the first task is a reminder that devices and data are not somehow morally neutral but are already implicated in activities and institutions that have to be judged on whether they promote or support good or evil.

In our case we should ask what prompts surveillance activities and how they fit on a spectrum of care-and-control – where they may also blur or overlap – or within contexts of other social relationships at home, work, school or play. Could one conceive of 'good gazing' as being surveillance-for rather than merely surveillance-of the other?[43] This requires some radically different thinking that places the person first, before personal data, and it is a properly ethical matter, not reducible to techniques for deciding what is best for this or that individual. It is a matter for public debate and deliberation.

Chapter 6 continues by revisiting the notion of surveillance practices. Once more, we find that surveillance practices are both responsive and initiatory. They evidence a certain kind of practical politics for an information-intensive world where data have become a source of both economic and political power. If 'good gazing' can be worked out in relation to fitbits, dashcams and home security systems, might this also work on a larger scale?

Much debate over surveillance, approached within abstract Western thought, focuses on legal 'harms' and modes of regulation. But how might wider questions of rights and responsibilities – based on that sense of humanness already mentioned – be worked out politically in the context of a reframed digital democracy? Again, if we examine actual practices that are currently appearing within digital domains, it is possible to find clues as to where things could go. This could be depressingly familiar if the filter bubbles continue to grow, courtesy of social media. But there are available alternatives, ones that still allow for conversation and debate over visibility, transparency and their connection with the common good.

Part I
Culture in Context

1
Crucibles of Culture

Today's emerging surveillance culture takes place in a process of social-technological 'melting' which, as it intensifies, is creating something new. Hence, 'crucibles of culture'. The liquefying metaphor speaks of changing relationships, both interpersonal and political,[1] and the contents of the crucibles themselves, of a novel mixing of elements – the technosocial – that portend some unprecedented outcomes. It has become possible to do and say things, using technology, that would have been unthinkable only a generation ago.

For instance, as a Pew study shows, 'Not only can internet searchers type in queries about someone who has aroused their curiosity, they also can seek pictures, videos, and real-time status updates online.' Here is do-it-yourself surveillance. The researchers go on, 'Location-based awareness in mobile devices adds another layer of information that can be searched.' But immediately, they also expose the other face of the coin: 'Avid users of mobile devices may voluntarily reveal their identity and location to certain websites, thereby allowing almost anyone to learn their whereabouts.'[2] Ordinary users watching others, surveillantly, and also providing the data for such surveillance.

This quote propels us directly into surveillance culture territory. It speaks of everyday roles in relation to surveillance. It is mistaken to see surveillance today simply as something that is 'done to us'; surveillance is experienced and also initiated by ordinary users. Many people do surveillance themselves, sometimes relying on complex technology to do so. The Pew report also points out that facial recognition technology is now commonplace in social media platforms, permitting some to engage in online identification of strangers. Non-visual identification is also easier for everyone, not just for corporations or police. Indeed, even at the beginning of the twenty-first century, 87 per cent of Americans could be identified with just three bits of information: gender, zip – or postal – code and date of birth.[3]

Once thought of mainly as the world of private investigators, police and security agencies, the means of surveillance now also flow freely through many media into the hands of the general public. This has helped to create an emerging surveillance culture – the everyday webs of social relations, including shared assumptions and behaviours, existing among all actors and agencies associated with surveillance. The symbolic and the material work together here, creating what is quickly becoming a significant dimension of social life. The culture of surveillance is about how surveillance is enabled not only by technical and political means but also by the enthusiasm, ignorance, and sometimes reluctant cooperation and even initiative-taking of the surveilled.

This chapter introduces a conceptual framework for considering the culture of surveillance. To grasp what is happening in the surveillance world today means extending our understanding of surveillance beyond common phrases such as 'state surveillance' or 'surveillance society' to think about the mundane ways in which surveillance has become an aspect of everyday lives. To achieve this, the concepts of 'surveillance imaginaries' and 'surveillance practices' are introduced, elaborated and placed in the context of a world of increasingly 'liquid surveillance'.

It is not just that daily lives are recorded, monitored and tracked in unprecedented ways, though this rings true. It is that in a culture of surveillance, everyday life routines themselves have an enlarged role in constituting surveillance, particularly through so-called interactivity, that is, through user-generated surveillance. Surveillance has become part of a way of seeing and of being in the world. It is a dimension of a whole way of life.

Today, surveillance is frequently fluid and flexible, in contrast to previous solid and fixed forms, and this resonates with the more liquid modernities of the present. Surveillance works at a distance in both space and time, channelling flows of data and sorting people socially. However, surveillance operates increasingly in consensual ways, dependent on how people perceive and act in relation to surveillance. These surveillance 'imaginaries' and 'practices' constitute each other; imaginaries provide the sense of what living with surveillance entails, while the practices enable actual initiation, compliance, negotiation or resistance to occur.

Once perceived as a peripheral aspect of life, limited to recognizable suspects or persons-of-interest, surveillance has become central to social experience, both as a serious security issue and as a playful part of mediated relationships. In the mid-twentieth century, many thought of government monitoring as 'state surveillance' of an Orwellian kind. In the later twentieth century, the language of 'surveillance society' was popularized, referring to a general social experience of cameras in public space capturing street scenes, or loyalty cards tracking spending habits and creating customer profiles.

Here, these concepts are rethought in the light of how surveillance becomes a way of life, a way of 'seeing' and 'being in' the world. Surveillance still happens in government, policing, intelligence and commerce and is hard-wired into streets and buildings, wirelessly present in smartphones and via internet platforms. It has also been democratized for mass participation through social media. Surveillance cultures emerge more obviously than ever as surveillance becomes more flexible and fluid, touching more frequently the routines of everyday life. Liquid surveillance seeps and streams everywhere.

In what follows, the characteristics of surveillance culture are pulled into focus. But this process is itself dynamic and constantly changing. Some conceptual clues are offered in this chapter, but these ways of seeing are themselves affected by the phenomenon that confronts us. Starting with the notion of cultural 'liquidity' is a way of warning that the solidity and stasis of some previous perspectives on social and cultural life are not what they were. I then explain the concepts of imaginaries and practices, each of which suggests movement and mutation.

Liquidity and surveillance culture

Liquid surveillance connects surveillance with major movements within modernity. For Bauman, who popularized the notion of modern 'liquidity', all social forms seem subject to melting and surveillance is no exception.[4] From once being more solid and fixed, surveillance is now increasingly fluid, which in turn contributes to the liquefying of everything from national borders to identities. The former were once thought to be imaginary but locatable geographical lines at the edges of national territories but, as we shall see, they are now as much in data processes remote from 'actual' borders.[5]

Equally, identities today are more fluid than fixed, especially in the fast-moving world of social media.[6] As I have noted, surveillance works in both space and time to channel the flows and thus to enable social sorting. One major result, elaborated by Bauman, is that power is globalized and harder to pin down, while politics seems to be primarily local and limited.

'Liquid surveillance' is less a complete way of specifying surveillance and more an orientation, a way of situating surveillance developments in the fluid and unsettling modernity of today. Surveillance softens especially in the consumer realm, as contrasted with policing and national security surveillance. Old moorings are loosened as bits of personal data extracted for one purpose are more easily deployed for another. Would all men guess when buying flowers or chocolates that eXelate, a data broker, sells this information to others as 'men in trouble', presumed to have relationship problems?[7] Surveillance spreads in a fashion hitherto unimaginable to non-experts in marketing, thus responding to and reproducing liquidity.

Without a fixed container, but jolted by security demands and tipped by technology companies' insistent marketing, surveillance spills out all over, just because it is an organizing principle of these activities. Bauman's notion of liquid modernity frames surveillance in new ways and offers both striking insights into why surveillance develops the way it does and some productive ideas on how its worst effects might be confronted and countered.

Surveillance, once seemingly solid and fixed, now twists and travels at speed, seeping and spreading into many life areas where it once had only marginal sway. Gilles Deleuze coined the phrase 'society of control' where surveillance grows less like a tree – relatively rigid, in a vertical plane, like the panopticon – and more like creeping weeds.[8] As Haggerty and Ericson observe, following this, the 'surveillant assemblage' captures flows of what we might call body data, turning them into highly fluid and mobile 'data doubles'.[9] William Staples also notes that today's surveillance occurs in cultures 'characterized by fragmentation and uncertainty as many of the once-taken-for-granted meanings, symbols and institutions of modern life *dissolve* before our eyes'.[10] Thus the bounded, structured and stable liquefies.

The liquidity of today's surveillance is not limited to the flows of surveillance themselves but also, crucially, to the kinds of social relationships that are possible within a surveillance culture. Shoshana Zuboff points out that the new 'surveillance capitalism' of internet companies systematically erodes what was left of mutual and contractual relationships between firms and both their production workers and their consumers. This may be seen at Amazon in Seattle, where the company states that their expected working standards are 'unreasonably high' and where employees are urged to send secret messages to bosses, based on their watching others, that prompts sabotaging one's workmates.[11] And in the world of social media, mutual expectations that users might have of each other are often full of uncertainty, shifting and mutable. Such liquidity is not so much *caused* by new technologies of communication as intensified within new social, economic and technological configurations.

Today's world is marked by a rampant individualism that debilitates if not destroys certain kinds of sociality. It is enabled and encouraged by online activity, something that can clearly be seen in the comments of young people interviewed by Sherry Turkle for her book *Alone Together*. As she says, 'These days, insecure about our relationships and anxious about intimacy, we look to technology for ways to be in relationships and protect ourselves from them at the same time.'[12] Similar topics are explored in Gary Shteyngart's novel *Super Sad True Love* Story, which also mulls the paradox of a culture of connection that has deep relationship troubles. Online performance is a thread running through Turkle's and Shteyngart's work, too. The media seem to encourage competition rather than cooperation and, as Bauman notes, seem to do so on marketplace criteria.[13] How such social relationships feel the impact of surveillance specifically is explored here.

Contrast all this with a classic model of surveillance, the eighteenth-century 'panopticon' prison design of Jeremy Bentham. The circular architecture placed inmates at the periphery, all visible to an 'inspector' in a central control tower. However, the inmates could not tell if the inspector, hidden behind Venetian blinds, was actually present. Though uncertainty existed about when the 'watching' was actually occurring, inmates and 'inspector' were very clear about their mutual relationships. The idea of panoptic surveillance became a key modern means of keeping control, by barring movement among inmates and promoting it among the watchers. But the watchers still had to be present sometimes. Of course, panopticon-style prisons were also expensive and entailed the inspector taking some responsibility for the lives of inmates. In many ways, today's world is post-panoptical. The inspectors can slip away, escaping to unreachable realms. Whatever mutual engagement might have existed is frayed if not finished. Mobility and nomadism are now prized, unless you are poor or homeless. The smaller, lighter, faster is seen as good – at least in the world of smartphones and tablets.

From panoptic to performative surveillance?

The panopticon is just one model – or better, diagram – of surveillance. The architecture of electronic technologies through which power is asserted in today's mutable and mobile organizations makes the architecture of walls and windows largely redundant, virtual 'firewalls' and 'windows' notwithstanding. Of course, the degree of flexibility varies, depending on many factors. Small start-ups are very flexible, but large organizations are often flexible too when it comes to quick market responses.[14] And the technological architectures also permit forms of control that display different faces. Not only do they have no obvious connection with imprisonment, they often share the features of flexibility and fun seen in entertainment and consumption. For example, airline check-in can be done, conveniently, using a smartphone, although the passenger name record generated with the initial reservation – also manageable with a smartphone – has to be shared with security agencies in the United States and other countries.

Not only that. Surveillance occurs across life spheres that once were in much more separate silos. Thus discipline – not to mention consumption – and security are actually related, in this view, something that even Michel Foucault failed to recognize. Foucault insisted on their separation at just the moment when their electronic connections were reinforced. Security now *uses* discipline, for instance, in border control. Security has morphed into a future-oriented enterprise – neatly captured in the novel and film *Minority Report* (2002) or in the widely watched US TV series *Person of Interest* – and works through surveillance by attempting to monitor and even to pre-empt what *will* happen, using digital techniques and statistical reasoning, often referred to today as Big Data.[15]

Less and less escapes the surveillant eye. As Didier Bigo points out, such security operates by tracking '*everything that moves*, products, information, capital, humanity'.[16] So surveillance works at a distance in both space and time, circulating fluidly beyond as well as within nation-states in a globalized realm. Reassurance and rewards accompany those mobile groups for whom such techniques are made to appear 'natural' and whose profiles promote them. However, parallel profiling processes and exclusionary measures await the groups unlucky enough to be labelled unworthy or unwelcome.[17]

However, while discipline and security are still significant, it is also important to consider other aspects of contemporary 'liquidity'. Social bonds become more brittle and novel forms of individualism come to the fore. While some speak of the 'me generation' or 'celebrity culture', a term that gets closer to the heart of the matter, as well as offering better links with surveillance, is 'performance'. It links together the idea that on social media we are all virtuoso performers before a – largely – unseen audience, with the accelerating expectations within any capitalist organization that measuring and tracking worker performance is the overriding priority. After all, the so-called post-Fordist employee assumes that virtuoso performance will be rewarded.[18]

The idea of surveillance performances animates John McGrath's work on *Loving Big Brother*,[19] which he prefaces by juxtaposing images of people leaping to their deaths from the World Trade Center on 9/11 and the trivial addiction to reality TV in its most famous form – *Big Brother*. He says that being riveted to the screen reveals how much we desire to watch – we may 'love Big Brother' – while at the same time the images of tragedy inform the ways that we encounter our mortality in the deaths of others. Understanding the ways in which watching is already a way of life helps to show why, as McGrath also observes, it is not just terrorism or television that restructures our world, but surveillance itself.

More recently, the concept of 'monitored performances'[20] has been mooted as a productive means of pulling together different threads of surveillance concern, from the performance monitoring of the corporation – 'this call may be monitored for quality control purposes' – to the monitored performances of anti-surveillance activists. In between, one might find, for example, the self-surveilling 'monitored performance' of the so-called quantified self. This is the use of health-and-fitness devices to collect data to check on our own bodily performances in ways that are, ironically, also monitored extensively by healthcare and insurance agencies. In the following chapter, the theme of performance is prominent, as well as its monitoring, often taken for granted.

Power and politics pull apart

Another aspect of contemporary liquidity is that power and politics are splitting apart. This is a key factor in Bauman's account of liquid modernity. Power now exists in global and extraterritorial space – think networked national security agencies or global internet companies. But politics, which once linked individual and public interests, remains local, unable to act at the planetary level. Without political control, power becomes a source of great uncertainty, while politics seems irrelevant to many people's real-life problems and fears.

Surveillance power, as exercised by government departments, police agencies and private corporations, fits this picture. As noted, even national borders, which once had geographical locations – however arbitrary – now appear in airports distant from the 'edge' of the territory and, more significantly, in databases that may not even be in the country in question. At Canada's Pearson Airport in Toronto, for example, a large sign indicates where bag-pulling passengers cross the US border, yet the airport is actually more than 120 kilometres from the land border.

Continuing with this example, the issue of mutable borders is a source of great uncertainty for many. Going through airport security, not knowing exactly whose jurisdiction one is in or where one's personal details may end up, is an anxious moment, especially for those who may be part of a suspect population. It is also a classic moment for performances. And if one is unfortunate enough to be detained or to discover that your name is on a no-fly list, knowing what to do is notoriously hard. Beyond this, effecting political change that might, for instance, make necessary travel more straightforward is a daunting challenge.

The melting of social forms and the splitting of power and politics are two key features of liquid modernity that have obvious resonance with surveillance, but two further connections are also worth mentioning. One is the mutual relation between new media and fluid relationships. While some blame new media for social fragmentation, Bauman sees things working both ways. He says that, within neoliberal regimes, power must be free to flow, and barriers, fences, borders and checkpoints are a nuisance to be overcome or circumvented. Dense and tight networks of social bonds, especially based in territory, must be cleared away. For him, it is the frailty of those forms that allows these powers to work in the first place.

Many activists see great potential for social solidarity and political organizing in tweets and messaging. Think of the Occupy Movement, or the Arab Spring, in 2010 and 2011, or the Umbrella Movement in Hong Kong in 2014. But this is an area to be carefully watched, not least because it is *already* being surveilled. Social media depend for their existence on monitoring users and selling the data to others. The possibilities for social media resistance are attractive and in some ways fruitful, but they are also limited, due both to the lack of resources for binding relationships in a liquefying world and to the fact that surveillance power *within* social media is endemic and consequential. The case for hopeful realism is made in the final chapter.

The final connection is that liquid times offer some acute challenges for all who would act ethically, not least in the world of surveillance. Bauman's recognition of the uncertainties endemic in a liquid modern world shapes the problem as he sees it. And his favoured stance, spurning lifeless rules and regulations, is seen in his stress on the significance of the lived encounter with the other person and the importance of the conversation.[21] Realizing our responsibility for the human being before us, as well as for our own humanity, is his starting point.

Components of culture

The emerging surveillance culture arrived with no fanfare. The world of surveillance is often seen – rightly, in many ways – as the domain of powerful organizations dependent on global corporations and utilizing cutting-edge hardware and software. The world of culture, on the other hand, is frequently associated with softer situations, the familiar, sometimes challenging, sometimes comforting, mundane details of daily life. These just evolve over time, often unnoticed, and are then taken for granted. Here, we pull them into view, to defamiliarize the familiar.[22] Or, as Dorothy Smith puts it, to 'see the everyday world as problematic'.[23]

Much of what might be thought of as surveillance emphasizes its *strategies*, the large-scale logics of technology and political economy. This all too easily obscures the role of the small-scale *tactics* of everyday life.[24] For instance, some academic discussions of 'internet users' have been infected with an abstract, centred, rational view of the self. As Julie Cohen says, they have lost sight of the embodied, social, creative selves who actually encounter, use and experience information.[25] Or, as N. Katherine Hayles puts it, information has lost its body.[26] This does not demand a return to a simplistic, 'humanist' view of the person, but it does mean that more attention should be paid to human action, now more and more mediated through digital technologies. The performance dimension, so important for sensing surveillance culture, has everything to do with embodied experience.

Surveillance culture exhibits forms that are varied and constantly mutating, but they have some common features that I begin to explore here. It is these common features that I refer to in the singular as surveillance culture, which despite the singular-sounding concept is nonetheless multifaceted and complex. As an increasing proportion of social relationships is digitally mediated, subjects are involved not merely as the targets or bearers of surveillance, but as more and more knowledgeable and active participants.

There are two main aspects of this. One has to do with widespread compliance with surveillance. Although attempts to resist surveillance in certain settings are relatively commonplace, in most settings and for most of the time, surveillance has become so pervasive in today's world that the majority comply without questioning it.[27] Much of this is a matter of sheer convenience. Of course, this general collusion with contemporary surveillance is particularly puzzling to those who have lived through the surveillance regimes of authoritarian governments.[28] But much compliance may be explained further by reference to three rather commonplace factors – fear, familiarity and fun.[29] I comment briefly on these here, but they are also closely related to the themes of chapters 2, 3 and 4, where they are more fully discussed, along with other factors such as trading 'privacy' for convenience, or finding more efficient or ingenious ways of using the internet.

On the first, fear has become more marked since 9/11 and it is apparent that the reported desire for surveillance measures relates to the ratcheting up of uncertainty in a media-amplified exploitation of fear.[30] All too often, it seems that politicians trade on fear of violence and terrorism to obtain support for the introduction of new security measures, and fear, of course, is a powerful emotion.

By familiarity, I mean that surveillance has become a taken-for-granted aspect of life, from loyalty cards in the supermarket, to ubiquitous cameras in public and private space, and to security routines in airports, sports arenas and many other sites of which many people are less and less aware. I think here of embedded sensors and the so-called data exhaust from our devices. This normalization and domestication of surveillance appears to account in part for the general level of compliance.[31]

Third, at the opposite end of the emotional spectrum from fear, fun also accounts for compliance, above all in the realm of social media and digital devices. While they are integrated into serious life in many self-evident ways, for many users there are many leisure-time and entertainment aspects of the same systems. Anders Albrechtslund suggests that, here, surveillance may be 'potentially empowering, subjectivity building and even playful'.[32]

All three cases, however, are reminders that today it seems entirely natural to many that life is lived online. Edward Snowden, a determined critic of the abuse of power by national security data-gathering, said without irony in 2015: 'I *live* on the internet.' Or, as Daniel Trottier suggests, social media exists as an environment for living, a kind of dwelling.[33] This is why the issues raised here are so vital. Everyday life is now enabled by and enmeshed in the digital. While users participated in the technological environments created by driving cars or watching television, there is a sense in which today the techno-social is not only participatory but depends for its character on user contributions. This leads to a further consideration.

The question of why certain populations would comply so readily with surveillance is important and has been widely discussed, but it does not tell the whole surveillance culture story by any means. The second, and larger, issue is why such populations might also participate in, actively engage with and initiate surveillance themselves. Of course, this may not even involve technological assistance. Consider the 'elf on the shelf'. Though apparently trivial, this cute little doll appears above child level – 'don't touch!' – in many American and Canadian homes before Christmas to assist Santa's determination of who has been nice or naughty. The doll has no battery, no electronic components, just a warning presence for children: 'you're being watched.' Just a toy, perhaps, but one could be forgiven for seeing it as early preparation for living in a surveillance-suffused world.[34] This is a common question of surveillance culture; how far do apparently innocent items intended for play and pleasure double as domestic surveillance?[35] Or domestic*ating* surveillance, where what might conventionally be thought of as an unusual activity of deliberate monitoring becomes normal, taken for granted, acceptable? Where habits, as Orwell observed, become instinctive.

Elves notwithstanding, the fact that many tools for doing surveillance are increasingly available is part of the reason for everyday monitoring. But that can hardly be the whole story either. After all, some such tools are adopted and used while others are ignored and neglected. Additionally, the markets are volatile, especially in social media platforms, with some erstwhile leaders such as Facebook losing customers to Instagram – until it bought it – or Snapchat. As in other spheres, social engagement with new technologies cannot somehow be read off technological capacities or availability. These are socio-technical phenomena.

Theorizing surveillance culture

To help grasp the components of surveillance culture, I use the concepts of imaginaries and practices to frame the discussion. Building on Charles Taylor's analysis of social imaginaries,[36] my term, 'surveillance imaginaries', has to do with shared understandings about certain aspects of visibility in daily life, and in social relationships, expectations and normative commitments. They provide a capacity to act, to engage in and to legitimate surveillance *practices*. In turn, surveillance practices help to carry surveillance imaginaries and to contribute to their reproduction. You will recall that the term 'surveillance culture' is not for a moment meant to be monolithic. Like any other, surveillance culture is diverse and constantly mutates. In this book, I have in mind primarily the surveillance imaginaries and practices of ordinary users of smartphones and the internet.

Surveillance imaginaries are constructed through everyday involvement with surveillance as well as from news reports and popular media such as film and the internet. They include the growing awareness that modern life is lived 'under surveillance', that this affects social relationships in many ways – for instance, 'will my employer look at my antics on this Facebook page?' – that the very idea of an expectation of privacy may be moot, and that everything from complacency to confrontation may be appropriate modes of responding to surveillance.

In a world awash with surveillance systems and tools there seems to be evidence that, over time, we build up a mental image of surveillance and how to respond to it. Building on Pierre Bourdieu, authors Michael McCahill and Rachel Finn call this 'surveillance capital', which 'refers to how surveillance subjects utilize the everyday knowledge and cultural know-how that is acquired through first-hand experience...'[37] Surveillance capital is closely related to what I call surveillance imaginaries. These latter offer not only a sense of what goes on – the *dynamics* of surveillance – but also a sense of how to evaluate and engage with it – the *duties* of surveillance. Such imaginaries, in turn, inform and animate surveillance practices; the two belong together.

Surveillance practices, then, are the things that we engage with, that we *do* in relation to surveillance. For McCahill and Finn, this includes, prominently, resistance to the power relations expressed by surveillance. I have in mind a range of activities that include but go beyond 'resistance'. Torin Monahan, among others, speaks of surveillance as a 'cultural practice', too, and his view is similar to the one I propose here. For him, this means the inclusion of features such as 'popular culture, media, art and narrative' and the attempt 'to understand people's engagement with surveillance on their own terms ...'[38] Each dimension is echoed in this book.

Surveillance practices include *responsive* activities that relate to being surveilled and also *initiatory* modes of engagement *with* surveillance. Examples of the former, responsive practices, include installing some form of encrypted protection from unwanted attention from national security agencies or marketing corporations, or wearing clothing – hats, hoods, masks, some of which are called 'glamou-flage'[39] – that limits camera recognition in public places, or eschewing the use of loyalty cards.

Examples of the latter, initiatory practices, on the other hand, include installing a dash-cam to record the activities of other road users while one is driving, using social media to check up on personal details of others, including complete strangers, or indulging in self-surveillance through monitoring heart rates or calculating activity duration and intensity with devices such as Fitbits – often referred to as the 'quantified self', discussed later. As noted, these are analytical distinctions, and some kinds of practices may include elements of each.

Exploring today's surveillance culture through the lenses of imaginaries and practices offers fresh ways of thinking about surveillance in general. It opens up a much more complex cultural landscape than can be captured with the concepts of surveillance state or surveillance society – though it does not supersede them – and simultaneously takes us beyond simple conceptual binaries such as power–participation, in/visibility, privacy–publicness or even the misleading us-and-them of much popular surveillance rhetoric. As noted, for example, for many users of social media, despite popular perceptions to the contrary, privacy is still a highly valued condition, but so also is publicness.[40]

It is also worth emphasizing that the term 'surveillance culture' does not for a moment signify any unified or all-embracing situation. It is merely an umbrella term for many different kinds of phenomena that points to the reality of a whole way of life that relates, positively and negatively, to surveillance. The emphasis on imaginaries and practices already indicates the variety of phenomena that exists in this context. At the same time, one can discern patterns, just as Michel de Certeau shows in *The Practice of Everyday Life*,[41] where the major strategies of consumption are reappro-priated in everyday situations. Similarly, I include examples of how strategies of internet corporations are mimicked in the tactics of internet users for their own purposes.

As this is a thread running all through the book, a further comment on the 'public' and the 'private' is in order. These are significant ways of construing the social world; ones with a long and fascinating history. Yet they are affected by and also affect today's cultural climate and, of course, they are affected by the new media that help to shape it. Such media permit a kind of publicness well beyond the co-presence of, say, friends arguing politics in a pub. Time and space no longer restrict visibility in ways they once did. Equally, privacy today is less about being 'let alone' than about trying to control the flows of information about users of these new media, a situation in which context is crucial. Notions of public and private are contested; vital and ongoing struggles exist especially around internet use. Seeking 'publicity', for instance, through social media or craving 'privacy' as a 'right' appear within the following pages, but a certain ambivalence will also be evident, both in everyday situations and also in the analysis and the politics of surveillance culture.[42]

Within surveillance culture, people both negotiate surveillance strategies – for instance, often seeing the giving of personal data as a trade-off for personal benefit[43] – and also adopt them as their own, modifying them for their circumstances and initiating forms of surveillance on themselves and others.[44] Everyday tactics might include getting around assumed limits on the use of some application – the most common has to be falsely claiming to have read the terms of use – to seeing how large-scale surveillance works and appropriating the practice for private use. Facebook users using facial recognition systems for checking on unknown others would be a case in point.

This complicates our understanding of and our responses to surveillance. The crude them-and-us of much popular surveillance opinion does not fit what is actually happening. One is obliged to ask, who's watching whom? As surveillance itself liquefies, the neat and simple one-way vision of surveillance becomes less relevant and even misleading.

Surveillance imaginaries

The surveillance imaginary, then, is my shorthand for how various features of what has been called the surveillance society influence how people picture themselves in their social arrangements and relationships, such that in ordinary everyday life they include and even embrace surveillance in their vision of how societies are ordered and their roles within that. The scripts – or 'treatments' to be improvised, if we think of screen rather than stage – for the dramas to which I have referred are provided by surveillance imaginaries. Again, this analysis resonates with performance.

On a larger canvas, Charles Taylor speaks of the modern social imaginary as a kind of vision of moral order, how people imagine society. It reveals facets of shared lives and also tells something about how people *should* live together and what is worth striving for. A social imaginary is not a theory; it is how in everyday life we *imagine* our social world. It is widely shared and is 'a common understanding which makes possible common practices and a widely shared sense of legitimacy'.[45] In an information era, one might add, it is also compressed, fragmentary and flowing.

Interestingly, an earlier and widespread social change in modern social imaginaries, suggests Taylor, was in the shift from hierarchies of personal links towards an impersonal, egalitarian order where 'direct access' is commonplace.[46] Modern individualism, for example, produced new forms of belonging, from what both Taylor and Craig Calhoun call 'relational' to 'categorical' identities.[47] More and more, people locate themselves socially in relation to impersonal entities. This connects with the idea of 'categorical suspicion' and 'categorical seduction' that refer, respectively, to policing and intelligence surveillance practices, on the one hand, and to commercial and marketing surveillance, on the other.[48]

Surveillance imaginaries include the following sorts of assumptions: to organize or oversee anything, data are needed, and using data is more efficient than previous methods or at worst a necessary evil. There are technical systems that will facilitate this, and indeed, that will do the job best. Security is a key driver and justification of extra surveillance. In the realm of communication – above all in social media – it is believed that such surveillance is far less significant than that involving state agencies.

Other shared assumptions that comprise imaginaries may include ideas about trading 'privacy' for benefits – 'I don't mind exchanging a little liberty for the convenience of a fast-track airport pass' – or that if one has 'nothing to hide there is nothing to fear'. Engagement with media, as producers-cum-consumers, is articulated with imaginaries. These are what Torin Monahan calls 'local practices with global significance'.[49] Media such as film and TV shows offer fresh understandings of social life, as Raymond Williams would have noted, as does understanding the varied meanings of surveillance in international contexts.

One way of thinking about surveillance imaginaries is to consider the ways that camera surveillance has become a familiar part of the urban landscape, and thus of everyday life. Public cameras are an inescapable part of our vision of the city and many are aware of the kind of view – grainy footage – they offer. So much so that Jonathan Finn suggests that, in Western cultures especially, people now 'see surveillantly'.[50] In this, he updates Susan Sontag's claim that 'In teaching us a new visual code, photographs alter and enlarge our notions of what is worth looking at and what we have a right to observe. They are a grammar and, even more importantly, an ethics of seeing.'[51]

Although others had experienced such things before, such surveillant seeing was viscerally visible to me at a protest march in 2010. Those attending the demonstration against the closure of prison farms in my own city, Kingston, knew to bring their phones to monitor police behaviour, just as the police used hand-held or body-worn cameras to record crowd behaviours.[52] In some situations, such as among the Palestinian population in Israel, bystanders are encouraged by the Israeli human rights group B'Tselem to shoot back, using video, so that evidence of police and military activities may be shared with others who are not present.[53] These examples 'highlight ways in which surveillance exists as an aesthetic concept, a rhetorical tool, and as a form of participation in social life'. Thus Finn concludes that 'surveillance is no longer the purview of police, the state and corporations' but that 'it is a constitutive element of life...' which 'requires a self-reflexive look at our own willingness and desire to watch, record and display our lives and the lives of others' – which is just what this book aspires to do.

It is also important, beyond our own engagement or participation in camera surveillance, to note the role of television – along with novels, films and music, of course – in providing components of a surveillance imaginary. For instance, the popular American television series *Person of Interest*[54] features a central character, Mr Finch, who has developed what is simply called The Machine, for the US government to sort information culled from public and private sources in order to predict future terrorist actions.

The Machine sorts events involving potential violence into important, that is, terrorist, and unimportant, interpersonal. Mr Finch has created a back door to The Machine, which provides him with a daily social security number of someone who is involved in an 'unimportant' crime. Viewers from the beginning of each episode do not know whether or not the person of interest is a potential victim or perpetrator of the possible crime. Mr Finch utilizes the data provided by The Machine to attempt to prevent 'unimportant' crimes. This show examines the moral dimensions of both surveillance and social sorting. Mr Finch admits, 'I'm a sucker for surveillance.'

Surveillance practices

Surveillance practices make up a growing repertoire of daily activities in the twenty-first century. Some, such as adjusting privacy settings, are obvious; others, such as donning a Fitbit or adjusting your online profile, may not strike one as primarily surveillant. This assumes that everyone is a creative actor, constantly drawing upon and reproducing cultural knowledge[55] – in this case, knowledge of surveillance. We all live in what Pierre Bourdieu calls a *habitus*,[56] which is how we do things, often unthinkingly, every day.

There is a logic to such activities, even if the 'actors' cannot necessarily articulate it, but this logic – from shielding a password at the cash machine to checking a Facebook friend's party-going – lasts over time and reappears routinely as it is repeated. And it goes beyond what each person does deliberately and with focused thinking. All sorts of unplanned events occur daily on micro-levels of human inter-action below the surface of conscious awareness or intention.

Technological systems – from tax forms and ID cards to public street cameras or cellphones – are themselves integral to everyday practices and are important components of modern myth and ritual. In this context, then, surveillance systems become inserted in everyday activities as one more thing to negotiate and are given meaning as people tap into their symbolic reservoirs, which, as Torin Monahan observes, can include narrative, media and art, among other things.[57] In this view, surveillance is embedded within, achieved by and generates many social practices depending on the context.

Surveillance appears more and more as an everyday activity as well as something orchestrated by organizations. As Michel de Certeau insists, so-called mass culture must be rethought in ways that take account of how ordinary people appropriate its various aspects and make them their own. Sometimes this still chimes with social and political expectations, but at other times people may be ploughing their own furrow, or altering an item to better suit their own purposes. When this occurs, the supposed shaping power of mass culture may not be quite so predictable: 'If it is true that the grid of discipline is becoming everywhere clearer and more extensive, it is all the more urgent to discover how an entire society resists being reduced to it, what popular procedures (also "minuscule" and quotidian) manipulate the mechanisms of discipline and conform to them only to evade them...'[58] How this applies to surveillance practices can be fruitfully explored in many contexts.

John Gilliom, for instance, draws our attention to the ways that ordinary people respond to what academics call surveillance.[59] His classic study of women on welfare shows how, in the face of the strategic, calculating and technical power of the casework software used by social workers, known as Cris-e, there are multiple and ingenious ways of responding. The women about whom he wrote never thought of themselves as engaging in resistance to surveillance so much as simply being in an ongoing struggle with powers that seemed set to stop them caring for their children as they saw fit. They had their own agendas and chose their moment

to subvert, dissemble, or even to cooperate with the function-
aries associated with the system – social workers – to make
sense of their own lives and to attempt to live beyond the
reach of power while not actually removing themselves from
or revolting against it.

This echoes de Certeau's insistence that it is mistaken to
assume that users, consumers or whatever are passive and
willingly guided by established rules. Everyday practices
should be explored to discover how people actually operate,
how they go on, faced by the strategies of power. Such
cultural practices add up to something significant because,
although there may be, among other things, dominating
systems of surveillance, those subject to them are unlikely to
be submissively docile.[60]

In the world of social media, however, new practices
become evident. They first become habitual, then instinctive.
Mark Andrejevic, for instance, talks of 'Lateral surveillance, or peer-to-peer monitoring, understood as the use of
surveillance tools by individuals, rather than by agents of
institutions public or private, to keep track of one another…'
He says it 'covers (but is not limited to) three main categories:
romantic interests, family, and friends or acquaintances'.
Thus the world of everyday is suffused with surveillance
practices in the 'everyday spaces of our homes and offices,
from law enforcement and espionage to dating, parenting,
and social life. In an era in which everyone is to be considered
potentially suspect, we are invited to become spies – for our
own good.'[61]

Interestingly, Daniel Trottier takes this further, uncovering
the 'mutual augmentation' of surveillance on Facebook, where
different users learn surveillance practices from others.[62] The
users in question are individual users, institutions (such as
universities, where Facebook began), marketers and police.
Trottier's research indicates that their own visibility on the
site is a primary motivation to watch others on the site. As all
parties engage in surveillance, so their ethical concerns about
covert scrutiny are dampened. The techniques of one group
may be appropriated by others in a constant upward spiral.
Equally, the surveillance strategies of Facebook itself are
enhanced by Facebook's attempts to understand what users
do to find out about each other. As users become more and

more aware of how Facebook keeps track of them, so they discover ways of keeping track of others.[63]

At the end of the day, though, does this mean that surveillance itself must be understood differently? Such everyday monitoring cannot merely be thought of in minatory, menacing ways, as if Big Brother were still looming behind it. When the roles, the imaginaries and practices of everyday users are taken into account, surveillance appears in more complex forms. While some surveillance is intrusive, undemocratic, disempowering, other forms seem participatory, playful, possibly empowering. Discerning which is which is a critical exercise.

Anders Albrechtslund suggests that social media offer fresh perspectives on surveillance. Characteristic of online social networking is the sharing, exploring and mutually checking-out of various activities, preferences, beliefs. He concludes that such surveillance practices cannot be adequately described within the framework of a hierarchical understanding of surveillance. Rather, online social networking seems to introduce a participatory approach to surveillance, which can empower – and not necessarily violate – the user.[64]

Surveillance culture takes shape

Surveillance is not static. The world of surveillance is constantly shifting, mutating, expanding, but not, at present at least, contracting. It is imperative that efforts to understand and respond to surveillance try to keep pace, not with every single new gadget or system, but with the key features of current developments. And it goes without saying that some new devices and assemblages *do* yield important clues about those 'key features'. One can trace the development of various dimensions of surveillance cultures through the twentieth century in particular, but now many societies seem to be on the cusp of further significant change.

Here, I am suggesting that surveillance should now be thought of, not only as relating to economic, technological, social or political realities, but as a highly significant cultural formation in the making. There is a growing awareness that watching and being watched are part of a whole way of life. Many in the later twentieth and early twenty-first century would have responded to the idea of surveillance societies, indicating how experiences of monitoring and tracking had strayed beyond state surveillance. All along, however, there was a growing tilt towards everyday life through information infrastructures and an increasing dependence on the digital in mundane relationships, all of which feeds into today's emerging surveillance culture.

Shifts may also be discerned from localized and enclosed surveillance to mobile and liquid surveillance, as embeddedness and ubiquity increase. State administration and security concerns have not disappeared. They are still very present as surveillance generators. But now surveillance – not only as done by vast agencies such as the NSA – penetrates the capillary levels of life. The move is beyond mainframes and personal computing, where computing machinery is embedded, more or less invisibly, in the environments of everyday life. This has given rise to phenomena variously referred to as 'ubiquitous computing' or the 'internet of things'. Paradoxically, these render the means of everyday visibility less visible. Cities are now being built or restructured as 'smart cities' – as seen in the futuristic city of Songdo in South Korea[65] – or in many plans for urban renewal.

Personal data are sought by multifarious entities, some having no direct relation to formal government, such that surveillance now affects everyday life in routine and profound ways. What began as database marketing in the 1980s and 1990s drew attention to the non-government use of personal data, although the trend really began with the spread of credit cards in the 1970s.[66]

As awareness grows of everyday surveillance, so it becomes more prominent in the picturing of daily life, in mundane surveillance imaginaries. And as different populations interact with it, complying, negotiating, resisting and even initiating surveillance practices, so the imaginaries are mobilized in action. Dealing with public space cameras has been one growing dimension of this, but securitization, especially of travel, has also prompted new practices. The rapid rise of social media is yet another – highly consequential – example of the same.

Let me stress once again that the culture of surveillance is not monolithic. Great diversity is evident across different populations and, as mentioned earlier, the very notion of surveillance culture is marked by fluidity rather than fixity. As we shall see, there are patterns that repeat across different cities and countries, but their prior experiences also contribute to the varieties of surveillance experience that are exhibited. Most of the research on which this book depends is from the English-speaking world and is primarily from North America and Europe. I tried to hear the voices of Asia, Latin America and Africa and also had readers from those parts of the world check my work. But this cannot possibly do justice to the variations available internationally, let alone in terms of class, gender and race.[67]

While much research now focuses on surveillance issues, few international comparisons exist, especially ones that are updated. An interesting snapshot of some dimensions of surveillance culture is seen in an international quantitative and qualitative study conducted in 2006, that showed a number of important variations around the world.[68] But while it could take account of changing views following 9/11, the attacks on New York and Washington, it is highly likely that these will have altered again after the disclosures of documents from the NSA by Edward Snowden in 2013. Nonetheless, it is worth noting some important variations from the study, if only to draw attention to their existence.

Globally, the majority of respondents worried about providing personal information online (Japan 82%, Brazil 70%, Spain 62%, US 60%, China 54%, Canada 66%). The majority of respondents did not believe that they had much say in what happened to their personal information (only 30% of Canadians, Americans, Spaniards and Hungarians believed they had complete or a lot of say; Chinese, Japanese and French felt they had the most say, at 67%, 62% and 61%, compared with Mexicans 40% and Brazilians 34%).

Those in Canada, US, France and Spain claimed to be more knowledgeable of the internet and other personal location technologies, whereas those in Mexico and Brazil claimed to be the least knowledgeable about these. Only a minority of people trusted that the government or private companies would do an appropriate job of protecting their personal information; in most countries, people trusted corporations more than government. However, Canadians and Americans were the most protective of their personal information.

People were ambivalent about businesses creating profiles of their customers and their membership in rewards-type customer profiling programmes. It seems that either people do not know or do not care. In a given population, the largest group (41%) assumed that government and business would protect their data and, while they might resist some activities as intrusive or unnecessary, in general they would comply. The next-largest group (33%) did not trust government or business with their data but they felt relatively powerless and fearful because they did not know what would happen to their online data. The third group (26%) did not trust government or businesses with their data either, but this was because they knew more about how they are used. They felt they lacked control over their data but would take steps to avoid surveillance.

Not only are surveillance cultures very varied and constantly mutating, they are also full of tension and ambiguity. While Bentham may have seen his panopticon prison as the midwife that would birth a modern utopia, Foucault queried this by noting that 'visibility is a trap'. Is this a dystopian way of interpreting the world? Such ambiguity provides for a creative tension in grappling with contemporary surveillance. What will the new cultures of surveillance mean for such ambiguities?

Surveillance culture certainly does not mean that new modes of monitoring and tracing will produce an orderly and efficient, let alone a just, society. As Walter Benjamin noted, 'there is no document of civilization which is not at the same time a document of barbarism',[69] and the same kind of Janus-faced developments are found in all kinds of surveillance. Even surveillance systems set up supposedly to mitigate the worst effects of poverty may end up simply causing more pain and problems among those they are intended to help, such as women on welfare. Good and evil are evident within all cultures, including the cultures of surveillance.

What do we know about so-called surveillance cultures? The mere fact that, for example, users of the internet and of social media divulge much information about themselves to corporations as they purchase online or present themselves through social media tells us nothing about how or why this occurs. It does seem that users generally say they want to have a sense of control over their information, but they often also choose the path of least resistance when making choices about managing their profiles. Young adult users are often more careful managing their reputations than older ones. However, many do not know what information about them is available to others, or do not mind information being connected with their names but will show concern about how it might be used, or may like aspects of customized marketing but dislike the online data collection and monitoring.

Conclusion

Alongside the more familiar state and societal surveillance, a surveillance culture is quietly appearing in which it is hard if not impossible not to participate. It is a fluid form of surveillance, constantly melting, morphing and merging, in ways that reflect the liquidity of data flows that characterizes what happens both in security intelligence agencies like the NSA and internet companies such as Amazon. But to focus on the cultural, our perspective must pull round from the panoptic to the performative, and to the roles people play across the spectrum from supporting to subverting surveillance.

To grasp all this means delving more deeply into the culture of surveillance in all its variety and variation. The succeeding chapters put more flesh on the bones of the components of surveillance culture. And we explore many surveillance imaginaries and practices that become visible – and are also about visibility – that appear as surveillance culture takes its distinctive shapes.

Part II
Cultural Currents

This second part of the book explores surveillance culture as an emerging phenomenon within the familiar worlds of surveillance. In chapter 2, 'From convenience to compliance', the kinds of surveillance carried out by government organizations, police and corporations are shown to be the soil within which new surveillance imaginaries and practices are growing today. The traveller at the airport or the internet user at the screen is not necessarily aware of surveillance from the outset. Once aware, however, the dawning realization forms itself into some section of the surveillance imaginary.

Once there, the imaginary informs future action, which may produce anything from compliance to contestation. Most will grasp the fact that the means of control and influence are vital characteristics of state and corporate surveillance even though the precise mechanisms by which they operate are largely unknown to them. The responses are to the experience of surveillance rather than to intimate knowledge of how it may affect them. The development of surveillance culture – especially through performance – produces possibilities for more nuanced and reflective responses to the patterns of power that predominate.

Chapter 3, 'From novelty to normalization', offers a similar analysis, in this case focusing on the ways that the appearance of a new surveillance culture is in part stimulated by the ubiquitous information infrastructure and the diffusion of digital platforms in today's world. Today's surveillance culture cannot be understood without remarking on the familiarity of things digital – they are taken for granted, normal, routine, domesticated – along with the surveillance mechanisms that they support and animate. As they become part of everyday life, so they contribute to the culture of surveillance.

This pattern continues into chapter 4, 'From online to onlife', where normalized aspects of surveillance culture may be viewed not just as a necessary evil, like airport security, but as something that may be enjoyable, desirable, even fun. The selfie is perhaps the archetypical illustration of this, where not only do participants welcome the watching eye of others but they also provide their own images and video for consumption by others. These offer the means that will contribute to the enjoyment of being watched, recognized and even celebrated, or at least 'liked'. Context turns out to be crucial; some watching eyes are as unwelcome, and read as intrusive or malevolent, as others are embraced and seen as adjuncts to identity and a positive self-image.

2
From Convenience to Compliance

'He showed devotion to all the rules, held at least one other security job, and went to night school. When he wasn't working or studying, he was watching cop shows, preparing himself for the latest threats. In other words, he was a true believer with big aspirations in the security field.' This is Lance, a transportation security officer (TSO) at Albany International Airport in New York State. He was assigned to tutor a new TSO, who had not yet perfected his performance, especially of pat-downs, those peculiarly intimate forms of surveillance-by-feel required since 9/11.[1]

Lance has a role to play and watching cop shows provides part of his preparation. For all that passengers may complain about the delays or even dehumanization during the security check, it is worth recalling that security officers are also playing a required role. In keeping with the theme of the growth of surveillance culture, however, this chapter explores the roles played by those experiencing surveillance. This yields rich clues about surveillance imaginaries and practices, from the ground up.

The focus here is on people experiencing fairly conventional forms of surveillance, first in the security field and then in marketing. The imaginaries and practices of those negotiating airport security or deciding whether or not to use certain search terms that could be incriminating vary according to many factors. National origin, gender and, of course, previous negative experiences make a difference. Similarly, choices about whether or not to use a loyalty card or even where to shop will differ depending on knowledge and experience along with gender, class and the like. This chapter offers some relevant illustrations without pretending to give comprehensive or systematic coverage.

Returning to the airport, then, hear a sample comment from a passenger, commenting on how it feels to go through security and how personal responses might be muted at Pearson International Airport, Toronto: 'I feel like they have all the control. If they don't want me to pass through then I won't pass through, and if they want to be rude to you they can be rude to you, and I can't say anything, because I want to go on my trip.'[2]

This aspect of a surveillance imaginary is a familiar one to many who travel by air, especially since 9/11. And the surveillance practice, in this case, is to say and do nothing that could be construed as suspicious. This even extends, as one researcher found,[3] to struggling to stay silent when a whole young family, not English-speakers and not 'white', are pulled aside not just for questioning, but for treatment quite different from that accorded to pale-skinned anglophones. Here we see caution and compliance writ large. Awareness of surveillance prompts particular kinds of attitudes and actions.

Because air travel for business or pleasure is such a familiar aspect of surveillance and one that often hits the headlines with stories about new systems such as automated biometric border controls or the use of full-body scanners, it is worth starting here, at the airport. I shall return to it in the next section, too. Compliance seems widespread. Are passengers simply governed by the gaze? What exactly is this gaze, and what does it mean to be governed? Recall that the gaze may generate anxiety.[4] And as passengers know from the airport experience, such anxiety may resurface all too easily as you divest yourself of your laptop, jacket and sometimes shoes onto the X-ray conveyor under the eye of the attending security workers.

However, parallel effects may be produced, or not, by a gaze that is not literally visual and that silences us in quite different ways. Passengers may find the full-body scanner at the airport threatening or potentially intrusive on their privacy, but in a broader context, what of journalists, bloggers and texters who discover that they are traced or tracked because of trigger words they have used? Such 'chilling effects' may be devastating. They affect not only the individual but also touch on the prospects for the journalistic profession, and indeed for democracy itself.

In each case, passenger or internet-user surveillance, emotions are aroused. Fear is a powerful means of obtaining compliance or of silencing voices. And because anxiety, fear and uncertainty are so easily and frequently associated with the term surveillance, they have to be brought properly into the picture. Academics in particular often tend towards dispassionate and distanced analyses but risk failing to recognize realities of life beyond the cool and rational. One colleague, reading an early draft of my book *Surveillance after Snowden*, exclaimed, 'where's the outrage?' An apt reminder that attempts to get the facts straight may forget that the facts are sometimes intolerably in your face. Needless to say, I revised the text.

Of course, not all surveillance automatically triggers fear-filled performances or debilitating chilling effects. It does not. There may be 'warming effects' too. Surveillance is not necessarily sinister. The purposes it serves may be positive ones. Not long ago I spent time in hospital and after surgery it was important that my vital signs be monitored. I noticed one day when the nurse came in to my ward that rather than asking how I was feeling she simply said she was pleased to see my healthy heart rate. But you haven't checked it yet, I replied. Oh yes, she responded, there's a remote feed to the screen by the nurses' station. We monitor you the whole time.

Surveillance is not only a constant and familiar fact of life, it is also in flux. The faces of surveillance alter over time and in different settings, and as surveillance expands our imaginaries and practices mutate as well. At the airport, to return there for a moment, the performances vary considerably for different passengers. Part of the script is given by the fact that travellers are already sorted and ranked by how much they paid for the flight, placing them in different queues and then in different seats in the aircraft cabin. But the perceived position of the passenger within that hierarchy will also lead to improvisation and even pre-security practising of roles. Again, at Pearson Airport, families that consider themselves to have a 'Middle Eastern' or 'Muslim' appearance take pains to tidy beards, speak no Arabic and to reduce the amount of conspicuous clothing.[5]

People know, in other words, that they are watched and modify their moves in ways that fit their imaginaries. At the same time, there are also contexts in which people try to watch back or at least watch as well. Such practices will again depend in part on the kinds of imaginaries within which constantly shifting experiences are placed. The use of smartphones to record police activities in traffic pull-overs or at protests is now answered by the rapidly rising use of police body-worn cameras. One could be forgiven for seeing this as a game, using developing devices, to outsmart the other in surveillance strategies.

At the close of this chapter, threads are drawn together by examining that frequently heard slogan, a routine phrase from many surveillance imaginaries, 'if you have nothing to hide, you have nothing to fear'. This seems to be taken by many as a sound basis for compliance, and its media-amplified repetition by government and corporations reinforces its apparent plausibility, not to mention its prominent place in many surveillance imaginaries. Is it really true at the airport or when you are pulled over by police? If not, then not only is its place in surveillance culture factually questionable, it is also ethically and politically so.

In a moment, I shall return to the airport and its security surveillance to consider more fully what happens there, from the passenger perspective. But first I want to highlight the significance of a term that has already cropped up several times in the introductory section: emotion. Ideas such as performance depend on a sense of how situations feel to those experiencing them. If you feel fearful, threatened or overwhelmed, this affects how you see yourself in a given situation – perhaps powerless, subordinate – and thus how you respond. Those surveillance imaginaries and practices are bound up with your 'performance'.

The emotional life of surveillance

The cases of airport performances and chilling effects discussed in this chapter should give us pause. They suggest that the impact of security-related surveillance is to create insecurity and with it anxiety and fear. These could, of course, be unintended consequences of augmented surveillance. But it is also possible that the so-called shock doctrine strategies of some governments may play into this,[6] in which case they may be rather more intentional. According to the shock doctrine, exploiting some natural or constructed crisis to introduce some new or controversial government measure is a deliberate strategy practised by many around the world.

Not only this. If experiences of airport security and of internet use are sources of uncertainty, anxiety and fear, then they also engage human emotions in profound ways. Needless to say, the scope of emotions is huge and the study of emotions sometimes overwhelming. Social scientists have not always been good at including emotion in their analyses; too often they are 'all mind and no heart'.[7] Yet surely human agency has to be thought of in terms of the heart and not merely the mind? More particularly, in the realm of surveillance studies, with some exceptions there is a surprising disconnect between descriptions of how people's rights might be 'trampled' or their privacy 'invaded' and the emotional content of how those people *feel* about such surveillance trampling and invading.

This disconnect is perhaps all the more surprising when one considers how emotions themselves have been placed under surveillance. One thinks, for instance, of post-9/11 efforts to use facial recognition technology in video surveillance to capture the micro-expressions – such as lip twitches when answering questions – on passenger faces in the airport. This is intended to yield clues about unusual emotional behaviour that might indicate a threat.[8]

Or, more recently, consider the 2013 experiment in which Facebook was accused of emotional manipulation for adjusting the positive and negative content of users' newsfeeds to demonstrate what was said to be a contagion effect. Many users were upset, saying that they were 'creeped out' by the experiment. Some cancelled their Facebook account; others angrily commented: 'you can't mess with my emotions; it's like messing with me!'[9]

The issue of trust also rings bells here. The breaking of trust is an emotional matter par excellence, whether mediated by security surveillance or social networking sites. Trusting relationships, as both Georg Simmel and Erving Goffman taught, depend in part on the person's ability to manage their visibility, however partially, before others, whether individuals or organizations.[10]

It is important not to forget that, while expressions of anger or irritation come from the lips of individuals, emotions are not only a psychological – still less merely a physical or chemical – matter. A sociological understanding places emotion in a social context. Of course emotion is subjective, but in this view it is also *inter*subjective, arising from encounters with others. Emotion is an aspect of daily life, as we interact with friends, associates, neighbours, family. In her classic *The Managed Heart*, Arlie Hochschild sees emotion as being rather like language and thus 'best understood in relation to its social context'.[11] In other words, emotion may helpfully be thought of in 'interactionist' fashion.

Thankfully, several scholars have addressed the question of emotion in relation to surveillance, from studies of how surveillance operators are affected by their work,[12] through to why questions of privacy should not only be examined in abstract, legal ways. On the latter point, the studies of Julie Cohen stand out, in which she stresses the need for considering how people under surveillance are embodied, subjective persons, in relationships with others and themselves. They are socially constructed selves who continually engage in efforts to manage the 'boundaries' between themselves and the surveilling eyes of government, corporation and, we shall suggest, other internet users.[13]

So-called boundary management is the way of limiting the visibility of others.[14] But this does not occur in universally similar ways. Both Valerie Steeves and Priscilla Regan take this up in discussing the ways that young people value opportunities to limit access to their online activities.[15] In this case, the emotional aspects of online users are threatened by unwanted surveillance because it exacerbates the sense of vulnerability to others within the general stresses of social interaction.

Negotiating airport security

There is little doubt that you are under scrutiny when you go to an airport. You expect to have your details checked at the airline desk or electronic check-in. You know you have to go through security. There, your boarding card is verified and your hand luggage goes through the scanner while you walk through the electronic archway and possibly get wanded as well. If you are at London Heathrow or some similarly equipped site, a biometric check is added to the mix. You have to stare into a camera for a second or two. And if your destination is in another country, customs and immigration services will also require more data. No one will be surprised to learn that you are also watched by video cameras, even though you may have been too preoccupied with the other searches to notice where they are.

In Canada, those video screens may be viewed by operators at the airport, but the images from major international airports are also available in the headquarters of the Canadian Air Transport Security Authority in Ottawa. So while you struggle through security in, say, Vancouver, someone 3,550 kilometres away may be watching. Not only that, they can also check their screen to see the X-ray of suspicious objects in your bag.[16]

In the US, successful tests of 'whole body imagers' led the Transportation Security Administration to decide in 2009 that these be phased in, in preference to walk-through metal detectors. They provide X-ray images of the unclothed body seen only, passengers were told, by operators at a remote location, unable to connect the image with the person being scanned.[17] These machines were later modified to produce clearer images of inanimate objects, less clear ones of the bodies. The same kind of equipment is in use in Canada as well, although across the Atlantic the European Parliament rejected whole-body scanners in 2008.[18]

The airport experience is very much one of performance. Not only is there a heavy emphasis on acting, but for some, notably so-called visible minorities, the performance must be practised beforehand to ensure that suspicions are not inadvertently aroused. Skin colour is a prominent issue here, with many passengers worrying that their brown skin or 'Middle Eastern' appearance will impede their progress through security checks.

Some families approaching the X-ray machines at Pearson International Airport in Toronto warn each other – 'OK, speak only English until we're on the other side.'[19] As Rachel Hall notes, these everyday surveillance rituals are part of a broader, coercive performance of risk management. Potential suspects are obliged to perform their innocence by showing that they cannot be construed as a threat to other passengers or to the aircraft itself.[20]

Hall's work shows how important performance is to how airport security works. What she dubs the transparent traveller exudes the imaginary and embodies the practice of submitting to surveillance. This is how it works. Airport security logic may be seen as what Michel Foucault calls biopolitics, where people are governed by determining if they fall into one or another population category. This is not the discipline of individuals, which Foucault also explores, but politics expressed as administration at the level of the population.[21]

The exceedingly small chance of death by terrorism is played up by the 'security theatre' logic of the airport such that passengers, in turn, are all encouraged to play their parts appropriately. Those who, for whatever reasons, but especially due to their racial differences, citizenship, age, ability or religion, are less adept at producing a convincing performance experience delays, detainment or even refusal to board an aircraft.

In terms of surveillance culture categories, surveillance imaginaries prompt practices that are not merely suited to the context but that also keep that context – airport security – functioning smoothly. Thus so-called security theatre is not merely a show for spectators. Hall shows that performance helps to constitute what is known of security measures. It is not enough for people to prove only once that they are trusted travellers; they have to perform each time they arrive at the airport. If imaginaries include a phrase like 'I guess they have to do it to keep us safe', then passengers are likely to continue with the idea that attacks can be prevented, even though proving that prevention occurred is ultimately impossible. In this way, says Hall, 'we become co-creators of a shared reality.'[22]

In other words, airport travellers become complicit in the security theatre with which all have become familiar. And for all the talk of 'clearing security', it is not obvious that this is ever really possible. Security is an ongoing performance, for the whole cast. Everything hangs on what Hall calls the 'aesthetic of transparency'. To appear transparent, passengers perform their innocence and show that they are willing to open themselves to inspection and checking. Who has not observed passengers who routinely remove their shoes and belts, even when there is no instruction to do so? Woe betide those who are less than transparent, for whatever reason. The cloudiness of their performance singles them out to wait longer in line, to be searched again.

Chilling effects

In the years after 9/11, many murmured about the chilling effects of ramped-up security surveillance. But that murmur became much more internationally audible after Edward Snowden's exposure of the NSA's intrusive surveillance, often carried out on people who were suspected of nothing. Among other things, it led directly to a lawsuit against the US Department of Justice and the NSA, in March 2015. The suit cited a chilling effect that stifled freedom of speech and the free exchange of ideas on Wikipedia, the collaborative online encyclopaedia, but was dismissed for lack of evidence of objective harms, just as earlier suits had been ignored for their 'speculative' character.[23]

Since then, however, it has become clearer that a chilling effect does indeed accompany the rapid expansion of pervasive surveillance of the kind that Snowden uncovered. Working against what some suppose, that intensified government surveillance would not have significant impact, given public accommodation to surveillance generally, Jon Penney sought evidence indicating that self-censorship does indeed occur.[24] He asked if search traffic for articles on privacy-sensitive topics decreased after the shock of discovering the nature and extent of the NSA's surveillance activities. The answer he found showed that there was a significant drop in such searches and that there was a lasting general shift in what Wikipedia users were willing to search, following Snowden's disclosures. In a sense, this could be read as pulling away from performance, so this section is more about imaginaries and practices that are cooled with caution.

The idea of chilling effects has been around for decades, especially since the Cold War years of the mid-twentieth century. It assumes that people may be deterred from expressing certain views in public for fear of punishment. Legal scholar Daniel Solove weighs in here to propose that chilling may not only be related to the possibility of punishment but also to being embarrassed, labelled or being further tracked by authorities.[25] Either way, such chilling would in principle have an impact both on individuals and on the democratic process in general, dependent as it is on open access to information of all kinds. Wikipedia is an ideal site for such research, given its huge popularity and widespread, everyday use.

Research like Penney's and Solove's contributes much, not only to the legal process of determining whether or not a 'chilling' challenge can be mounted in relation of self-censorship, but also to our knowledge of how government surveillance affects how people obtain and share online information. This is a crucial question for the health of any democracy. It has been explored in several contexts since the Snowden disclosures began, not least in relation to the writers' group PEN, and more generally among ordinary internet users. PEN – 'Poets, Essayists, Novelists' – was founded in 1921 to promote literature, literary cooperation and freedom of expression, as well as the freedom to write and to read.

First, in 2015, PEN International launched a report on post-Snowden chilling, based on feedback from almost 800 authors, living in fifty countries. Because of the importance of free expression to their craft, writers have been described by the novelist E. L. Doctorow as the 'canaries in the coalmine' when it comes to the impact of surveillance on privacy and free expression in society writ large.[26] It showed that concern about surveillance is nearly as high (75 per cent) in democracies as in non-democracies (80 per cent). Self-censorship reported by writers – now including bloggers and other internet users – in democratic countries approaches levels reported by writers in authoritarian or only semi-democratic countries. And writers in many countries say that mass surveillance has deeply damaged American credibility as a global champion of free expression. As one British writer noted, 'most UK citizens are now under levels of surveillance that would make the Stasi seem amateurish.'[27]

Accepting this as part of their surveillance imaginary, many writers now engage in self-censorship for fear that their communications will be monitored by a government authority. For an example of this surveillance practice, 33 per cent of US writers reported deliberately steering clear of certain topics in personal phone conversations or email messages, or seriously contemplated it. Similarly, the proportion of writers in free countries equalled that of non-free countries in limiting their internet searches or website visits for 'controversial or suspicious' topics. These were striking findings that the authors of the PEN report hope might lead to a curtailing of mass surveillance in the US and elsewhere.

Also in 2015, the Pew Research Center made an extensive study[28] of American attitudes that showed a very divided nation on the question of whether the US had gone too far in restricting civil liberties or, as was previously the view, not far enough in protecting from terrorism. In 2013–14, however, the proportion switched to concern for civil liberties for several months, following the Snowden revelations. Curiously, at that time, both Republicans and Democrats were equally concerned about the impact on civil liberties. After this, however, with the emergence of 'Islamic State' or ISIS and actual attacks in the US, the proportion of those saying not enough is being done to counter terrorism has risen, especially among Republicans.

Interestingly, a large proportion of internet users (86 per cent) were taking steps to remove or mask their digital footprints, and many wished to do more but were not sure which tools to use. They clear their cookies, avoid using their real names, mask their internet protocol (IP) address or, in some cases, encrypt their email. And quite a sizeable group (55 per cent) sought ways to avoid observation by specific people, organizations or the government. This included worries about social surveillance as well as what corporations or government might be doing with their personal data. Generally, there was a lack of confidence in the security of everyday communication channels and a lack of trust in all kinds of organizations to protect their data.

The chilling effect may also be seen through the lens of ethnographic studies with particular groups, for example Muslim Canadians. In Tabasum Akseer's study of the chilling effect of security surveillance on this particular minority group, young people freely expressed their sense of chilling. The kinds of experiences they have reflect the unevenness of treatment that exacerbates the chilling effect on some segments of the population, but also drives home both the gut feeling involved and the surprising buoyancy of some responses:

> You know you just have to watch yourself. Don't be too loud, don't hang out with more than 3–4 Arabs, [laughs again] and don't grow your beard too long! Those are typical things that scream – I'm a Muslim, look at me so watch out, and control the image that you give up.[29]

All of which suggests that the chilling effects of so-called mass surveillance are real and widespread and lead to uncertainties and fears that disturb the normal routines of everyday life. Canadian Muslims certainly worry about how their internet use might erroneously incriminate them:

> You don't know who is watching you [on the internet] ... Now that you know that someone's listening to you, or someone's recording you, how are you going to react? Now people have to think of what they post, they can't just be free ... I try not to be one of those people ...[30]

The clear majority of Americans polled by Pew were keen to be in control of what information is collected about them.

At the same time, most also admitted that they struggled to understand what information is collected on them or how it is used, although this is less a feature of younger respondents. The latter also do more than others to restrict their online visibility. In general, the chilling effect seems to promote a state of fear that is hard to pin down and appears to ebb and flow in unpredictable ways.

The data dragnet and surveillance culture

So, passengers expect to be watched at the airport; this is a commonplace aspect of surveillance imaginaries. The airport is a peculiarly focused surveillance zone. You are obliged to go through security and you cannot but be aware that you are under observation at several levels simultaneously. And it is not surprising to hear of 'chilling effects' of surveillance, especially among writers and journalists. After all, their very livelihoods and often their sense of identity are bound up with how they work with words, seeking their stories and crafting them for their audience. Surveillance does elicit emotional responses, and it does provoke performances of various kinds.

But some people might perhaps be surprised to discover both how much is seen and the ways in which ordinary people are seen, and how they – wittingly or unwittingly – allow themselves to be seen, playing a role in what is actually seen. If it were not for the fact that novelist Franz Kafka's *The Trial* is about a mysterious police probe into his life, for reasons that he cannot fathom, and that leaves him increasingly frustrated and frightened, it would be a good image for consumer surveillance in the twenty-first century.[31] Consumers may have a vague sense that they are profiled and tracked but generally lack inside knowledge of how their data are collected, compared and calculated, let alone why and with what effect.

Thus what can be known about consumers' surveillance imaginaries and practices is more limited than the literature on those of either airline passengers or journalists. What evidence there is often comes from sensational stories about massive data breaches – even though these are more often in public services – or highly intimate disclosures that embarrass family members or those with romantic attachments. I shall refer to one of these later, but the 2015 case of Ashley Madison, where hackers published details of 30 million users who were using a dating site for people who were already married, is a case in point.[32]

When security agencies defend their data-gathering strategies of vacuuming up data and 'collecting it all', the notion of a data dragnet sounds plausible. Yet you never need to go close to an airport or complain publicly about the government to be under scrutiny. Surveillance is ubiquitous. Some is literally visual, done using cameras, but much surveillance does not involve literal watching at all. You are 'seen' in your bank records, cellphone calls, bus passes, workplace IDs, loyalty cards at the supermarket, passports, credit cards, healthcare and social security numbers, on Google, Facebook and Twitter, only some of which have any visual dimension. But a lot of personal data can be seen. Some, as from airport security cameras, are fine-grained, or, as from whole-body scanners, quite intimate.

However, the data-dragnet metaphor applies just as much – if not more – to the corporate sphere of consumer surveillance as to security agencies. In order to grasp how the emerging surveillance culture develops, it is vital to have some sense of how personal data became so valuable, so avidly sought after and so difficult to imagine or respond to. Today's watching is driven by new dynamics. In part, it is an economic logic: personal data are assiduously sought by consumer corporations and marketers, making them valuable as never before. An organizational logic also plays into the mix, for example, moving management from risk to precaution. Plus, of course, a techno-logic; many organizations as well as, now, individuals have access to the means to amass and process personal data that was never available to the legendary little old lady behind her net curtains. Behind all these lies a cultural reliance on watching and visibility; to see – and, as discussed in chapter 4, to be seen – is to be sure. Supposedly.

In a world of much-hyped Big Data, fine-grained fragments of information are sucked up, stored, combined, analysed and interpreted in ways that do reveal patterns of life but are also subject to much potential error, especially when they are used in an attempt to predict behaviour. A classic example is when the megastore Target inferred from purchases of lotions, supplements and cotton balls that a Minnesota teen was pregnant. Her father, displeased, complained, but it turned out that Target knew better than he did. She was indeed pregnant.

However, as maths professor Jordan Ellenberg points out,[33] the creepier scenario is when the algorithms get it wrong. As he argues, Netflix and Amazon do not have a very high rate of success, but it is enough to satisfy, usually. If similar algorithms are deployed by predictive policing programs or 'homeland security', the dangers are obvious. At the same time, as we shall see, the customers' own imaginaries and practices play into this, especially but not exclusively as people perform on social media.

Supermarket surveillance

The same kind of social sorting logic applies in supermarkets and superstores as in airports. To get a sense of this, I look at a British, an American and a Swiss supermarket chain and a Canadian hardware chain, before turning to how consumer surveillance is experienced, understood and responded to by customers.

Tesco, a major British supermarket chain, runs a database, through a subsidiary, called Crucible that profiles every consumer in the UK with personality details, travel habits, shopping preferences, degrees of greenness and levels of charitable generosity.[34] Crucible says that in a 'perfect world, we would know everything we need to about consumers ... attitudes, behaviour, lifestyle. In reality we never know as much as we would like.'

The Tesco subsidiary uses a software system called Zodiac for 'intelligent profiling and targeting' so that, together with Crucible, a map is generated of how individuals think, work and shop. Consumers are classified into one of ten categories: wealth, promotions, travel, charities, green, time poor, credit, living style, creature of habit and adventurous. The Clubcard is used as one data source, but added to that are huge international data brokers such as Experian, Claritas and Equifax, and public sources such as the electoral roll, Land Registry and the Office of National Statistics.

Why is all this worthwhile? Just because the company knows better where to focus its energies, which customers to court with offers and which to ignore. Data Analytics has become a watchword at Tesco, with an increasingly complex set of categories into which customers are placed. It is widely viewed as a leader in the field. The company organizes the databases carefully, to avoid conflict with the UK's Data Protection Act, but it is amazing just how fine-grained their data are.[35] And curious how such an inscrutable scheme is constructed in the name of 'care for the customer'.

In Canada, an executive at Canadian Tire, the electronics, sports, automotive and kitchenware chain, decided back in 2002 to make a precise inventory of all credit card sales.[36] What could this show? Well, people buying generic motor oil were less likely to pay debts than those buying brand names. People buying carbon monoxide monitors or felt feet for furniture to protect floors would also pay back quickly, unlike those buying chrome-skull car accessories. Drinking in a particular bar in Montreal was associated with bad risks, while buying premium birdseed was not.

Psychological profiling was the next step; folk who buy felt feet protect their belongings and their credit scores as much as their hardwood floors. This way, the company knows who to spend time on when they register for baby showers or weddings and whose credit lines to cut when they see their credit cards used in pawn shops or for marriage therapy. The latter uses could easily flag bad risks if they also lose their jobs.

The use of personal data for all manner of purposes, often well beyond what might be imagined, shows that it makes sense to speak of this as surveillance. Personal lifestyles can be 'seen' in fine-grained and intimate detail through the profiles constructed not only by police or security officials but also by corporations. Of course, the customer may not agree that hanging out in a particular bar is associated with not paying credit card bills, but to the company that shopper is part of a statistical set that cannot fully be trusted. Here, too, we can discern those three logics at work, the economic, the organizational and the technological. Those personal data are surprisingly valuable (there is an extremely big market for them), especially to organizations keen to reduce the risks they face (like defaulting credit card holders), and smart software and statistics are available to help maximize their use (this is part of the 'techno-logic').

Customers of all kinds inhabit a closely watched world, both visually – think of those ubiquitous video surveillance cameras, frequently in stores – and virtually – think of the digital profiles by which customers are seen metaphorically. The video image has its consequences but so, equally, does the digital image. Today's surveillance imaginaries are often aware, but hazily, about the fact of ongoing surveillance, and fuzzy about how it actually operates. Interestingly, however, when chain stores started involving customers in their own monitoring, this opened a crack in the door through which those who took up such opportunities could see better what was happening. So why do companies use these kinds of surveillance?

Along with security agencies, database marketing was perhaps the most obvious site for surveillance to be found from the 1990s onwards. One data source for this was loyalty card programmes, a domain where data appetites mushroomed.[37] Such surveillance appears as a form of biopower, where data mining is utilized to reveal patterns of consumption, as in the Canadian Tire example. Recall that biopower is Michel Foucault's term for the means used by institutions of all kinds to regulate people's lives. As he explains, it is the 'administration of bodies and the calculated management of life'.[38] It is how populations and groups are dealt with, beyond the individual disciplining power of surveillance of which he wrote elsewhere. What is more, this marketing biopower is strengthened by emerging projects which aim to use consumers' data for purposes beyond pure marketing, such as obesity prevention or monitoring the intake of food additives.

In 2008, for instance, the American retail store Safeway launched the now discontinued Foodflex programme, an initiative enabling consumers to monitor their own nutrient consumption.[39] The technology was able to make personalized product suggestions so that participants could improve their diets and consumption profile. These recommendations were in accordance with US Department of Agriculture dietary guidelines. In a similar way, Migros, the major retail chain in Switzerland, uses what they call a Famigros programme.[40] This scheme offers advice on how to achieve things such as consuming healthily, losing weight or feeding a newborn baby. These recommendations are derived from official governmental sources. In these ways and others, biopower, based on data derived from both government and corporate sources, may be coupled with data from those enrolled in performance-improvement schemes to enhance that 'calculated management of life'.

All such schemes, now also seen in various available apps, depend increasingly on consumer interaction with the analyses. Feedback loops are created in which the data collected may in turn be appropriated by those who are the subjects of the data, thus leading to fluctuations in the datasets themselves. As consumers discover how the corporations work, so they join the game. A curious twist to this, from the point of view of the social sciences, is the way that those whose behaviour is analysed may alter their practices to the extent that the original analysis must be modified. In the later part of the twentieth century, this kind of process was used to show how the social sciences differ from the natural sciences. In the human, rather than natural, sciences, research subjects have the chance to learn of the research and modify their behaviour accordingly.[41]

Despite some legal and technical limits, personal data streams went from a trickle to a flood such that it is now impossible to follow all the conduits and rivulets back to their source. As well, new techniques of data capture and, especially, analysis were developed, often under the 'Big Data' banner. 'Metadata', a term not noticeably in the public domain until Snowden's leaks, became a crucial source not only of security-related intelligence but also of commercial surveillance. Where some might once have worried about the content of specific photos, videos, texts, messages or calls being publicly displayed in contexts where they might be compromising or embarrassing, now the data dragnet gathers all kinds of apparently trivial fragments of information, including dates, times, locations or call durations relating to communication or transactions, that can be analysed for patterns and trends more easily and sometimes more accurately than combing through content itself.

We know you're watching

Surveillance imaginaries only exist insofar as there is some awareness of being watched and what that might mean for one's place in the world, one's opportunities or one's limits. While some watching is surely surreptitious and while there may be some spheres of surveillance about which internet users are unaware, few have missed at least some signs of surveillance culture. One does not need that sixth sense that alerts us to a hidden watcher; the cameras' tinted domes decorate the ceiling and advertisements pop up on the screen relating directly to some keywords in the freshly sent email. And, as in the case of weight-watching or healthy eating, some surveillance data are modified in real time through the data subject's conscious responses to it.

If, for instance, you drive onto the toll highway ramp, like Highway 407 in Ontario, without going through tollbooths (because there are none), the cameras will capture your licence plates. Even though the car carries no windshield transponder, the bill will drop into your mailbox anyway. You may order a pizza from a big chain but be aware that they know your topping preferences just from the phone number. Indeed you may have to make it quite clear that this time you do *not* want 'the usual'. There is, in other words, some knowledge of being under surveillance that prepares you for a bill from the toll company or reminds you to be specific in ordering pizza.

So knowing that you are watched is an important aspect of surveillance culture. Surveillance today may in some cases be covert but in many situations the subjects of surveillance are aware of what is happening. The data-entry clerk or call-centre operator knows that keystrokes are counted and that calls are monitored for quality control purposes. The trucker is aware that the truck carries a 'How's my driving?' sign on the back, by which passing motorists may call the employer when some particularly bad – or good – driving is observed. The consumer wandering the street, window-shopping, can clearly see the sign saying that the store is under video surveillance, just as the internet surfer is aware that the sites visited often include their privacy policies that explain what personal data gleaned by the owner may be used for.

Among those who are aware they are watched, changed behaviours may result. My local drug-store clerk never fails to ask if I have an Optimum Card – a loyalty programme membership – when I make a purchase, to which I invariably reply, no, and then, no thank you, when I am asked if I would like one. Other stores often ask for telephone numbers and postal codes, and again, one can hear varied responses. Some simply comply, while others ask why it is necessary or just refuse. Such refusal depends, of course, on prior knowledge – an element in a surveillance imaginary – that such apparently innocent data may become a key for connecting with other personal data. And questioning such everyday surveillance – a surveillance practice – is, from a privacy perspective, a commendable response.

However, such acts of questioning or resistance, while important, are unlikely to be very effective in themselves, given the huge imbalance of power of organizations that carry out surveillance, compared with the solo refusenik. Without doubt, some acts of citizen surveillance may be significant on a larger scale, as when photos or video are shot by protesters during demonstrations, such as those following the queried election in Iran in 2009, or in the spate of police shootings of black men in the US that became notorious from 2012 when a neighbourhood-watch volunteer killed teenager Trayvon Martin.

But, more often, acts of self-protection – which are also signs that people are aware of surveillance – such as putting privacy settings on 'high' on Facebook, covering the laptop lens with tape or having the phone camera at the ready downtown 'just in case', are unlikely to have much effect. While citizens are often encouraged by many means to protect themselves, the larger, truly political question is whether or not ordinary citizens can challenge surveillant organizations to care appropriately about the personal data they handle. The accountability for doing surveillance is far more significant than our personal preferences and practices relating to whether or not we are surveilled.

We have more to say about resistance to surveillance, but at this point it is worthwhile examining another phenomenon; the ways in which surveillance may be not so much avoided as adopted. Surveillance cultures seem to spawn other levels of watching. Rather than eschewing surveillance, some seemingly embrace it.

You can watch too

You are watched and you know it but do you care? Another dimension of surveillance cultures is that people respond intentionally to surveillance. As we shall see, some even do surveillance for themselves. Perhaps as a response to the question of why large organizations should have a monopoly on monitoring, but more likely for mundane reasons, ordinary people start to watch too. The technologies for so doing are already at hand. This includes using smartphones to find others using GPS technology, checking through social media networks such as Facebook to discover details on neighbours, colleagues or friends, installing nannycams to keep an eye on the babysitter, or snooping into your children's internet surfing.

Extreme ways of reversing the gaze, or watching back, include Steve Mann of the University of Toronto who has a camera secreted in his glasses or, even more imaginatively, Rob Spence, also in Toronto, who dreamed of having a digital video camera installed in his artificial eye. Mann is a walking history of prosthetic technologies for extending his visual and audio capacities; he has spent more than twenty years perfecting the craft. He will turn his wearable camera lens on, say, overhead shopping mall cameras and record his consequent exchanges with retail staff. Rob Spence, originally from Belleville, Ontario, is a filmmaker who aspires to be what he calls an 'eyeborg', watching and recording those in his field of vision in order to make people more aware of the surveillance that is everywhere.[42] He has had several upgrades to the original video 'eyeball' such that it now resembles any prosthetic eye.[43]

I suspect that few aspire to be eyeborgs, but this does not mean that people never engage in do-it-yourself surveillance. If you google the word surveillance, and even more, if you add the word camera, plenty of suggestions come up about why you need your own surveillance system and which company will sell you the equipment for installing your own. 'Protect your home and business from vandals,' offers one. 'Free shipping, free tech support,' sirens another. And of course, for bargain hunters a 'discounted selection of new and used surveillance cameras at low prices' is promised on eBay. The idea is to be able to check on who is at the door or on the property, or alternatively to keep an eye on those you know are there, such as your children's nanny or your pets. Harold Hurtt, former police chief in Houston, Texas, thinks that domestic surveillance cameras are such a good idea that they should become part of the building code.[44]

While Harold Hurtt may have public safety as a priority, in North America most people deploying their own surveillance systems do so from simple self-interest or to protect family members from harm. There is much activity in the realm of what might be called snooping or spying on the others, especially where parents are concerned. According to a Pew internet and American life study, more than half the parents surveyed said they used either monitoring software to inform themselves about their children's online activity or an internet filter to block access to inappropriate sites.[45]

In Brazil, however, setting up one's own surveillance system may have much to do with your opinion of public surveillance organized by the police or the city. Many Brazilians opt for private security systems because they do not trust the public ones. They are suspicious of the motives and operations of the police and the judiciary. Doing one's own surveillance seems better suited to the interests of the family and the community.[46]

So the surveillance culture not only becomes visible in the large corporations using high-tech means to track and monitor the daily activities of consumers, but may also be seen in consumers' awareness of and responses to surveillance. Even more strikingly, the culture of surveillance is evident when ordinary people start to use surveillance themselves in order to organize their lives, protect their homes or family members, or to check up on what their partners or children may be doing. Or parents. Some families in the US have agreed to have aged relatives who are suffering from Alzheimer's or some other memory-inhibiting disease implanted with a radio-frequency identification (RFID) chip to try to prevent them from wandering too far or to find them when they are lost.[47]

At the same time, popular media may ring some warning bells about the limits of aping the collect-it-all mentality of government agencies or consumer corporations. In the 'Entire history of you' episode of the *Black Mirror* series, it is precisely exploiting the capacity to record and play back everything that makes relationships unravel, devastatingly.

Today's surveillance culture is unprecedented. Never before has so much time, energy and money been invested in watching others, and never before has such watching been so consequential.

Now we have surveyed some of the key dimensions of surveillance culture, what may we conclude? In our everyday lives, people are watched in an extraordinary number of ways and contexts. But they are also increasingly aware that they are watched and in some respects appear to have made their peace with this. Indeed, inspired perhaps by the prevalence and availability of new surveillance devices, many are even prepared to adopt some surveillance strategies for themselves. This is clearly not merely about 'us and them' where the watching is all top-down. This is why we can speak of a surveillance culture. Surveillance has become a way of life, a key aspect of how we think about the world and operate within it on an everyday and sometimes almost unconscious basis.

Nothing to hide, nothing to fear?

At the start of this chapter, I promised to comment on a common phrase – nothing-to-hide-nothing-to-fear. Probably originating in a biblical text – rendered in contemporary

English as 'Decent citizens should have nothing to fear'[48] – it features prominently as government propaganda in many countries, encouraging the 'innocent' to believe that however surveillance systems are reinforced, their lives will not be affected. And judging by opinion polls and anecdotal evidence from everyday conversations, many accept this as part of their surveillance imaginary. It follows that their surveillance practices will also reflect such ideas.

Because the nothing-to-hide-nothing-to-fear phrase is intrinsically attractive, because people have become accustomed to surveillance, and may have come to terms with aspects of the new reality and are complicit in user-generated surveillance, and because many even set up their own private surveillance systems, this does not mean that some basic questions are not in order. The idea of a surveillance society was once associated with police states, with repression, and was rightly seen as repugnant. Within these, having nothing to hide certainly did not keep fear at bay. Orwell's classic novel *Nineteen Eighty-Four* begat the language of Big Brother to describe a state of affairs of impugned innocence to be resisted at all costs.

But, Orwell notwithstanding, the surveillance society arrived, not wearing the heavy boots of brutal repression, but the cool clothing of high-tech efficiency. It came not from an authoritarian state[49] but from companies claiming to know their customers better so that they could provide just the goods and services they wanted. It showed up not as a looming telescreen with the fearsome face of Big Brother, but on a million screens of social networking sites and of handheld devices marketed as convenient, cost-effective and customized. Surely in this world, having nothing-to-hide-nothing-to-fear makes sense?

The fact is, today's surveillance is deeply ambiguous. Efficiency, convenience and customization are not generally seen as enemies. And nor are they just a Trojan horse, to trick people into thinking a gift conceals an enemy. No, to some degree genuine social benefits are available from the new surveillance technologies that also promote and extend questionable modes of monitoring and tracking. This is true of surveillance systems run by both government agencies and consumer corporations. The crucial question to ask about the new visibility is how the system actually works and how it operates in different contexts.

Once, in societies that accepted the rule of law, in which the vital presumption of innocence was upheld, it was fairly safe to assume that if you had nothing to hide, you had nothing to fear. Authorities had the right to search out and make visible only those who might be hiding something. Of course, no system is perfect, but in general and in many countries this rule could be trusted. Today, the assumption that if you have nothing to hide you have nothing to fear is being systematically undermined by the new surveillance.

Of course, even such undermining is not a uniform process. If we return to the kind of Canadian experiences that informed the earlier discussion of airport passengers, it is clear that opinions about surveillance differ. While more open and flexible outlooks have grown in Canada generally over several decades, now more than isolated pockets of the population worry about the risk of terrorism and associate such risks with newcomers.[50] A third of Canadians now say they change their travel plans due to potential attack risks, and one in four think that police should be allowed to listen in on phone calls or read texts without special warrant. The same people are more deferential to traditional authority.

On the other hand, two-thirds of Canadians are more open to immigration, less accepting of police snooping and believe that seeking crime-and-justice responses to terrorism is more appropriate than augmenting police powers of surveillance without increased accountability or turning to violent measures. These are also more willing to learn from diversity and do not automatically defer to authority. Clearly such shifts in what pollsters call values also lie behind evolving surveillance imaginaries and practices.

Remember the case of the bar and the birdseed? Where you choose to drink in Montreal may flag you as a bad risk in seeking credit. You are simply caught in the wrong company according to Canadian Tire. Remember Tesco-Zodiac's 'intelligent targeting and profiling'? The whole point of this is to place people in consequential categories so that they can be treated differently. The same goes for the 'webwise' software that classifies people by browsing habits, not just by their visits to one page. You are where you surf. From such automated assessments, decisions are made about everything from creditworthiness to levels of after-sales service, and from internet speed to the ability to keep a bank account. And if you are already marginal or disadvantaged, the system will ensure that these vulnerabilities are magnified, through the effects of what Oscar Gandy calls 'cumulative disadvantage'.[51]

But it does not stop there. These kinds of classifications are also used by police, intelligence services and other authorities. After 9/11, the agency that would become Homeland Security made a priority of calling customer relationship management companies to help them locate and identify not potential customers but would-be terrorists.[52] Classifying, clustering and excluding certain groups work here too. And the same strategies trigger the inclusion of innocents on no-fly lists and watch lists, ordinary homes within police hotspots in the city, and peaceful pedestrians as 'possible suspects' as they walk under cameras, shopping or simply coming home from work. This is how Canadian high-school students like Alistair Burt have been refused permission to board planes when on family holidays, and innocent citizens like Canadian 'suspects' Maher Arar, Ahmad El Maati, Muayyed Nureddin and Abdullah Almalki ended up in Syrian torture chambers in 2002 and 2003.[53] Even without reasonable grounds, and with nothing to hide, you can still end up as a suspect.

Yet, because there may be apparent benefits of some kinds of surveillance and because it is so hard to know how some kinds of seemingly trivial data – birdseed? – could possibly make a difference, there is relatively little outcry against surveillance overreach, allowing it to grow almost unimpeded. As well, the positive effects can benefit some people, and their negative effects are predominantly felt among those who, because of their economic situation, ethnic background or gender, are already disadvantaged. On the other hand, as the examples of Montreal drinkers or teenage holidaymakers show, anyone may be affected negatively. There are some real safeguards, such as privacy and data protection laws, but they tend to be effective only in extreme cases, when there is some obvious or well-known violation or intrusion.

Most of the time, the real risks of this new surveillance affect people negatively when those systems are working correctly, for their intended purposes, and within the limits of law. Social sorting, especially when it uses searchable databases and networked communications, works through automatically categorizing people's data so that different groups may be treated differently. Simply being in a statistical group sets you up for inclusion or exclusion, access or denial. Having nothing to hide simply does not help to protect you from any negative effects that surveillance might have.

Conclusions

Starting with performances at airport security and the chilling effects of state surveillance for internet users and journalists, this chapter has explored some facets of surveillance culture in relation to some rather familiar forms of convenience, caution and compliance. Clearly, it is not just state agencies but also corporations that are involved in surveillance of rather extensive and intensive kinds. The latter, corporations, may well be more, not less, significant than surveillance by state agencies. Many understand this, too, but also comply, this time for the sake of convenience and the possibility of reward.

In the following chapter, I examine the ways that surveillance is far less obvious than in airport security or loyalty card systems. In much-hyped ideas such as the internet of things or smart cities, surveillance seems to change character to become much more taken for granted. It becomes, as it were, part of the furniture, and as it does so, aspects of the culture of surveillance mutate as well. This is not just because the part played by the machines has become less perceptible. It may be because the very contexts within which surveillance occurs are metamorphosing, in ways that it would be unwise to ignore.

3

From Novelty to Normalization

In 2016, Nest, part of the Google family, was awarded a patent for a smart crib, embedded with sensors, that lets parents know what the baby is doing and what the baby needs or wants at that moment.[1] It sends an alert to the parents' phone if the room is too warm or too cold, and even responds to the baby's mood with appropriate music or a cartoon screened on the ceiling. Now, patents frequently do not produce the goods, but this one is plausible, given popular interest in using the internet of things in pregnancy and child-rearing. In surveillance culture terms, it reflects beliefs about the efficacy of digital monitoring of children and the growth of practices involving parental reliance on embedded devices that alert parents to children's conditions or activities.

Critics of many stripes may well worry about such devices, and serious warnings are already available. Tama Leaver, for instance, observes that such 'intimate surveillance' is in line with other already available products and potentials for parental monitoring and also for mediating information about their children online. He cautions that the use of such systems could normalize the idea that intimate surveillance is a necessary part of caring for children today, and that parents not taking advantage of smart cribs or platforms for sharing information about their children online could be seen as failing in their responsibilities.[2] The novel opportunities offered by digital technologies may be attractive to some, but they may also come with a negatively normalizing price tag. The smart crib exists at present only as a patent. The smartphone, however, is an everyday reality. The smartphone is an iconic symbol of the present era of digital communication. It began with the Blackberry's mobile email device in 1999, to which voice calling was added in 2002. The meteoric rise of the iPhone after its launch in 2007 has set the pace since. However, that 'since' is only a decade to the time of writing, 2017, ten years of massive competition between Apple's iOS and Android devices, where Samsung is the biggest player. The novelty lies in cleverly combining desirable features into one pocket phone. The normalization that occurs lies in their use becoming commonplace, taken for granted, within those few short years and in the fact that their surveillance aspects – whether for watching or being watched – are so seldom seriously considered.

I sometimes feel a bit foolish when I think of a phone as something you use to call others, to hear the voice of the other and to, well, chat. Of course, they are still used for that purpose, on which I was raised with landlines, but it is no longer their primary use. Texting, taking and sending pictures, finding one's way in a strange city, even tuning your guitar – any of these and more is what phones are now used for. Old telephones could be tapped by police or intelligence agencies or, more prosaically, operators with their plug-in switches could not only connect you but listen in to the call – these were the limits of audio-surveillance by phone.

Today, smartphones are central to the emerging new attitudes and activities that I have dubbed the culture of surveillance. They have a captivating cachet with their addictive apps and at the same time are so ubiquitously familiar that *not* to have one is in some contexts to be marked as a curiosity. Basically, the smartphone is the embedded medium par excellence that connects users with data in everyday life. They are not just familiar, they are in many ways indispensable to contemporary life. They are used for many commercial transactions, including ticketing and online banking, as a way of being informed about breaking news, working out the ideal route for a trip, and checking what bodily symptoms might mean for personal health, among multiple other tasks. The commonest uses in the US, as in many other places, are for text, voice, internet and email.[3]

The explosion of awareness that smartphones are a treasure trove of data led to their uptake for predictive policing, security intelligence, consumer data analytics and the like. They are surveillant at several levels, in terms of the data they display. Just as 'loyalty' programmes that earn profits for businesses are promoted as 'rewards' systems, so what one might call these 'personal tracking devices' – PTDs, for short – are marketed as 'smartphones'. At a basic level, they are 'logjects'[4] – objects with embedded software that monitors and records their own operation. In a so-called data-driven world this is highly significant because much of the users' data is available to both telephone and internet companies, through data brokers to other companies and, under certain conditions, to government and policing agencies as well.

Social media data mining is explored more fully in the following chapter, but the factors propelling its development are important here. Data on users and their online behaviour are critical whether for commerce or for policing, especially as more and more transactions, communications and social activities generally occur online. Targeted advertising is the commonplace consequence; spectacular disclosures about the NSA and other 'Five Eyes' members is another. Each requires analysis, including explorations of how these apparently diverse spheres of government and commerce are linked with each other. And they are sometimes linked together, as house-holder Pauline Cook discovered when she asked 'Alexa', Amazon's Echo digital assistant, if she was connected to the CIA. Instead of answering, Alexa simply shut down – twice. It became evident that the connections are indeed strong and serious.[5] 'Alexa' could not deny that Amazon and the CIA have connections.

To grasp what is going on, however, one has to move beyond the level of alarmist approaches and paranoid predictions to examine the ways in which data accumulate, with the rapid proliferation of sensors in smartphones and many other contexts and the ways in which human behaviour is affected, for better or worse, by deliberate attempts to manipulate outcomes. As Sara Degli Esposti cautions, the really important issues are how certain approaches to data analysis become standard, what assumptions are implicit in these data management systems about human beings as persons, and how human identities and mutual relationships are affected by these developments.[6] This also stretches to the political level, discussed later in the book, of data justice. Some things may be discovered by interrogating the systems, others by examining everyday life experiences that are at least partially shaped by them.

This chapter looks at ways that people have become culturally familiar with rapidly growing surveillance under the signs of mobile communications – typified by the smartphone – 'smart cities', the 'internet of things' and 'wearables' such as health and exercise devices like Fitbits. I look first at the example of facial recognition technology. Then, after seeing how fascination and then familiarity with the new are a longer-term phenomenon, we examine some explanatory factors such as invisibility, fascination, convenience – that can be understood in terms of surveillance imaginaries.

Beyond that, we examine some possible consequences: not noticing surveillance as such, becoming inured to surveillance, taking it for granted, going along with or even engaging in surveillance. These emerge in practices whose significance as surveillance starts to fade from view. This in turn has larger consequences: namely, the development of new modes of organizing everyday life where algorithms play an expanding role, and the clustering, classification and class divisions and other inequalities that result. In other words, our imaginaries and practices may contribute to the needless enlargement of large-scale surveillance as well as the emergence of user-generated surveillance.

Facial recognition: normalizing the questionable?

Clearly, some surveillance technologies may be used in quite different contexts and user experiences of them might thus be very different. A case in point is facial recognition technology, FRT, which has been popularized online through its use on platforms such as Facebook but which may also be used by an officer in a police cruiser to check on someone who may be a suspect. Put like that, it is difficult to see how the two could be considered in the same frame, of surveillance. But what if using FRT in the one, social media, context made a difference to how it is viewed in another, policing, context? Might the playfulness of one context produce a downplaying of its seriousness in the other? Could the novelty of one lead to normalization of the other?

This is explored by Ariane Ellerbrok, who asks under what conditions previously controversial or unacceptable technologies might be made palatable, or even embraced?[7] She responds by highlighting the role of play in accounting for the social life of surveillance technology. After all, play has a marketing logic as well as being an important cultural practice. Could play help to ease the way for controversial technologies that may have very serious implications? If so, this puts a twist into Johan Huizinga's classic analysis of play, which he saw as something different from everyday life, and from profit-making or politics: a separate world.[8] In the case of FRT, the play, the game, becomes a part of everyday life yet serves to support wider commercial and governmental goals.

FRT is a biometric technology that uses algorithms to match unknown faces with previously existing images of known persons in a database. It is used by police and security agencies and was widely marketed after 9/11 as a key tool in anti-terrorism initiatives.[9] But as Ellerbrok observes, FRT has more recently become available in consumer contexts for photo-networking and organizing personal digital images. It is best known in Facebook tagging. In this context, pleasure, convenience and entertainment are much more in view.

FRT is controversial in its original military, policing and security contexts, not least because there is evidence of its use in subordinating certain groups along racial, ethnic and class lines. It is also viewed by some as being redolent with both criminality and with state control of a 'hard' kind. But when Google Picasa and iPhoto Faces started offering FRT opportunities to customers, it seemed to have few if any threatening or negative features. On the contrary, it was convenient and facilitated fun – it was even 'feminized', suggests Ellerbrok, in contrast with its original 'masculinized' uses.[10]

Ellerbrok also makes the telling point that the photo 'tagging' now used extensively on Facebook and other platforms seems to have no associations among users with electronic 'tagging' of offenders as a means of criminal identification and tracking. Indeed, the potential for errors in photo tagging is seen as a source of humour – they are funny as well as fun. In this case, even mistakes are entertaining, quite beyond the convenience of photo-organizing programs. FRT may be associated in this case with lightheartedness, escapism and even fantasy.

The errors made in tagging may amuse, but in fact Facebook's recognition rate is high because each time a face is viewed, say, from different angles, the machine learning program improves recognition efficiency. An agency such as the US Federal Bureau of Investigation (FBI), on the other hand, has only a limited number of images, often taken face-on, like a driver's licence photo. Their recognition rate is, understandably, lower than Facebook's. Some have objected to the facial recognition dimension of some apps such that, for example, Facebook's 'Moments' was launched in Canada and Europe in 2016 without FRT.[11] It is far from uncontroversial.[12]

It may be a short step from tagging friends on Facebook or using iPhoto's recognition system to seeing the technologies themselves, in this case FRT, as relating to play and from there to the role of play in obfuscating, normalizing or marginalizing the technologies. 'Soft' FRT may appear far less ominous than 'hard' and thus contribute to a certain dissociation of FRT from the hard contexts, says Ellerbrok. Play may also help to foster normalization by making FRT more acceptable through photo-sharing and the like. Lastly, play may also permit the marginalization of certain groups as games involving 'spying' offer pleasure from placing members of such groups in a subordinate position to the user.[13]

Of course, the serious and the playful are mixed messily in practice – games may be played in serious contexts and play may also take a more sombre tone in others. Play could well have a role in legitimating once controversial technologies, a situation that appears again in the following chapter. Playfulness lends weight again to the notion that surveillance imaginaries and practices are implicated in how surveillance of certain kinds may have a fascination through association and then become acceptable where once they may have attracted scepticism or disapproval.

More needs to be done to grasp how play relates to surveillance. This requires close, ethnographic studies of everyday social situations. But the Ellerbrok proposal is plausible, that the use of facial recognition in the context of playful checking of photos could reduce the seriousness of issues raised by FRT both in this and in other – policing and security – contexts. In this case, the enjoyable surveillance practices associated with tagging and related apps may help to inform surveillance imaginaries in ways that yield a more sanguine attitude towards FRT in other contexts. There is, however, some evidence from large-scale studies about how the public's attitudes to surveillance might change. This is examined later in the chapter.

Part of a bigger picture

Whether it is the smartphone itself or some function or app that allows for checking the identity of someone in a photo, these are historically unprecedented possibilities. The devices and what can be done with them offer new potentials. Novelty attracts attention and may even be expressed as *neophilia*, a term popular with some hackers for the 'love of the new'.[14] It may be seen in the way that smartphone users may queue up for a new version of each smartphone. Over time, people may become more familiar with what once seemed amazing, normalized to possibilities – including the ongoing potentials for surveillance – available using such devices.

But fascination with the new is not itself new. One wonders, for example, if today's fascination with so-called driverless cars is as big as was awe around horseless carriages a century ago. Even *Brave New World* writer Aldous Huxley seems to have been thrilled with the latter when he noted in the 1930s that the 'drug of speed provides the one genuinely modern pleasure'.[15] Are there digital equivalents to Huxley's apparently avid attraction to the 'drug of speed'?

Just as the horseless carriage took time to develop, so too the shift towards 'assisted' vehicles has been in process for a long time – at least since power-assisted brakes or steering. The actual slow progress does not stop enthusiasts such as Tesla chief executive Elon Musk from claiming that the 'Autopilot' function is 'almost twice as good as a person'.[16] Many seem to be intrigued about these possibilities, especially if they already have features in their car that hint at further automation to come. Such openness to the new plays a role in informing imaginaries and, because of that, practices – which, as we have argued, then become carriers of the imaginaries, sometimes in a widening spiral.

What is not so often considered is the way that the assistance, in vehicles as elsewhere, comes primarily from computer systems that have steadily been colonizing cars and trucks for many years, and what this might mean for surveillance. Because such systems are constantly recording and reporting where the machine is, how it is operating, as well as what the user might be doing, they are highly surveillant in practice. But they are surveillant in ways that differ from earlier forms of surveillance – they depend on the continuous collection of data through sensors.[17]

Autonomous vehicles are in the news, and the safety of passengers has been a recurring theme in discussions of their likely impacts. This is appropriate, of course, and must remain a priority for makers of self-driving cars. However, the computer systems that assist such vehicles, rendering them increasingly autonomous, have many dimensions. A key aspect of this is how instructions are given to the car, not to mention how the car communicates with the user. In order to work well, much data have to be entered, in an ongoing way, about potential routes, stopping places – for coffee or other errands – time, pick-ups and the like.

Those data necessarily reveal much about so-called self-driving cars and their users, which it may be possible to keep 'self-contained' inside the vehicle, as with the experimental Google car. Such vehicles contain a mother lode of personal data on their users, such as where they travelled, for how long, at what speeds, where they stopped. However, one suspects that a more likely scenario is one involving interconnected vehicles in a road-user network, where information is shared in order to keep the whole system running smoothly.[18] Information may circulate about other users, road conditions, weather, along with GPS location data. Indeed, these data may be advertised as contributing to the enhanced safety of the vehicle. In the US, the Department of Transportation already has a Connected Vehicle Program to coordinate existing forms of assisted driving in preparation for their further development.

The autonomous car may seem like a dream for harried drivers, but the draw, convenience, also comes with possible drawbacks, including unwanted surveillance. This is nothing new, of course. Precedents were set with the Uber car-hailing service, an app that allows users to hail a ride remotely, but also collects tremendous amounts of data with the familiar rationale – to improve the service for users. For instance, in 2015 Uber initiated a new data-gathering technique that involved continuing to collect information on passengers' whereabouts even after their ride was over. This prompted a complaint in the US from the Electronic Privacy Information Center (EPIC) to the Federal Trade Commission, on the grounds that it 'far exceeds what customers expect from a transportation service'.[19]

This raises questions about how some are drawn to new technologies, from the digital computer to the internet of things, with a sense of wonder and the thrill of the new. And how these things soon become familiar, taken for granted, especially when they are invisible and do not fit traditional definitions of surveillance and privacy. In Orwell's twentieth century, a vehicle deemed to be surveillant would have been deliberately bugged. In the twenty-first century, it is commonplace for vehicles to be surveillant in the sense that they record their own use, and those data are available for scrutiny, even before autonomous vehicles are common. It would be easy to become blasé, assuming that new, self-driving cars are safer, part of today's world and therefore basically beneficial or at least neutral. In the case of smartphones, clearly, many enjoy the convenience, the contact with others, even the aesthetics and feel of the devices. Desire *for* devices is significant. They offer status, approval, enjoyment.

Sexy surfaces

Such sentiments are also true of the main player in this drama, the smartphone. The ways in which users are fascinated with their digital tools vary considerably, but Apple aesthetics give some interesting clues. No Silicon Valley company has managed to achieve quite the status of Apple when it comes to design. It appeals to what began as 1960s countercultural values that are both stylish and empowering. Apple was non-conforming and clearly aspired to the imaginative and even to liberation. What the iPad or iPhone can do is important, but the medium, the device, is itself designed to delight.

The lure of the seductive surfaces is acknowledged, for example, by *Guardian* writer Jonathan Jones, who admits that the iPad is not the easiest machine for writing – yet that is how he uses it. He admits that 'I am captivated by the beauty of this piece of technology'.[20] As he says, it was the 'soft machine' aesthetic that succeeded from the start. At a time when science fiction was foreboding, worried about a dark, inhuman future of disembodied users staring into screens, Apple offered what seemed to be a simple, human alternative, machines that accompany us in daily life, to whatever location we wish – on public transport, in the café, in the street.

While computing machinery has been seen as sexy and attractive and has been given personal names for a long time, this has been particularly true of the iPhone era. They are seen as objects of desire, even, says Deborah Lupton, as 'edible' or 'delicious'.[21] They may also be thought of as being intimately attached to their owners, as extensions or prosthetics for the body, associated with personhood. Users may even think of themselves in cyborg-like terms, particularly when the iPhone is unlocked with a fingerprint or with facial recognition rather than a password.

Interestingly, British psychological researchers found that the very choice of phone may be a predictor of some traits.[22] While iPhone and Android devices each have roughly half the market, it is younger people, more frequently female, who own the former, seeing it as a status object and not caring that so many others use the same device. More men than women use androids, however, and they appear to be less extroverted and less likely to seek personal gain. The researchers point out – of course – that from their findings one could predict who might buy an iPhone or an Android device, but also that our devices may become more like us, leading to unease when someone else uses our phone. How far your image of yourself matches the profile created by those with access to your data is a question of imaginaries meeting analytics and what happens to each when they do.

At the same time, the sheer convenience of computer machines is also part of their fascination, and how they become so familiar. As a Pew study of so-called millennials found, this first 'always connected' generation depends on convenience: 'Steeped in digital technology and social media, they treat their multi-tasking hand-held gadgets almost like a body part – for better and worse. More than eight-in-ten say they sleep with a cellphone glowing by the bed, poised to disgorge texts, phone calls, emails, songs, news, videos, games and wake-up jingles.'[23]

But this is about more than being excited about new technologies. It is also about how so many new technologies are embedded as sensors in the routines of everyday life and how inconspicuous they are. Once, sociologists spoke of 'cultural lag',[24] meaning that cultures take time to catch up with technological change and that some dislocation or distress may occur in the process. The notion does still have some resonance with what is happening today. Except that with the consumerist pressures to embrace the new, the idea of cultural lag now seems more complicated. And, of course, the responses to the new technologies vary depending on factors such as age, gender, race and class. Not everyone lines up for the newest phone; many users are actually quite ambivalent about them, even before questions of surveillance are raised. In the Pew survey of smartphone use, while 46 per cent of American users polled said they 'couldn't live without' their smartphones, 54 per cent agreed that they were 'not always needed'.[25]

But more is going on than just some acclimatizing to the new. The context itself is shifting. While the familiar may become 'normal', it also happens in this case because surveillance institutions are changing – notably with consumer monitoring and tracking and the growth of the data industry – and this in turn may portend a larger-scale shift. Building on past developments, dominant cultural expectations now incline many populations to individualism, and towards self-exposure and self-promotion, topics considered in the next chapter. Here we are concerned with issues of how new technologies are often seen as boons to convenience or security, but how they are also imperceptibly surveillant. It may turn out that fears of potentially damaging surveillance in vehicle computer systems, the subtly normalizing effects of features such as facial recognition on Apple or Google devices, or worries about how users' own surveillance may negatively affect others play little role in surveillance imaginaries and practices. Ignorance or unconcern may be just as important.

But these features of digital modernity are still worth considering and studying carefully. Given the substantial political-economic role of these new devices and systems, ignorance and unconcern may well have negative consequences, not only for individual users but for wider issues such as democratic participation and human flourishing itself. So the focus requires sharpening.

We turn next to reflect on how far this may portend the rise, not only of those much-hyped smart cities, the internet of things, and 'wearables' carried on your own body, but of a new way of organizing consumption and of modelling business. It may one day be widely seen as knowing capitalism,[26] or perhaps better for our purposes, surveillance capitalism.[27] This view, too, deserves more than a passing thought.

Part of the furniture

A defining feature of surveillance culture is the state of technology. The use of interactive and smart technologies shifts the focus from fixed to fluid surveillance, from hardware to software. Data from the smart electricity meter show whether or not you are at home. Your smartphone logs your location and your 'likes' as well as whom you contact. But this occurs within a wider cultural context in which gauging risk and opportunity are central, anticipating the future is a key goal, and of course where economic prosperity and state security are locked in a mutual embrace. The result? Smart surveillance and social sorting go hand in glove. And together, they inform and inspire surveillance imaginaries and practices, which in turn help to enable or constrain the further development of smart surveillance.

But what sorts of imaginaries and practices emerge from the increasing ubiquity of computer-based things? Having a sense of the cultural meanings of things like the smartphone and anticipating futures are contributors to surveillance culture. They are undoubtedly modern, 'rational'. But what of the ways in which such things become part of the *Lebenswelt* or lifeworld? How do they affect surveillance imaginaries and our practices? This is a much less modern-rationalist kind of question. It relates to a shift that occurs when we think less of these computer-things as 'tools' – where function and efficiency to 'users' are paramount – and more as 'presence', where the specific user and context are crucial.

The smartphone is an ideal example of a technology as 'presence'. Things like this enter our lives; some people sleep with their devices by their beds, showing that they have fully accepted, welcomed and domesticated them. They do not simply exist, out there. For some, they are like prostheses, artificial body parts, on which the user depends and which the user treats seamlessly as a taken-for-granted and necessary part of the body.[28] Philosophically, we are now thinking in a more phenomenological fashion about how people 'dwell' with computing machines, rather than merely 'interact' with them.[29] We are asking what they *mean* to us, not just what they 'do'.

Embedded, wearable and mobile technologies slip easily into the routines and regimes of everyday life. They are purchased by people for whom they often offer seductive, convenient benefits, including personal enhancements. Most obviously, with mobile and then smartphones, the device becomes a part of life, a personal object not just a communication tool. But more generally, as ubiquitous computing and the internet of things develop, both designers and 'users' become more aware of the need for appropriate 'interfaces' that diminish the 'distance' between users and their machines. Hence, for instance, the items of clothing that contain sensors that are otherwise in personal tracking devices like Fitbits.

One good question is, how do users start to use the device or system? How is it 'invited' into daily lives, consciously or not? It depends in part on how it is presented, or presents itself, to potential users. Is it an appliance with functions, or does it represent a particular expression? When people see others' things, especially their devices, and what they do with them or to them, they get a sense of what they mean to them and how they are part of their lives. Albert Borgmann contrasts the 'device paradigm of modernity' that works by commodifying wants and desires with what he calls 'focal things' that ask for attention or involvement; they are engaging centres in human practices.[30]

In these ways, aesthetics become important in considering smart technologies of surveillance. What the machine expresses is significant. This depends on its location in time and space much more than the mere technical specifications that it possesses and which the retailer will play up. The machine may be built to be fast but in the world of 'dwelling' it is not necessarily so. Its 'presence' is likely to be long term. Users may even develop ways of using phones that are distinctively theirs; they have been invited and welcomed into their lives in particular ways. Of course, the machine may then become, paradoxically, no longer unique, just another building block of users' lives, like things made of wood or metal. In this sense, it is not only embedded sensors that 'disappear' but also the thing itself, the computer.

Smart cities and surveillance culture

Embedded sensors and the computer-communication systems that support them are also (dis)appearing in urban environments. They often do so under the banner of 'smart cities', which are described as built environments – both new and retrofitted – integrated by such computer-communications systems along with the internet of things. Enthusiasts think of them as intelligent platforms for the life of the entire city. And there are, doubtless, benefits for citizens – note the connection between this word and city life – to be gleaned from more creative uses of available data. However, critics worry that the ancient and complex task of city building cannot be reduced to computation.[31] Data are always collected in particular contexts and all such cities are bound to be surveillant, whether in obvious ways using street cameras or drones, or through less than obvious data centres and smart meters.

In such contexts, it is easy to see how smart cities could become incubators for surveillance culture. If you live in an urban area described as smart, then the informational infrastructure will be taken for granted and its novel features will be normalized. The disappearance of more familiar markers of surveillance activity will be matched by the seeming ordinariness of monitoring and calculating the 'optimized' city. Watching and being watched are hard-wired into the smart city. To explain what I mean, we may travel to the long-promised green-field smart city of Songdo.

This new, built-from-scratch city nearing completion near Seoul, South Korea, is intended to be a high-tech and international business hub for North East Asia.[32] Some proposals that have been made for Songdo are to fit public recycling bins with RFID sensors so that people are credited when they throw in their bottles, and to provide pressure-sensitive floors that alert emergency services when older people experience falls.[33] Smartphones, with early popularity in South Korea, store health records and may be used to pay for prescriptions.[34] Children may be tracked – for their safety – by microchips embedded in bracelets[35] and no doubt, when they happen, smart cribs will be available for younger siblings.

This is the world of ubiquitous computing – indeed, Songdo is described by promoters as a ubiquitous city. However, bottles, floors, cellphones and even children's safety bracelets are all very tangible, concrete phenomena, and it is easy to be distracted into thinking only about them. Ubiquitous computing environments also depend on embedded sensors, mobile technologies and, crucially, relational databases. These may be less visible but they are part of what makes 'ubicomp' work.

Take relational databases. These connect the bottle with the consumer, the elderly person with emergency services and, through the cellphone, the patient with the prescription. The database can very quickly sort through a range of digital tables to make the appropriate links. Indeed, such systems sense the environment, create a context for the information, communicate internally among the relevant components, draw inferences from the available data and draw some conclusions.[36]

Behind the relational databases, of course, are management decisions – of business, policing, security, healthcare or whatever – that guide the 'conclusions' arrived at by 'intelligent systems' in smart cities. As Shannon Mattern notes, smart city pundits depend on calculating the 'effectiveness' of cities using key performance indicators – clearly a very business-driven approach.[37] But what, for instance, if the consumer, elderly person and patient were one and the same, and access to healthcare was dependent on evidence of moderate alcohol intake, as judged by which bottles were tossed in the bin? How simple and subtle surveillance could be, and how innocently associated with smart business acumen.

Without the hype of smart city utopianism, however, similar changes are occurring elsewhere. There is a push to 'informate' cities and to offer new services and benefits from electronic networks connecting previously separate functions into large-scale systems. The shift to online communications and to dependence on tracking and sensors has been a steady one and is felt every time one obtains a medical prescription, tries to contact city hall, or even attempts to park a car.

In the last case, the urban area of Santander, Spain, boasts wireless in-ground sensors that are supposed to reduce the stressful search for a parking spot and optimize the usable spots, thus also helping to reduce pollution.[38] Such systems are always likely to be ambivalent. Living there, one may well be grateful for such a system while at the same time being made aware that the system, and perhaps even someone running it, must be aware of where you are when. Another component is added to the surveillance imaginary.

In many minds, such a question immediately connects ubicomp and sensors with surveillance. Rob Kitchin, for instance, notes that would-be smart cities have surveillance systems from smart cards to automated licence plate recognition cameras, 'intelligent transportation systems' to smart meters for electricity consumption. In addition, he says, 'Urban places are also now full of objects and machines that are uniquely indexical that conduct automatic work and are part of the internet of things, communicating about their use and traceable if they are mobile.'[39] They transfer data between themselves, producing more derived data.

Because of this, some believe that so far from being utopian – as in hyped depictions of Songdo or Silicon Valley-type dreams for American cities – RFID and other wireless technologies may well have dystopian aspects. Or, at least, smart cities may end up resembling state and corporate priorities – Songdo's context of conduciveness to bicycle friendliness and urban farming notwithstanding. If everyone is observed, automatically and constantly, questions about surveillance deserve to be raised. These novel cities may foster the normalization of surveillance, to which ordinary urban dwellers contribute simply by communicating, commuting or caring for their elders.

The questions with which one is left have to do with the intensified scrutiny under which smart city dwellers live, and how this is seen and experienced by them. Will they accept the reassurances about safety and security, convenience and comfort? Or will they be brought into public debate as matters for discussion, contestation and community-based solutions that might be relevant and acceptable to all? As we build our case, we turn our attention from smart cities to another area where there is much promotion and few clear markers – wearable technologies for self-tracking. Here again, surveillance novelties may be subtly normalized.

Prêt à porter

Imagine. You show up for your first day at your new job, only to be informed that you will be wearing a device that will track your movements, your fitness and your health, perhaps even a body-worn camera or a biometric authenticator to check that it really is you who wishes to enter a secure area. The company will have access to the data you generate but you are not told a lot about how they will analyse and interpret it.

Yet it is you who will be doing the surveillance. The employee is involved in collecting, analysing and sharing information on herself. Researchers at the Surveillance Studies Centre produced a 2017 report showing that workplaces widely promote the use of wearables.[40]

Wearable technologies such as Fitbits are rapidly becoming commonplace, at least in some countries of the global north. The ubiquitous computing and internet of things mentioned earlier touch not only vehicles and buildings but, with 'wearables', human bodies as well. They enable the body to carry electronics, software and sensors. Fitness devices or activity trackers are probably the most common, along with smart watches and smart clothing. They may be straight-forward consumer goods or, increasingly, gadgets that are supported or even required for certain jobs or activities.

Wearables measure aspects of our behaviour, data that they also record, track and transmit. Fitness and wellness data are checked through the use of devices that are worn as bracelets and armlets or in clothing. However the actual electronic thing is configured, the point is that it depends on complex computer and communication technologies as well as on the user – who often imagines herself to be the chief beneficiary. In the case of wearables, it is clearly the user who is in view, regardless of who has access to the wellness, fitness, movement and other data.

However, another potential beneficiary – apart from the health and fitness corporations – is the employer. There is a market for wearables to enhance the productivity and safety of workers, both in more traditional heavy industries and in desk-based occupations. They may also assist people with disabilities or heighten the sensitivity of workers to their tasks. Of course, in workplace settings specific concerns may be expressed, such as that the employer may use the device for 'spying' on employees' whereabouts or checking that breaks are limited to the agreed times.[41]

Those who use wearables for their own purposes may do so with a degree of seriousness that goes beyond earlier forms of keeping a journal or diary. Indeed, the Quantified Self movement that began a decade ago with meetings and conferences is now a term in more general cultural use. Although more will be said about self-surveillance in the next chapter, it is worth noting here that wearables take this to a high level. They include practices such as life-logging and self-tracking in a quest for self-improvement. By knowing more about oneself, one can monitor one's health or one's personal performance in many contexts.

Users of wearables display surveillance imaginaries that raise questions about the normal – 'Am I doing this correctly?' 'Is my diet regime paying off as expected?' 'How am I performing in relation to my peers and my past?' Their actual practices, then, follow from this; an assiduous wearing and checking of the devices to be sure that one's performance is indeed up to or beyond par. It takes little imagination to see how this, too, may well have normalizing effects as the role of data is raised to a high level, perhaps eclipsing other ways of being aware of how well – or not – a user is doing.

Deborah Lupton describes these entanglements of humans and digital data as 'lively data'.[42] She does so for several reasons, among them that the data are always on the move, shifting, changing and subject to modification based on the goals of the end users and of the parent corporations. She has in mind the whole range of smart devices and contexts and describes the emerging data practices of such users. Again, because we are considering the digital, all these practices have surveillance implications, from the interpersonal through to the monitoring activities of corporate and government organizations.

One finding common to a number of research programmes is that while people may be aware of the apparent benefits of the circulation and analysis of data for national security or healthcare, they do not know what happens to data collected from them. They may even personally value the same kinds of data when self-monitoring or fitness tracking is involved but be less than sure about why it might circulate and with what effects, on them or on others.[43]

There's an algorithm for that

In this emerging world of ubiquitous computing, smart environments and always-on devices it is hardly surprising that few know what happens to personal data – if they can still be described thus – or what effects others' use of it has on us or on others. The use of sensors, which is a large part of what makes cars, buildings or clothing smart, has to be considered in relation not only to how they respond to human presence or activity, but also to how they are programmed to function in the ways that they do. The hidden element in all this is the algorithms, the codes that guide the workings of the system.

If, as I am proposing, surveillance imaginaries and practices attend many commonplace devices, systems and situations today, it is important to find out what is being 'normalized' and how it becomes so. Digital lives are inevitably under surveillance and surveillant in some respects, but is it possible to know exactly how this works? Where does the definition of 'normal' come from, that becomes the rule by which users measure their adherence, their degree of congruence? In the digital world, it is often quipped that 'there's an app for that'. Behind the app, the wearable, the smart crib, city or phone are algorithms.

In his book *The Black Box Society*, Frank Pasquale homes in on *reputation* as a key area for considering what algorithms do. This refers to the reputations of businesses but also especially to the personal reputations of ordinary users of the internet. As he says, 'In ever more settings, reputation is determined by secret algorithms processing inaccessible data.'[44] While the internet companies and others who use algorithms claim that they are scientific and neutral, this is hard to substantiate. And when matters such as credit scoring and social ranking, not to mention decisions as to who gets onto no-fly lists, are achieved using those algorithms, it is at least clear that much hangs on how they are constructed.

There is little doubt that algorithms and indeed the Big Data practices that require them involve power relations. After all, they are used to identify potential terrorists as well as generating credit ratings or parole recommendations. In 2016, for instance, ProPublica, a non-profit, public interest newsroom, exposed how a correctional tool used for informing sentencing decisions overestimated the recidivism rate of black defendants.[45] Thus, who has access to datasets, what Big Data correlations really mean, how data are obtained and what inequalities and injustices might be caused by the use of certain algorithms are all vital questions. These are the large context in which lives are organized today. While ordinary users may rely on various devices to keep track of personal progress, at home, at work, at play, such practices are also subject to wider scrutiny.

In the end, as John Cheney-Lippold avers, 'we are data'.[46] In other words, the systems and platforms described here view their users only in data terms. From the elderly person who might fall in their smart city building to the worker who is required to wear a tracker in the office or manufacturing plant, each is known to the system as data, organized and analysed by algorithms. The same is true, of course, of the more intimate-sounding dating sites or some 'caring' infant-monitoring systems. The potential lover or crying child is understood only as data.

That power relations may be discerned in those algorithms is, in this sense, beside the point. Their ability to control, to govern is not circumscribed by rights or legal require-ments. Such 'algorithmic governmentality', as Antoinette Rouvroy explains it, ignores the embodied individuals it affects because its supposed subject is actually a 'statistical body'. As she says, individuals 'are considered as temporary aggregates of exploitable data at an industrial scale'.[47] How does this work out in practice?

Durable differences

In the effort to understand contemporary forms of surveil-lance, particularly from the perspective of those who experience it, it is difficult not to conclude that some of what happens today is quite different from the kind of surveillance normally associated with the word. The fascination and familiarity with embedded sensors or body-worn trackers takes us to a world of rather voluntary, open and even participatory surveillance that goes beyond that of national security or policing surveillance, which is often secretive, covert and coercive.

All the same, in a time of liquid surveillance, digital data flows allow the former to mix and mingle with the latter. Predictive policing, for instance, draws upon just those 'voluntary and open' sources for data that will then be repurposed for surveillance of the more conventional kind. Such policing practices are becoming popular in Europe, North America and elsewhere. They depend on using algorithms for Big Data analysis to indicate geographic shifts of crime in a city, or to second-guess who is likely to reoffend.

A perennial preoccupation of sociologists has been to discover how societies are divided and why. In modern times the idea of social classes has been prominent. If Karl Marx saw social classes forming in relation to production – those who own the means of making money over against those who have nothing but their labour to sell and nothing but their chains to lose – then Max Weber, more subtly, conceived of class in relation not only to production but also to the marketplace, to purchasing power, status and the like. But by the later twentieth century, none of these categories seemed satisfactory. Certainly, the rich were getting richer and the poor, poorer, and both situations were increasingly globalized.

While some sociologists seemed to turn their backs on class analysis and to focus on other divisions, another process was quietly under way that had everything to do with classifying populations. Its outcomes were not a bit less portentous for people's life-chances and opportunities than those explored by Marx and Weber. That process began to flourish in the 1990s with geodemographic marketing, which divided populations into clusters according to their purchasing and preferences, before morphing into an information-intensive system generally called 'relationship marketing'. The earlier phase made much of postal and ZIP codes as a means of categorizing consumers – 'birds of a feather flock together', they observed – and this process persists to this day.

The Claritas Corporation, for example, divides cities into 'urban uptown', where you might find the 'young digerati' but also a 'bohemian mix', or the 'urban core' where 'low-rise living' – 'a transient world for young, ethnically diverse singles and single parents' – or 'city roots' – 'lower income retirees' – reside. This means, significantly, that such classifications are connected with place. As Claritas Corporation put it, back in the 1990s, 'you are where you live'. By which was meant, data about you correspond with similar data about others living in the same neighbourhood.

Territory is emphasized as a means of differentiating between social groups. It helps to dissolve a common distinction, seen especially in Weber's work, between class as economic situation or as material property, on the one hand, and status, as lifestyle choices and consumption, on the other. Although the hierarchies of classification, say, from 'urban uptown' to 'city roots', are clearly economic and relate to wealth, they are based on consumption patterns as the means of distinguishing between different social groups. The geodemographic analysts build on popular phrases that describe city zones, from 'SUV-friendly' to 'granola belt' to 'gritty neighbourhood'. But they turn them into classifications that have very real effects on people's opportunities.

Pierre Bourdieu wrote in the 1980s about the importance of such 'distinctions',[48] which include an aesthetic dimension which subtly sorts differences between social groups, keeping the 'lower orders' in their place. The right to classify others bespeaks considerable power, according to Bourdieu. As Roger Burrows and Nick Gane observe, while Bourdieu thought mostly of classification as a decisively government activity, such classification is now, at least initially, very often in the hands of major corporations such as Choicepoint or Experian.[49]

However, it is worth noting how, with the spread of surveillance across different domains, but often using similar codes, both state and commercial entities are involved in the process.[50] Either way, the geodemographic dimension connects such classifications with locations, places where people may feel they 'belong'. And in an increasingly individualized world,[51] such a sense of belonging is also experienced as a positive benefit. As Burrows and Gane say, where people (desire to) live, and especially where they consume, means a lot for who they are. People choose to group themselves with others with whom they believe they have features in common and this is reinforced by geodemographic and, today, social media marketing methods. Embodied individuals, in other words, began to interact with their data doubles, as an evolving aspect of surveillance practice.

Processes of social sorting are constantly in play. Some people are excluded altogether; some classified in negative ways, such that 'personal and group data are used to classify people and populations according to varying criteria, to determine who should be targeted for special treatment, suspicion, eligibility, inclusion, access...',[52] are deeply involved in the somewhat 'liquid' social classes of the twenty-first century. As Joseph Turow observes, we have to move beyond thinking only that individuals can be identified and harmed using data. Corporations construct our reputations, which in turn determine what information, consumer deals and other surveillance attention we receive. These affect our opportunities, our view of ourselves and the world we are presented with.[53] Our surveillance imaginaries and practices, in other words.

More than a decade ago, a *Report on the Surveillance Society* in the UK concluded that 'surveillance varies in intensity both geographically and in relation to social class, ethnicity and gender'.[54] 'Individuals are seriously at a disadvantage in controlling the effects of surveillance' because of wide differentials in access and influence. And, at the same time, 'Individuals and groups find it difficult to discover what happens to their personal information, who handles it, when and for what purpose.' But it is equally true, as argued here, that surveillance itself helps to create those classes in the first place.

That report noted that social sorting 'affords different opportunities to different groups and often amounts to subtle and sometimes unintended ways of ordering societies, making policy without democratic debate'. Of course, every administrative system aims to sort through differences between different groups in the population in order to ensure, for example, that taxes are paid appropriately or that benefits are distributed according to agreed criteria. And in so doing, they contribute to orderly governance. By the twenty-first century, the growing dependence on risk management and the rapidly expanding use of information and communication technologies were driving significant changes in surveillance as social sorting.

While contemporary organizations have become dependent on surveillance as their key modus operandi, surveillance, in turn, is increasingly characterized by social sorting. A focus on risk and opportunity management underlies such social sorting, and the widespread use of new technologies and their associated statistical techniques facilitates it. With the decline of shared risks within state-sponsored welfare systems, for example, risk becomes increasingly an individual responsibility and the management of those risks becomes an industry in itself. In order to streamline and organize such risks, private corporations – such as Accenture or Experian – are engaged. They use Big Data analytics to sort risky individuals into categories for differential treatment.

Data are increasingly drawn on to make inferences about persons and groups. The personal data of some may be used for the financial gain of others, raising social justice and civil liberties questions. Scoring is a key way of deciding who should receive what in terms of goods and services, or who might be a suspect or a criminal. The scoring is done using algorithms that process personal data in order to make predictions that may produce negative discrimination just because individuals are categorized as a member of a particular social group. This can affect access to healthcare, credit, insurance, social security, educational institutions, student loans and employment options. This is turn creates vulnerabilities such as unfair targeting by policing and security agencies.[55]

For example, a few years ago the UK government was concerned with so-called 'high cost, high risk' groups in British society who are vulnerable to 'social exclusion'.[56] One such group is young people classified as 'NEET' (Not in Education, Employment or Training), and according to one study a NEET seventeen-year-old is likely to cost the British taxpayer ten times more by the time he or she is twenty-eight than their counterparts in education, training or work, just because they may claim benefits, use health services, be involved with the criminal justice system or not pay taxes. Social intervention, even from the onset of pregnancy, is required to avoid social exclusion.

Thus locating, targeting, tracking and mapping the distribution of such groups is vital, as is extensive data-sharing to classify more carefully and to organize the necessary surveillance. In other words, once socially sorted, such groups – homeless people, drug users and previous offenders are viewed similarly – can expect greater and ongoing scrutiny, which may either exacerbate or ameliorate their situation.

One example does not tell the whole story, of course. Other government departments work in different ways, contributing to different outcomes. But the same basic processes are at work. In applications for a driving licence, the social sorting is fairly subtle, and produces different kinds of layering effects for persons with varying credit and purchasing histories. It is unlikely, of course, that licence applicants would guess that the speed of service received depends on apparently unconnected details like whether or not they have dealings with mail-order companies. What this does demonstrate is the increasing reliance of one agency or unit on data – and even data analysis – from another. Apparently trivial commercial data may be used to sort and make judgements about behaviours, both current and future.

On the other hand, decisions may be made to find data to control crime and violence in which some very telling judgements are made. Muslims living in Birmingham, UK, for example, found in 2010 that they were the particular targets of a relatively novel use of cameras set up for automated number plate recognition of their vehicles. These were disproportionately deployed in areas of Birmingham with high Muslim populations, under the rationale of attempting to combat antisocial behaviour, vehicle crime and drug dealing in the area, but actually paid for out of a Terrorism and Allied Matters Fund – a fact that was not made clear to the local population.[57]

Social sorting draws attention to the ways in which the processing of personal data for surveillance purposes of various kinds contributes to the drawing of social distinctions. People are sorted into social categories (these may include gender, socio-economic, religious and ethnic/national) so that their classification may be used to distribute opportunities and risks according to the criteria of the surveillant organization. The 'pie slices' are cut in a number of ways, sometimes subtly and complexly, but with very real consequences in the everyday world of work, travel, consuming and relating to official bodies. As the examples show, the distinctions are often reinforced in the process, as well.[58]

It is important to recall that, as the *Surveillance Society* report says, 'no one voted for such systems. They come about through processes of joined-up government, utility and services outsourcing, pressure from technology corporations and the ascendancy of actuarial practices.' Social sorting is nowhere an official, legislated process. It is one in which statistical categories determine differential treatment for different population groups, directly affecting their life-chances and opportunities. But while it clearly affects social ethics and justice, it is not in any sense subject to democratic participation.

What Charles Tilly once called 'durable differences' are now enabled by the 'smartness' of the internet of things and Big Data applications. The rules are now embedded in software protocols, making them even less visible to those whose daily lives are affected by them. But it is not impossible, as the geodemographic marketing example shows, that aspects of their data doubles may be made visible to the embodied persons that generate them. If this were to occur, it would bring new factors into the surveillance imaginaries and, potentially, new surveillance practices.

Conclusions

This chapter has explored some ways in which items that start life as attractive, even seductive, novelties end up contributing to a process of normalization of surveillance. In everyday life, people respond to surveillance as it is increasingly embedded in the contexts and routines of everyday life. The flagship of this process is the ubiquitous smartphone, but it is also evident in more abstract-sounding processes of smart city development, the internet of things and wearable devices in which communication between objects, and between objects and persons as well as between persons themselves, is creating new sorts of relationships between data and people.

One important way in which surveillance imaginaries and practices have taken on a new dimension is that they have become decidedly participatory. This is not to say that earlier forms of surveillance require no participation – you still have to be on the street for the camera to detect your presence or at airport security to have your bags and details checked, and to play your role. But today, participation is a much more obvious feature of surveillance – users know that their phones, wearables and other gadgets and platforms are interacting with their activities, even if they do not understand the extent of that interplay.

Participation has been noted here in several contexts beyond smartphones – facial recognition technology, building sensors, self-tracking devices, even semi-autonomous vehicles – but it is always negotiated between various actors whose intentions and actions still have to be explored and translated.[59] This 'participatory turn', as Julie Cohen calls it,[60] becomes even more evident in the world of social media and gaming that the following chapter explores. As yet, its implications are hard to understand by those involved with it, not least because the algorithms that guide their operation are opaque to users.

Conventional forms of surveillance, seen in national security or policing, are not generally associated with aesthetic pleasures and tend to elicit instead various kinds of caution and compliance. With the ongoing levels of innovation in new media, along with growing familiarity with everyday forms of baked-in surveillance, cultures of surveillance develop that are less anxious, often because they are consumer related and play on features such as convenience or conviviality. This means that they may themselves become quickly taken for granted as necessities for everyday living or that they may serve to domesticate aspects of more obviously law-and-order-producing surveillance.

But the key innovations of the twenty-first century, seen here in smartphones and social media, are associated with some deeper changes. On the one hand, so-called soft surveillance has some subtle ways of ensuring compliance, for instance through social sorting, that reduces the options open to consumers or users. And on the other, explored in the next chapter, is evidence that surveillance practices increasingly include more conscious complicity in our own surveillance and engaging in do-it-yourself surveillance. We look at each of these, and other aspects of participation, in the next chapter.

4
From Online to Onlife

You do not have to be in security or policing to conduct serious surveillance. Any laptop offers access to intimate, business or criminal aspects of almost anyone's life. Ada Calhoun, for instance, found out early that as someone often given the tabloid task of finding out about people who had just died, social media were a boon. As news broke of the 2011 shooting of American Democratic member of Congress Gabrielle Giffords, for example, she quickly found the alleged shooter's MySpace page, a photo in a local newspaper and a YouTube manifesto. Indeed, 'any original trace of information ... could be a place to start tracking down someone's bitter ex-girlfriend or paranoid self-published novel'.[1]

With no training in private detection, anyone can easily find out a lot about people not known to them, for whatever purpose. This chapter explores how this happens, from the viewpoint of those for whom watching has become a way of life. I doubt that a large proportion of those who do the kind of 'social surveillance' discussed in this chapter have a professional – or even macabre – obsession with finding out about recent deaths. But many internet users find that social media are a key means of finding out about what is happening in the lives of their friends, not to mention strangers with whom they had no prior connection. It is a mundane matter.

However, while social media do supply the much-needed means for keeping in touch with others, the research indicates that face-to-face contact is still vital to deeper relationships. Indeed, the order of events is often the other way round: people use the technology to maintain contact with those already known to them. As for checking out strangers, more investigation is needed. Some of this may be idle curiosity or the fascination of following apparent links. Another part relates to so-called fandom, snooping on celebrities. In neither case will there be any intention to attempt developing a friendship with those under such private surveillance.

Watching is now a way of life, and nowhere is this more clearly seen than in everyday online activities. As we shall see, this did not come from nowhere. Television culture in a sense prepared the way. And, of course, it is not just 'watching'. Communication occurs, especially on sites that permit direct messaging – above all, texting. Watching others is part of the story, but becoming visible to others watching is the other part. Chatting, playing or arguing about politics or religion are ancient pastimes. What is new is the wider audience for such activities, with members able to join in or comment.

Social media writ large, including sites where people create personal profiles, post photos and videos, participate in networked gaming, share links to memes, comment on news stories and gossip with friends and family, are a key context for considering the devices and desires relating to such watching. True, in the early days of digital exploration, cyberspace was often conceived as a separate sphere from 'real' life. Within a few years the conceptual gap narrowed as it became apparent that cyberspace had actually taken root within everyday life. In the shift from online to onlife, rather than thinking of digital communication as an activity where wariness of being watched was warranted, it became a zone where people wanted to be watched. To be watched was to be seen, acknowledged, perhaps even recognized, a space where status could be affirmed.[2]

As people become immersed in life online, or – as networked devices have become embedded in the lived environment and taken up within the context of everyday interactions – onlife, their sense of the social is being shaped in new ways, and surveillance is just one aspect of this. On the one hand, surveillance by commercial organizations is in tension with their consumers' behaviour, where being free to choose is the watchword. On the other, 'social surveillance', initiated by users, expresses, among other things, consumer behaviour, where desires to look good to or compete with others or even to be a celebrity are prominent. The cultural currents from online to onlife are thus marked by profound ambivalence.

So the surveillance imaginaries and practices associated with onlife differ only in some specific ways from those that might be met at the airport, in the workplace, or simply when walking down the street. You may assume that they are or feel like quite different contexts, until the US border official wants to check your Instagram account. The changes here connect most clearly with issues of what human life entails in a digital era, how subjective experiences are tweaked and how identities are formed. The ambiguities of being watched and watching others, now digitally deepened, affect social relationships and responsibilities in ways that are just becoming apparent.

This chapter begins with the turn towards more participatory activities online and its possible consequences for surveillance culture, particularly in the ways that desire features so strongly in a world of devices. There are initiatory as well as responsive practices here. The former are associated with social surveillance, the latter with consumer surveillance. So the question is not just why so many users allow their data to be seen and used by others but, also, why people engage in high-tech but small-scale surveillance themselves.

In order to understand this properly, however, a bit of background is needed. Conventionally, the sorts of issues discussed here – under what circumstances should personal data be available to others and how far is it appropriate and possible to limit such access? – were thought of, at least in the Western world, as questions of surveillance and privacy. How did this change during the twentieth century, in everyday imaginaries and practices surrounding earlier technologies of communication such as radio and television? This background offers some insights into why social media and gaming have been taken up so enthusiastically today.

Even with such a background, however, some find it hard to imagine why, when social media and gaming seem so surveillant, ordinary users would apparently give up their personal data so freely and fully. This, which we have already met earlier, is often called the 'privacy paradox'. Once again it recalls the language that became culturally important in widespread ways in the twentieth century. Here, while we recognize that, for some, the privacy paradox seems real, we shall also try to relieve it of some of its paradoxical character.

In the first quarter of the twenty-first century, the privacy paradox must be re-evaluated. The stimulus and incentive to share all manner of texts and images online despite what we now know about the organizational appetite for personal data may seem paradoxical. Here is the central question: Why do people permit their personal data to circulate within internet companies, especially in social media, when those data are made available to both marketing corporations and to government departments or police agencies?

To answer this question we shall focus on social media and gaming to discover the specific directions that they have taken. So we examine 'social surveillance' as a phenomenon in which the opportunities for watching others are appropriated by users. Who is doing surveillance – if that is the right word – now? And as for gaming, we explore this briefly, too, to discover the commercial driver that also uses the coin of personal data in yet another realm where desires are patently powerful and devices facilitate their fulfilment.

Having done that, we shall be in a better position to consider the meaning of these shifts. There are two key areas to consider. First is whether the desires, such as to be seen, really mean that we now 'love Big Brother'. John McGrath argued an important case, that surveillance may be both enjoyable and desirable,[3] but we also have to ask about the relevance of other concepts, to be explained in a moment, such as scopophilia, narcissism, soft surveillance and the outsourced self. Each has been proposed as a way of thinking about the privacy paradox – of why people so freely give up their personal data in a surveilled world.

The second area to return to is this: in the world of social media, where apparently voluntary engagement with checking and tracking is commonplace and therefore unexceptional, is it still correct to speak of 'surveillance' and 'privacy'? Are there other ways of understanding this that help us grasp the actual imaginaries and practices of social media and gaming?

What happens when ordinary users have their say about what they are doing and thinking? Do these signal a new era of 'post-surveillance' and 'post-privacy', or is that going too far?

A participatory turn?

The realization that some might knowingly and willingly participate in surveillance began to dawn before social media were invented. One of the first to comment on new ways of thinking about surveillance in which people play an active role in the production of images was Hille Koskela, writing about reality TV, mobile phone images and, in a phrase that already sounds quaint, 'home webcams'.[4] Without diminishing the need for traditional analyses of surveillance, she proposed that the novel practices – 'empowering exhibitionism', she called them – associated with these new media present strong reasons for rethinking surveillance, in terms of new forms of looking, seeing, presenting and circulating images.

Not long after, when social media were still a novelty, some started to note the 'fun features and entertainment values' of surveillance[5] and also drew attention to the participatory forms of surveillance that were becoming available on social networking sites.[6] They also concluded that in such contexts, surveillance could be 'potentially empowering, subjectivity-building and even playful'. Rightly critical of views that separate online from offline social life, Anders Albrechtslund suggests that, in this context, surveillance is seen not as controlling or disempowering but in much more positive ways that are wrapped up with the socializing that gives social media their attraction.

While acknowledging that other assessments of online surveillance see possibilities for amplifying already-existing commercial or state surveillance, Albrechtslund shows that social media users are likely to see things differently. They are constructing their identities through self-revelation – even exhibitionism – and through monitoring others in an ongoing way. Checking up on information that others share is vital to the social life that makes social media hum. In other words, online surveillance as understood through the imaginaries and practices of its users is not necessarily as sinister or coercive as its critics might think.

However, the participatory turn may also be seen in a rather different light. For instance, while Julie Cohen freely accepts the futility of trying to regulate online surveillance without taking note of the playful sociability of social media, she also demands that such participation be viewed in a larger context.[7] For her, the participatory turn occurs within a political-economic shift from the surveillance-industrial complex in which surveillance was seen as a necessary evil, to what she calls a surveillance-innovation complex in which it is viewed as a force for good. With the former, efforts were made to regulate and contain surveillance as something that might constrain civil liberties or invade privacy. But in the latter, surveillance moves into a context where it is seen as exempt from social and legal control.

Commercial surveillance environments are positioned as places of play and gaming. Foursquare, Groupon and Nike+ are all examples used by Cohen to show how game-playing encourages the engagement of users to increase their level of data-sharing via rewards systems, to facilitate targeted marketing and to keep them returning to the site. And, of course, other kinds of social media also rely on similar strategies to retain their users. Facebook and others send constant reminders to intermittent or occasional users, telling them that their activity level is low or that they have missed many messages or posts.

So what are appropriate ways to evaluate the participatory turn? Clearly, cultural shifts include the apparent collusion, at least with consumer surveillance, by ordinary users who may seek the best deals or simply engage with new media to position themselves favourably in their social world. A certain playfulness has to be acknowledged along with actual game-playing that has also become a leading online pastime. Failing to appreciate the ways in which participation is a central feature of online practices, framed by fresh imaginaries of what online life signifies, will mean missing the meaning of surveillance today.

At the same time, everyday involvement in social media in their multifarious dimensions does not occur in a political-economic vacuum. There is a price to pay, even for 'free' services and platforms, and that, as many warn, is that those users and consumers may not realize that they are in fact the commodity or, in another realm, the suspect. Their surveillance imaginaries and practices also make a difference to how well the systems that construct subjects as commodities or suspects actually work. So the question then becomes, with what sorts of knowledgeability do so-called users participate in social media and gaming. What sorts of concerns characterize their assessment of the media that absorb social life today?

First let us look at the ways in which desire is expressed, before considering how this point was reached, historically.

Devices and desires

Little did Thomas Cranmer, sixteenth-century author of the General Confession in the Anglican *Book of Common Prayer*, imagine that five centuries later a 'device' would be a common noun for an electronic gadget carried in one's pocket. In his day, it meant something negative, an underhand stratagem, a trick or a falsehood, a mask, rather than a machine. Thus it twinned neatly with 'desires', which could also hold sinful significance – it was in a confession, after all – in the prayer: 'We have followed too much the devices and desires of our own hearts'. By the end of the twentieth century, P. D. James's brilliant detective thriller *Devices and Desires* made the engineering connection with 'devices', but the desires still connote the dispositions of the possible murderers.

The story told here is one in which apparently negative surveillance stratagems can become the object of very strong desires. Culturally, there is a turn from a much more Orwell-inflected watching-averse world to one in which being watched is welcome, even to the point that many social media users especially start to watch others more deliberately. Context, as we shall see, has become a critical factor. Our grasp of this will be helped by a key article by Kevin Haggerty and Richard Ericson, on the surveillant assemblage,[8] in which they in turn invoke the insightful studies of Felix Guattari and Gilles Deleuze.

Haggerty and Ericson maintain that it is mistaken to think of surveillance only in terms of centrally organized systems, as the Big Brother and panopticon metaphors often do. Rather, fluid forces or 'flows' work with mutating 'assemblages' of items that come together simply to operate systems of power – Facebook and the US Department of Homeland Security would be examples – quite unlike traditional political science models of government. The flows of the surveillant assemblage are secured by desire, which for them is an 'active, positive force' – not just a 'lack' – in Deleuze and Guattari's work.[9]

All sorts of desires come together in today's surveillant assemblages. As Haggerty and Ericson note, 'surveillance is driven by the desire to bring systems together, to combine practices and technologies and integrate them into a larger whole'.[10] And it does not deal in bodies, traditionally construed, but is seen as a series of signifying flows, brought together so that the body – itself an assemblage – can be known, or rather, reduced to information. Such information, as Mark Poster pointed out, becomes our data double[11] which is how we are 'known' by marketing companies and government departments. What Poster might not have guessed is the extent to which people are now willing to trade on their data double, to accept benefits of convenience from the loss of control of their double.

As Haggerty and Ericson also note, in what is almost a footnote, wanting to ensure order, control and management may not exhaust the list of desires relating to surveillance. Its 'voyeuristic entertainment value', seen in CCTV footage or TV shows like *America's Dumbest Criminals*, indicates other dimensions of desire. However, those dimensions are visible in another work by Deleuze and Guattari, *Anti-Oedipus*, where 'desire is a machine and the object of desire is another machine connected with it'.[12]

This can translate into a situation where users themselves are desiring machines, connected with other desiring machines, their devices and the apps and platforms found there, suggests Bernard Harcourt.[13] Constantly checking for new messages, posts and images, driven to more than nine hours a day online, having a hard time pulling away from the pressure to be always available, always alert to pings and vibrations, these are signs of a culture of desiring machines. For Deleuze and Guattari, the source of much desire lies in this realm as in others; it is consumerism that 'liberates the flows of desire'.[14]

Thus all those devices become increasingly present in daily life; users dwell with them, and they want them. As Harcourt says, people enjoy playing with their videos and texting and Facebooking so much that surveillance of all kinds is permitted and fostered. 'We just *want*, we just *need* to be online, to download that app, to have access to our email, to download that selfie.'[15] If this is explained by desire, then it must be desire understood as *interests*, in this case those unleashed by association with consumerism.

Accordingly, desire plays a prominent role in this surveillance imaginary, something unsurprising from the psychoanalytic perspective of Lacan, for whom desire is the very dynamic of human agency.[16] This is important, says Charlotte Epstein, because it may, paradoxically, be the reason why privacy remains both a personal and political goal, even though, as Nissenbaum insists, it must be construed contextually. This is discussed further, later in this chapter.

The alluring or alarming eye

Surveillance often sparks responses relating to privacy. The twentieth-century era of state surveillance, especially read through warnings like Orwell's, made being watched seem negative, undesirable. Apparently, many aspire to escape, to hide, or just be private. But this approach seems myopic in a world of mass media and now social media. The world of celebrity makes being seen a matter of privilege, of desire. And if the chance for Andy Warhol's '15 minutes of fame' was limited by TV, social media open the floodgates. The consequences for surveillance are far-reaching – from the unwanted eye to welcome watching. The desire to be seen may help to naturalize and legitimate surveillance of all kinds, to encourage new modes of cooperation of the surveilled with their surveillors. This is facilitated by emerging surveillance imaginaries and practices.

So surveillance culture becomes the new normal. Surveillance is no longer the exceptional circumstance, the last resort, the specific probe it was assumed to be in liberal democratic societies that rely on judicial oversight to protect citizens from overreach. The desire to discover, seen in large-scale surveillance, meets the passion for publicness in social media. How to account for the apparent willingness to be visible to all, especially when there is a growing awareness that our daily routines and whereabouts are tracked and traced constantly? What kinds of desires are visible here and what role do they play in surveillance imaginaries and practices?

Later, we shall look at a range of possible explanations for the new online openness and the supposed shrinking of privacy concerns. As mentioned earlier, they include *scopophilia*, a love of being seen, *narcissism*, an excessive interest in oneself or one's appearance, *soft surveillance* by consumer businesses, and what Arlie Hochschild calls the *outsourced self*.[17] Here, we consider how this may be part of a larger issue, in which public life has become successively less significant compared with so-called private life, particularly within societies oriented to consuming and celebrity and when assisted by new technologies – especially our ubiquitous devices.

Some historical background illuminates these shifts in earlier surveillance imaginaries and practices. Richard Sennett, for instance, describes large-scale, long-term changes that have occurred since the lively public life of eighteenth-century Paris, where connecting with strangers was seen as a key to becoming 'social' or 'civilized'.[18] Such flourishing urban, public life is also visible in nineteenth- and twentieth-century London and New York. But gradually, within increasingly capitalist, secular and urban societies, the idea of the private individual becomes more significant, the personal becomes more 'authentic'[19] and people think they have a right to be 'left alone' in public.

In this way, properly public life shrinks as self-absorption expands and as aspects of the private – such as judging the public figure by some 'true self' standard – intrude into public performance. The private deflects attention from the importance of involvement in the public realm. Sennett says that the resulting confusion means that people try to work out in terms of personal feeling things that previously belonged in the world of public, impersonal codes.

Today, however, the public, paradoxically, has altered again. Public and private realms merge in new ways online and in social media. What was once considered private is now shared in the public realm. Performing, even play-acting, are vital here.[20] The trend probably began with television, however. As Joshua Meyrowitz suggests, mid-twentieth century communication technologies facilitated a fresh sense of social space, separated in new ways from physical space.[21] Other people's living spaces and domestic relationships could now be viewed in one's own living room, for instance. You did not have to be there to see it.

Erving Goffman's old assumptions about roles having two sides, a 'public face' to the audience and a 'private face' in the 'backstage' area,[22] had to be revised, along with Marshall McLuhan's on 'informational contexts'.[23] It is not now the urban space so much as the electronic space or the informational setting that becomes significant. Social positions – such as age, gender and authority – become much more fluid. How could parents persuade children that 'this is the way things are done' when radio and television told a much more varied story? The new media, as McLuhan insisted, make a difference to social behaviour; Meyrowitz seeks to demonstrate how.

This electronic blurring of public and private spaces[24] and the weakened link between physical location and social experience contribute to the increasing liquidity of contemporary culture. As well, Meyrowitz suggests, it stimulated the eventual use of much more interactive media, including self-display on social networking sites. A further telling insight is that familiarity with television as a watching machine helped pave the way for greater tolerance of 'pervasive government, corporate and populace surveillance'.[25]

The same process, then, could be responsible for both permitting pullulating surveillance and, suggests R. Jay Magill, making privacy seem 'somehow miserly'.[26] Magill also points to radio and television as a means of bringing things that are far away, or known only to the imagination, into the public sphere. This allowed President Roosevelt to have 'fireside chats' with the American people, or the British King George V to broadcast a Christmas Day message to the people in 1932 – thus paving the way early on for what would one day be called social media.

At the same time, other analogies and analyses throw additional light on surveillance imaginaries and practices seen as sharing, publicly. Zygmunt Bauman, for instance, has a slightly different take on the business of online display and the creation of a fuzzier line between public and private. For him, certain TV shows amount to a cult of confession. They encourage participants to 'open up', to wear their hearts on their sleeves, sharing in the TV studio things that once would have been seen as necessarily intimate.

While for Sennett this would destructively destabilize the public realm, Bauman suggests that, today, the group actually obliges public confession by individuals. That would be seen as the route, paradoxically, to true community.[27] Bauman sees the confessional society as both the triumph and the betrayal of privacy. While privacy may have invaded the public realm it has also arrived there shorn of secrets, especially in the world of often intimate 'sharing'.[28]

Welcome watching?

Few first-time social media users realize they are signing up for surveillance. But it happens and is soon apparent. People seeking flexibility, mobility and connectivity through social media also find themselves tracked and recorded using the same media. They soon see banner ads on the screen that eerily relate to a site they sought only a short time earlier. Social media may offer a broader 'community' of sorts, but individuals are also tied into abstract systems that track and monitor consumption, mobility, behaviours. Little wonder, then, that in the wake of 9/11 the newly minted US Department of Homeland Security (DHS) quickly moved to using Facebook as a source of personal data, very soon after the fledgling platform was launched.

Homeland Security surveillance exists in the same space as Facebook surveillance. Each is a product of the late, or, better, liquid[29] modern world and in this environment surveillance is both organizationally and culturally central today. This liaison expresses how both government and commercial organizations work but it is also how we have come to think and to live. Today's culture of surveillance goes far beyond fearing no-fly lists or being aware of terrorist hotlines. It lives, equally, in social media. While these two may appear to be quite different realms of life, they grow in the same soil, thrive in the same conditions and, crucially, are vitally connected.

One way of thinking about the relationship between Homeland Security and Facebook involves the television connection again: in Homeland Security, the few watch the many, in TV the many watch the few,[30] but in social media, the many watch the many. When in an early phase of Homeland Security activities the idea of 'total information awareness' was initiated, the rather sinister image used was of an eye in a pyramid whose vision radiated out to the globe. The message? That this all-seeing eye will detect your presence wherever in the world you are. However, if you opened Facebook at that time you saw another map of the world, but with individual figures dotted over it and a little line drawn between each, creating a web or network diagram.

It is a mistake to imagine that these two media, Homeland Security – in whatever country and under whatever name – and Facebook, are unconnected products of the same liquid, digital modernity. True, one has the protection of territory, trade and, possibly, citizens in mind, receives its mandate from the highest level of government and can call on the full might of military engagement to support it, while the other is the brainchild of a university undergraduate imagining new ways of letting students network electronically with their 'friends', which mushroomed in a decade to boasting more than a billion users. But Facebook hosts a Homeland Security page and Homeland Security makes extensive use of Facebook data.

The DHS finds Facebook and other social media very useful in its investigations. As an Electronic Frontier Foundation freedom of information request revealed in 2010, a memo from Citizenship and Immigration Services, part of DHS, states:

> Narcissistic tendencies in many people fuels a need to have a large group of 'friends' link to their pages and many of these people accept cyber-friends that they don't even know. This provides an excellent vantage point for FDNS [Office of Fraud Detection and National Security] to observe the daily life of beneficiaries and petitioners who are suspected of fraudulent activities.[31]

In the run-up to President Obama's inauguration in 2009, the DHS monitored social media sites for 'items of interest', and although they claimed not to collect personally identifiable information, they also say that anything publicly divulged is fair game.

And on the flip side, Facebook cheerfully states, mimicking, it seems, other Homeland Security practices, that it 'collects information about you from other sources, such as newspapers and instant messaging services'. Read the small print! Note too that 'this information is gathered regardless of your use of the Web Site'. Indeed, Facebook says it 'may share your information with third parties, including responsible companies with which we have a relationship'.[32] This is regardless of how high you place your privacy settings.

So much so, in fact, that when Jennifer Stoddart, then Canadian Privacy Commissioner, became aware of the fact that 'third-party developers of games and other applications on the site had virtually unrestricted access to Facebook users' personal information' she launched an investigation into Facebook's practices. This resulted in a 2010 agreement with Facebook that 'Applications must now inform users of the categories of data they require to run and seek consent to access and use this data'.[33]

So Facebook and Homeland Security work similarly. The search model used very successfully by Google, and matched by DHS, was in some ways upstaged by Facebook. Google depended on 'rigorous and efficient equations' whereas Facebook saw – and sees – the potential in the 'social graph' provided by networks of 'friends'.[34] Google monitors search histories and browsing activities using tracking cookies but Facebook connects with people who use their own names, with real friends, with actual email addresses and users' real tastes, ideas and news, tracking user profiles.[35]

Facebook has frequently been questioned or criticized for its privacy policies such that from time to time it upgrades them to 'allow more user control over the settings'. Naturally enough, those who are concerned about privacy are sure to push all the settings to high. Thus, those beyond friends and family may not learn much directly from what is available on your page. But marketers, and others like DHS that use similar methods, do not care what you yourself say.

You have Facebook friends, perhaps hundreds of them, who unwittingly betray you to whoever has access to Facebook data, such as those corporations that Facebook has told you it shares with. When people use real names and reveal their real preferences, politics and personal beliefs, those using Facebook data believe that they have tabs on you even with your own privacy settings at max. True, few people friend others with whom they have nothing in common. Quite the contrary. At the same time, the 'realness' of preferences, politics and personal beliefs may well be qualified by users sharing what they think is expected or, in the case of young people especially, what will display them in a good light. Many of the latter dread being judged for being different. The performance is staged by the site design, imagined or real expectations, and the individual keen to satisfy both. Thus Facebook surveillance meets social surveillance.

At this point, we have to think beyond twentieth-century theorizing such as that done by British sociologist Anthony Giddens. He presciently placed surveillance squarely in his diagram of key institutional areas of modernity,[36] and also argued that 'free speech movements' act as its countervailing force. But he neither reckoned with the already growing influence of new technologies nor did he foresee the resilience of the neoliberal turn towards consumer capitalism that had been unleashed by US President Reagan and UK Prime Minister Thatcher just a few years before his book came out.

These new technologies and neoliberalism have worked together since to render redundant older notions of surveillance as primarily relating to state activity. It is, as Giddens rightly surmised, a central dimension of modernity but emphatically not now centred solely in the state, although governments everywhere still seek access to personal data, however gathered. And as it happens, as if to confirm part of Giddens' thesis, contemporary state surveillance has indeed turned out to be a serious threat to free speech. The chilling effects after Snowden are felt by both journalists and ordinary internet users.[37] Part of today's surveillance culture involves, as we saw in chapter 2, convenience, caution and compliance.

But another aspect of surveillance culture involves consumer devices and related communicative desires. No social thinker could have guessed at this departure, though some, such as Philip K. Dick and Herbert Marcuse, came close. Social media exhibit some technological precedents that in hindsight can be seen as preparing the way, but the advent of social media as a communicative platform also presents quite new possibilities and problems. The fact that, viewed with some political-economic and ethical realism, social media must also be thought of in relation to processes such as Homeland Security only adds to the complexity.

So, the later twentieth-century development of information technology reduced labour intensivity and facilitated communication, simultaneously permitting greater surveillance capacities all round. As James Rule observed in his early sociology of surveillance, looking at social security, credit cards and drivers' licensing,[38] new surveillance methods were characterized by greater numbers being surveilled, the amount of information available about each, the subtlety of decision-making achieved, the centrality or interconnectivity of data in the system, the speed of information flow and the points of contact linking systems and individuals.

However, such practices started to spill over into everyday life, although that process of 'spilling over' is itself far from innocent. It does not necessarily mean that massive surveillance capacities are open to people in their daily lives. While it is obvious that social media facilitate very sophisticated surveillance by ordinary users, checking personal details of friends or strangers remotely and in real time, such tools do not necessarily empower users in other ways. Hence the mistake of imagining, as some do, that simply to turn cellphones or laptops against established authorities such as government or police somehow redresses an imbalance of power. They are undoubtedly a source of real power, but the equation is a complex one. As we shall see in chapter 6, an examination of actual imaginaries and practices is needed to indicate what possibilities exist for new media in struggles for political power.

People with no experience of using high-tech surveillance may see surveillantly partly because they have been empowered to do so through their own interaction with new technologies. This applies both to visual surveillance and dataveillance, from video cameras to social media. Information technology use expanded massively in twentieth-century organizations, but new media of all kinds also diffused quickly into the minutiae of daily life. In many societies, a large proportion of the population is connected, not only through workplace machines and home computers, but in a major way through cellphones and other devices. This is sometimes more, not less, true of 'developing' societies that leapfrog past first adopters.

Social media and electronic games are seldom sold as means of doing 'surveillance', but some systems, such as FourSquare and other platforms enabled by GPS or cell towers, such as Facebook's iPhone app 'Places', cheerfully allow people to find their friends in real-time locations. As well, all social media sites encourage users both to circulate personal information and simultaneously to track and trace the activities of others. The implications of this were dramatically thrust into public awareness when Snowden demonstrated that personal information transmitted and stored by internet and telephone companies is accessible to intelligence agencies.

But what sorts of surveillance occur using social media and how does gaming fit into this picture? Curiously, social media are used in several different but not unconnected ways, and gaming, too, has its unexpectedly surveillant side. Social media users as well as the service providers engage in surveillance using social media. Games may facilitate involvement in surveillance under the rubric of fun.

Social surveillance

Today many are aware of social media surveillance. The debates are strung along a spectrum from cheery assurances that would please Mark Zuckerberg, Facebook's founder, who thinks that privacy is passé – unless it affects him personally: he takes great pains to guard the privacy of his own home![39] – through to others who see inescapably sinister signs of influence and control. This is a contradictory trend whose controversial character shows no sign of abating. It is worth reviewing the debate in order to get some perspective.

Several early commentators on social media noted that in this context, while certain classical forms of top-down surveillance are present, other activities also proliferate, involving more mutual forms of surveillance and what Alice Marwick calls 'social surveillance'.[40] However, many question what privacy might mean in a world that celebrates *publicity*. For instance, in what sounds like an oxymoron, danah boyd speaks of 'networked privacy'.[41] Users upload images of others or share information about others in a routine way, and tools for finding out about others, such as Facebook Graph Search, are available. These are used to mine others' data and search for patterns. This complicates further the debate over social media and surveillance.

Some of the most interesting studies of this are carried out on the largest user category, twenty- and thirty-somethings. However, social media use often starts with a younger crowd, teens and pre-teens. Valerie Steeves's findings on children, young people and social media are telling. It is clear that the necessary skills are learned early. They 'try on new identities and connect with friends',[42] and while actively seeking to avoid the surveillant gaze of parents and teachers, these eleven- to seventeen-year-olds welcome lateral surveillance as a means to discover their identities.

Turning to parental surveillance online, the younger group continues to accept this as 'care', whereas the older teens may have their hackles raised against 'control': 'My mom keeps on [posting] me, "You're on Facebook! Get off! Do your homework!" And I'm like … de-friend.'[43] Even though they might be able to see that their parents are trying to protect and support them, they feel they have to work out some things for themselves. But responses to parents are mild compared with their attitude to school filters and other blocking devices. The teens sensed that they were just not trusted within this almost panoptic situation. They liked the networked spaces of social media for the visibility that they offered but baulked at the monitoring.

For Marwick, it is important that what actually happens on social media is understood. She insists that when users closely examine content uploaded by others and look at their own content through others' eyes, this is surveillance. While acknowledging that this is a variant of more classical under-standings of surveillance – in terms of power, hierarchy and reciprocity – it very much counts as surveillance. Everyday social differences contribute to the micro-relations of power, social roles are altered, and people are included and excluded from networks through deliberate sharing or sequestering of information.

As Marwick and others show, users 'monitor their digital actions with an audience in mind'.[44] This is key to the surveil-lance imaginary in this case. People are watching others and are aware of being watched. Most analysts agree that the latter is a strong sense that other users are watching. They are not necessarily aware that other levels of surveillance – primarily commercial – also affect participants.[45] Marwick explores three key areas: the significance of what Nippert-Eng calls 'boundary work' – such as home-and-work – where contexts collapse on social media; Facebook stalking, where users do digital digging through others' material to buttress their position or undermine others; and how participants use social media to be seen.

The effects of such surveillance are not as direct as conven-tional surveillance effects but social surveillance undoubtedly produces *self*-surveillance of other users. That the surveilled gaze is internalized may be seen as behaviours are modified with the realization that specific watching occurs. And sometimes the behaviours are simply reinforced. As one of Marwick's respondents, Mei Xing, observes, 'with Facebook you know that at that moment a portion of your friends are doing the same things that you are'.[46]

Social surveillance may seem fairly innocent until one considers the power relations evident within social media surveillance. These become obvious when matters such as gender, race, or the intersections between different kinds of vulnerability are considered. These are magnified in social media settings, as Valerie Steeves and Jane Bailey clearly show in their studies of young women online.[47] While they feel the burden of unequal treatment – 'Boys get away with murder!' – they also seem to acquiesce to the gendered gaze, and the overvisibility of the feminine body by packaging it as a form of 'sexual feminine liberation'.

Such insights are valuable as they indicate other ways that surveillance may occur, even without major institutions or organizations being directly involved. The power of the gaze is still evident at this interpersonal level, because it makes a difference. And users who are surreptitiously checking out others, for example, are fully aware of those power relations. A study carried out using international polling showed that up to 30 per cent of social media users in Canada, the US and the UK not only engaged in such 'stalking', but imagined that those whose personal information they were poring over would be embarrassed or upset if they knew they were under surveillance in this way.[48]

However, while it is tremendously important to understand surveillance as it occurs in many domains beyond its classical, conventional sites, it is also vital to note what facilitates that surveillance. Social surveillance is *done* by ordinary users of social media but is still *enabled* by some very complex high technology from some of the largest corporations in the world, which use, among other things, algorithms, machine-learning software and facial recognition technology. The opportunities for these kinds of surveillance are provided externally, not from the users and their own capacities to 'gaze' or 'drill down' into the others' records, but from organizations with their own purposes and business models.

We drew attention earlier to Daniel Trottier's Facebook investigation[49] where he observes that living in a social media environment is like a dwelling place, somewhere a lot of time is spent doing things with people known to users. But Trottier follows Michel de Certeau's distinction between owners and dwellers in which the former, unlike the latter, have the capacity to shape and regulate spaces. The dwellers' tactics describe how the space is used, but in the end the owners determine how the space is known and experienced.[50]

Trottier looks at four levels of social media use, starting with the lateral or peer-to-peer information exchange known to all users and described by boyd, Marwick and others. But the other levels are the institutions, both corporate and governmental, that monitor populations of interest to them, using social media; the aggregated data-mining of marketers that turns social identities into sortable data; and lastly, police and other investigators such as security agencies, who are covert in their practices. However, the levels are not separate, sealed. They interact dynamically with each other, often 'mutually augmenting' their capacities.

All this reveals something of a tension within studies of social media and surveillance. Whereas some, such as Albrechtslund and Dubbeld, highlight the pleasurable and empowering dimensions of such networking, others, notably Mark Andrejevic and Christian Fuchs,[51] stress the 'digital enclosures' within which all such surveillance, however enjoyable for some, takes place. In this case, the lighthearted fun that is surely present occurs against a less freewheeling backdrop that is also understood by many social media users.

The approach taken here is that, rather than taking sides in a debate that may still involve some talking past each other, it is more constructive to try to understand how the genuine enjoyment of social media may be tempered by the recognition that one also has to negotiate constantly with the medium in order to minimize its negatively surveillant features.[52] Might the same be said of online games and the gamifying of other everyday activities?

Fun and games

All sorts of activities, including academic work, may have gamified[53] aspects. For instance, ResearchGate, the online scholarly network, operates in game-like ways, offering incentives and rewards for participation. The metrics of academics' participation are constantly on display and every milestone, such as a hundred reads, twenty-five citations or the periodic addition of new 'followers', is greeted with a congratulatory message to the researcher.

At the same time, strong pressure also exists to play the game for everyone's benefit; you may be a solo operator but you are not alone in the network. If you fail to offer downloadable copies of your work, for instance, constant reminders pester you to do so. And few will have failed to notice that the world of ResearchGate closely mirrors that of the corporate, performance- and metrics-driven university – a reminder that it is not *only* a game. How long until universities require their faculty to participate in such academic media?[54]

Play is the name of the game, as theatre director John McGrath observes. While much surveillance is framed in popular thought by fear and risk, relating to crime control, security measures and privacy, this does not exhaust the possible frames. As Jennifer Whitson points out, 'empowerment, seduction and desire' are important candidates today.[55] She shows, following Erving Goffman, how games should be considered as serious social interaction. They are encounters, with rules and rituals.

Online games such as World of Warcraft or Angry Birds, however, have some unique features, such as the hiddenness of the rules. You discover them through experience with the game, which itself may alter as it progresses, in response to your own involvement. Players become part of the cybernetic feedback system, based on opaque algorithms. In this way and others, games themselves as well as gamified elements of 'serious' sites such as Academia.edu and ResearchGate also echo wider processes of capitalistic organizations.[56] With the academic gamified sites, non-transparent scoring systems use mysterious metrics to give academics a supposed rank within a world of self-branding. Like any other 'free' platform, what is really free is the labour of the academic as she contributes to the profit of the platform.

Gamification occurs as enjoyable game-like features appear across different activities, and all depend on quantified scoring. Whitson comments on the kinds of self-surveillance entailed, giving personal examples from running devices, and others that she has analysed such as those for struggling with obesity or improving financial planning. They all work on the same premise, that minutely analysing data and giving feedback will increase both pleasure and performance for their users. Such systems measure and chart what previously was private. Inducements for desire are thus built in to the product and can easily become part of the surveillance imaginary. My own doctor has suggested – in vain, as yet! – that I consider obtaining a tracker to check my swimming, biking and running performance. He himself is an avid user.

Whitson concludes that this amounts to 'quantifying the care of the self'.[57] Users may constantly adjust their activity levels or behaviour depending on the incoming data, improving on their personal best in whatever field they 'game'. It is not difficult to see in this case as well, however, how in certain areas, especially those associated with the workplace, such devices are also of interest to employers.[58] The engrossing and pleasurable aspects of this may blur our vision of how this might also make us easier to manage, more administrable.[59] Thus what we do as self-surveillance may also offer potential for others to surveill us as well.

Foursquare, which advertises itself as the 'local search-and-discovery service mobile app which provides search results for its users', is a somewhat different entity, says Whitson: 'gamified networking'. Using maps for locating others, it enables social activities that move through space, finding friends in bars, clubs or coffee shops. Participants have to check in and become involved in tagging others to make the gaming aspects work. And, of course, if those participants are less than willing, the game aspects become moot.

This is where gaming and especially gamification become fuzzy. As noted a moment ago, employers are not slow to see the advantages to the organization of using quantified feedback to improve real-time productivity. Some will encourage the use of games, including Angry Birds, in the workplace as a way of motivating workers;[60] others may adopt certain gamified self-surveillance as a part of their management strategy. But when is a game not a game? Probably when the employer *requires* you to 'play'. Few workers will fail to recognize when the game is not offered as fun so much as to increase their efficiency and thus company profitability. Function creep, as desire is appropriated for different ends, is always a possibility.

But even when the game has no connection with employers, suggests Whitson, its 'game' qualities may be limited by its unique feature – the hidden rules. There is no way that players can see if the algorithms governing the game are fair and impartial, or if they are slanted in a specific way. Such games offer no spaces for negotiation or mutual agreement, and value judgements are always embedded within them, which may not favour all players equally.

Another way of considering the issues of games and surveillance is to see how important game metaphors have become within the surveillance scene. Multiple players with varied motives engage in surveillance, and power and discipline do not seem to be its key characteristics. Hille Koskela and Liisa Mäkinen discuss the metaphors of cat and mouse, hide and seek, labyrinth, sleight of hand and poker where enjoyment and control merge in surveillance today.[61]

For these authors surveillance-as-game, as play, offers the chance to challenge some standard surveillance definitions and thus re-evaluate some theories and highlight civil liberties concerns and perhaps unexpected forms of resistance. As an example of cat and mouse, they cite Internet Eyes, a British site for registered viewers to watch camera feed from stores and other businesses and to alert the camera owner of possible thefts. They comment, 'As our lives become saturated with surveillance, new forms of social action will take place. We will have to recognize new forms of resistance and new moralities yet unknown.'[62]

Surveillance saturation, especially seen through the surveillance culture lens, definitely does call for new modes of alertness within emerging imaginaries, along with, one hopes, new modes of action in everyday practice. The challenge of the gamifying aspects of commercial surveillance is placed in a somewhat more sombre light by Julie Cohen. She argues that they mobilize 'participation in our own construction as cultural subjects according to a very specific behavioral model'.[63] By this she means that technologies of the self turn into quantified, monitored, feedback-driven 'trajectories of self-improvement'. The story of the self thus constructed is one which network users cannot themselves shape.[64] So the apparently pleasurable dimensions of such games both encourage their migration from one context to another – function creep – and potentially come at a high cost to the user.

For Cohen, then, the playfulness of these kinds of surveillance is a smokescreen. The algorithms that remain hidden from the user actually 'constrain and channel evolving subjectivity, guiding individual action along more predictable lines'.[65] Gone indeed are the sterner rationales for surveillance, to be replaced by light, even laughing, themes of play in the new narrative arc. But the 'gamer-self' now discovers new, socially reinforced notions of virtue. Maintain your high scores, outdo your personal best. In this case, they originate in online commercial platforms. They may be genuine fun but at a deeper level that fun is framed by others.

In this view, the participatory turn is a typically neoliberal stratagem that echoes entrepreneurial freedoms. The idea that games players are autonomous and consenting wears somewhat thin when the likeness of the system to other neoliberal distributions of privilege and entitlement is brought into the light.

If desire appears, through gaming, as a basic element of surveillance imaginaries, contributing to the creation of the self as a subject of carefully camouflaged criteria for forming identities, does this mean that gamers are just dupes of the system? Do gaming and related activities reduce down to loving Big Brother? This may seem bewildering for those who catch the reference to Winston Smith's confession at the end of *Nineteen Eighty-Four*, understood as the final chilling capitulation of self to the surveilling state.

For John McGrath, surveillance proliferates in part because we desire it – enjoy it, play with it, use it for comfort – and through 'repeated viewing we reposition ourselves, our psyches, in relation to ... surveillance space'.[66] And unlike Orwell – or Julie Cohen for that matter – McGrath does not think that we concede defeat or lose our selves when we admit to loving Big Brother. The games about which he writes have more to do with TV than the internet, as his investigation is, among other things, of the famous *Big Brother* shows that did most to launch the reality TV genre.

What does McGrath mean by 'loving Big Brother'? Importantly, he sees the subjects of surveillance engaging in experiences not intended by the surveillors. He speaks of a 'repositioning' towards surveillance, perhaps like Koskela and Mäkinen's 'new forms of resistance'. In performance within surveillance spaces, he promotes the possibility that the desires of the powerful will be turned back and that an active social self will emerge, unafraid of surveillance and able to live creatively with it. The difficulty here, suggests Keith Tester,[67] is that McGrath ignores the fact that the Big Brother lovers depend heavily on capital, both cultural and economic. The performers depend on their theatrical experience and also need the means to perform, however subversively.

McGrath discusses the *Big Brother* TV series, but these characters, too, know that they have nothing to lose in terms of subsistence. After all, their daily needs will be met. They do not know scarcity, poverty or put-downs as those who live in the wider world of surveillance certainly do. As Tester notes, 'For the marginalized groups of contemporary capitalism, surveillance is not so accommodating or supportive.' Beyond this, it is worth recalling that it is not just any capitalist social relations that are at play here, but a particular kind of relations, what Zuboff calls surveillance capitalism.

From contesting to complying

Readers of Orwell, used to contesting privacy invasion and lost liberties, may scratch their heads when they realize how data-careless some social media users seem. Why would you comply so readily, so unthinkingly, with this system that seems geared to sucking up personal details as a basic feature of its operation? Up pops the privacy paradox again. Orwell readers might well think that social media users seem seldom to worry about this, whereas, as danah boyd puts it, 'it's complicated'.[68]

The Department of Homeland Security rather coyly – and condescendingly – refers to the 'narcissistic tendencies' of social media acolytes.[69] Perhaps its agents were required to read Christopher Lasch, whose critique of *The Culture of Narcissism* long pre-dated the advent of social media but who, according to some, foresaw the expanded self-absorption of new media culture.[70] Lasch's indictment of American culture, now over thirty years old, struck out at this pathology in which people's grandiose ideas about themselves lead them to use others for their gratification even while craving their love and approval. Lasch worried about the deformation of character in a bureaucratic world that put a premium on the manipulation of interpersonal relations and discouraged the formation of deep personal attachments. Does DHS hear echoes of this today?

Whatever the case, the DHS reference to broader cultural tendencies is a useful antidote to the kinds of hype that assume that what we see in the world of social media is merely the exploitation of technical potential. Mark Zuckerberg is a product of the culture excoriated by Lasch, and analysed sociologically by figures such as Richard Sennett and Zygmunt Bauman. Homeland Security capitalizes on those supposed narcissistic tendencies in order to glean information on potential threats to safety. But the capacity to garner such data from social media depends on the same technology infrastructure as the social media sites themselves. They are simply different dimensions of the same liquid modern culture.

One useful way of thinking about the connection between DHS surveillance and 'narcissism' is captured by the concept of exposure. As Kirstie Ball suggests,[71] surveillance exposes people in various ways, but in the world of social media the inner life, or 'interiority', is exposed in ways that involve the activity of subjects. And as well as possibly resigning themselves to such exposure, it is possible that they enjoy it as well. The concept of exposure offers analysts the chance to think about the contents of the interior that are exposed, how they come to the surface, and how they may be examined by others.

Ball develops the concept of 'exposure' to draw attention to the ways in which a combination of media cultures and psychotherapy imperatives may encourage subjects to believe that they ought to divulge things about themselves. She suggests that surveillance may not only be tolerated but even sought after because 'the giving of data satisfies individual anxieties, or may represent patriotic or participative values to the individual'. People may also be 'ambivalent towards surveillance because there is sometimes no identifiable "watcher" or perceivable "control" being asserted, or because the pleasures of performative display override the scrutinies that come hand-in-hand with self-revelation'.[72] Ball's pioneering work may be seen alongside others'.

Of course, the context of consumer 'soft surveillance' may itself encourage exposure. Soft surveillance, as described by Gary Marx, is less intrusive and giving body data may be less controversial where particular forms of language are used and where there exists a particular media and cultural climate. This gets compliance by persuasion, yet denies meaningful choices, emphasizes community, not individual interests, and scans at a distance rather than crossing intimate body boundaries. It may also be associated with a cultural tendency to desire exposure for the gratification it affords. In such a context, personal exposure and the capture of increasingly private aspects of the self may be accepted as 'desirable, normal and harmless'.[73]

Frank Furedi argues that a rise in 'therapy culture' normalizes public displays of vulnerability.[74] For him, the climate creating the erosion of boundaries between public and private has everything to do with therapeutic confession. Public sharing of private troubles was already well developed on television – think Oprah Winfrey – long before social media simplified, expanded and globalized it. If emotions and feelings become the core of personal identity, then, says Furedi, bringing them to the surface and sharing them is seen not only as personally healing but as socially responsible. Once out, they can be managed. One sees this in support groups such as Alcoholics Anonymous, as well.

Sharing may make a person feel good, even if it places them in a position of recovery rather than a return to health. Thus sharers are taught their place in society, suggests Furedi. Perhaps it is no accident that a stronghold of this kind of therapy is in California, in the work of figures such as the family therapist and psychologist Paul Watzlawick at the Mental Research Institute in Palo Alto. Encouraging intimate sharing becomes part of the imperative of communication and may be seen as defining what it is to care. Chapter 5 comments on this in relation to a compelling fictional account that connects sharing and caring, surveillantly.

Connected with this, others are impatient with what they see as a myopic view of social media. They will assert that it is contemporary economic arrangements that encourage sharing of information in general, not just private problems. Jodi Dean argues that the need to be informed in the climate of endless amounts of information 'catapults the repeated exposure and disclosure of secrets into the public domain'.[75] So, in this case, the apparent willingness to be exposed may have to do with the ways in which today's technoculture valorizes the production of better, faster, cheaper information, where the onus is increasingly on 'going public'. The corollary of this is that otherwise there may be things you want to hide. According to Dean, contemporary communicative capitalism and state arrangements together produce the conditions promoting revelation and self-disclosure.[76] The compulsion to disclose meets the drive to surveill, reinforcing the politics of the personal – or at least of personal data.

But yet another possible explanation of why social media users feel so free to allow their personal details to circulate freely online is that it represents a logical outgrowth of what Arlie Hochschild calls the 'outsourced self'. Hochschild talks of twentieth-century America as a place where massive dislocations and disturbances occurred and where families, once dependent on local communities for support, now had to fend for themselves. With women and men in the labour force in almost equal numbers and an increasing incidence of divorce, a gap yawned between family and market provision of care. With no prospect of European-style government support, Americans turned to the market for making clothes, cooking and, of course, for growing produce in the first place. Old services became democratized and more specialized, but they also reached 'into the heart of our emotional lives, a realm previously more shielded from the market'.[77] Not only nannies and babysitters but also marriage counselling and 'love coaching' are services for sale.

When the self is outsourced in these ways, the market steps in, making incursions into many aspects of intimate life. If social life is already structured around such services, then the appearance of apps and sites where such services are also offered makes sense. In general, if there are already existing contexts in which highly personal details are readily shared, in a market context this could be seen as preparing the ground for internet versions of the same kinds of services. Willingness to part with personal data becomes routine in such settings. Why not?

Needless to say, online marketers may also benefit from these newly available kinds of data. The world of the emotions and of familial and romantic relations has long been a rich source of revenue and to tap into it remotely would have seemed an obvious next step. Mark Andrejevic calls this 'affective economics', which emphasizes the role of the emotional commitments of consumers when they make purchasing decisions.[78] The aim is to code and analyse emotion to control modes of sociality and thus to turn 'affect' into a basic resource for exploitation within a very 'soft' version of surveillance capitalism.

Of course, this too could be taken even further in ways that distance even the user's emotional content from the process of online participation. A curious story caught my eye, of an 'autonomous self agent' that can be hired to manage your social media without the tedium of constant checking, monitoring, liking and posting.[79] The bot will do it for you for a small fee. Presumably, if the affect algorithms are correctly calibrated, the system will be able to second-guess your emotional state not only for making specific purchases, but also for lining up appropriate relationships. How handy.

Users speak

We have heard many voices in this chapter, many views of what goes on in the world of social media and gaming cultures. From the DHS assuming that narcissism explains things, to scholars speaking of desire, scopophilia and, more straightforwardly, 'loving Big Brother'. Each makes sense, in a way, but few actually refer to how users themselves think about their online activities. Yet those users have developed diverse and sometimes complex surveillance imaginaries and operate with online practices that make sense to them but do not necessarily fit the categories provided by commentators.

This is partly because the world of internet involvement is often thought of as a way of finding information or, more likely, a way of communicating, or networking, with others. Parting with personal data in the world of online activity is not necessarily thought of as a result of surveillance, for which privacy protections are needed. Thus if researchers start by asking social media users about their experiences of surveillance or their concerns for privacy, they are unlikely to get very far.

When social media users are interviewed or speak in focus groups about their online experiences, without the prompts of surveillance-and-privacy language, the results are diverse and complex. However, it becomes quite clear that, so far from not caring about what happens to their personal data, they are often very sensitive about such matters and consider some marketing and corporate activities highly inappropriate and simply unfair. That is not to say that all agree, by any means. Indeed, the context makes a difference to how institutional uses of personal data are construed, as does one's social position, in terms of gender or age, and how much time is invested in online activities.

One fruitful way of considering this is what Helen Nissenbaum calls 'contextual integrity'. She says that in an age when personal data flow freely through various channels and when all sorts of uses are made of them, it is important to know what really matters to those to whom the data refer. Many social media users, for instance, are much more concerned about what their online contacts can see of their posts and pages than about what corporations can see.[80] Of course, this may be a sign of lack of awareness rather than lack of concern, but it could well be the case that different standards would still be applied to the different contexts.

Nissenbaum proposes four classes of context: the flow of information, the capacities in which the users are acting, the types of information in question, and the principle of transmission.[81] The last case includes variations such as receiving information because a LinkedIn contact sent it, or Amazon chose to suggest a purchase, or a doctor's office was obliged to inform the patient, or the recipient had agreed to keep a secret. For her, these contexts help to show why some kinds of data are seen as more revealing or controversial than others, and why some data collection methods provoke ire at least within certain groups of people. Indeed, Nissenbaum goes on to argue that disclosing certain kinds of details amounts to a denial of data rights if it is contrary to the expectations of the data subject.[82]

When users in England, Norway and Spain were asked by Helen Kennedy and associates to discuss their responses to online data-mining practices, many took a dim view of information shared with third parties, such as when an internet company like Facebook sells data to another company.[83] A large proportion (81 per cent) disapproved of sharing information without their consent, and a similar percentage objected to companies monitoring social media to find out what employees were saying about that company. Some felt that there is a trade-off between connectivity and tracking and some were under the impression that, when they set their privacy setting on high, social media platforms would not share their data with other organizations.

'Fairness' is the word that appeared most frequently in these discussions about personal data mining on social media. A user might expect to divulge some personal details when, say, setting up an account, but would not assume that the company would then sniff out other intimate details for unadvertised uses. Users often noted that they wished for their consent to be meaningful, to be told in simple transparent terms what they were signing up for. Overall, this study suggests that while users may not pepper their parlance with 'privacy', they are concerned about 'whether social media platforms operate within users' normative expectations of what is ethical and just'.[84]

Towards a conclusion

What can be learned from the fact that surveillance and privacy do not hold the same power as they might once have done for discussing issues of the handling of personal data, especially in the social media world? Does this hint that we now have to go beyond these concepts and argue that the onlife world is a post-surveillance or a post-privacy situation? Two things are worth saying here. The first is that if we are to understand appropriately the culture of surveillance, this may well mean accepting that surveillance may not be the top-of-mind word that users draw on to describe what is happening, any more than privacy is the first word they use to complain or claim some right.

In tension with the first, the second comment is that the language of surveillance and, yes, privacy has to be retained because these terms still point to the broader realities of what is happening in the world of social media and indeed of personal data generally. Power relations are inevitably involved, whether in corporate or government contexts. If our concern is not only to comprehend but also to be critical of today's surveillance culture, then that concept is still crucial. This does not for a moment require denial that social media and gaming aficionados have fun, that their desires are expressed in being drawn to sharing and playing. But it does mean that such emotions and engagements must be viewed in context.

Enough has been said by now for the nature of that context to be fairly clear. Technically, it is the broad context of digital modernity with its distinctive, rapidly developing departure – surveillance capitalism. But as I say, this is merely a technical way of describing it. Others are available, notably the one that enlivens the next chapter. Although the chapter title refers rather abstractly to 'total transparency', its guiding topic is a novel, now a movie, *The Circle*. This piece of popular culture explores through near-time sci-fi a Silicon Valley corporation that epitomizes aspects of surveillance capitalism. Switching to a literary offering is a good way to complement the social science approach that we have engaged thus far. But it also offers the chance to stand back and appraise the situation in a more critical fashion – is it utopia or dystopia?

Part III
Co-creation: Culture, Ethics, Politics

Considering surveillance as cultural imaginaries and practices places debates over surveillance in the realm of everyday life and not just in the high-level world of businesses and government agencies, critically important though that world is for surveillance. Our social and cultural worlds are the products of conflicting currents, opposing flows. Of emotions, play, commitments and experiences.

The towering institutions and processes of high technology and global government that seem to overshadow our daily life-paths are not relentless and invincible. Opportunities still exist not only to slow the pace of the blundering beast but also to tame and even humanize some of its activities. To deny human agency is to deny hope.

The notion of 'co-creation' may be illustrated by the ways in which, after Snowden, millions of ordinary internet and cellphone users became aware that their own imaginaries and practices are implicated in today's surveillance. The internet is itself a mutating assemblage that is subject not only to corporate and government pressures but also to the activities of ordinary people, often acting in concert, sometimes contributing constructively to its reimagination and reshaping.

Here we look first at a fictional world – eerily on the edge of ours – where total transparency is not merely the organizational goal, but where ordinary participants join in willingly and even enthusiastically to the heightened visibility of the digital world. Many themes reappear: the convenience that conceives compliance along with dwindling calls for caution, the online personae and performances that mark online involvement, the novelties that are normalized or that help to reassure that other kinds of surveillance are acceptable, and the ways that the self is subtly shaped and identities formed through seemingly innocent innovations that feed fascination and drive desire.

Reading *The Circle* offers the chance to decide for ourselves how far to go with transparency, given that, in a sense, today's users too are already, inevitably, part of the digital world portrayed there. How do the novel's characters comply, cope with or question the seductive and subtle surveillance situations that are the nub of the novel? How do we – the readers – decide whether utopian or dystopian perspectives are appropriate for our times?

Then finally, we consider new surveillance imaginaries and practices to figure out what a culture of 'good gazing' might look like. And this is no abstract, armchair reflection, either. Surveillance imaginaries are constructed from many sources, and in the activities of younger users of social media, among others, worthwhile approaches are already being developed. What are the components of a constructively critical way of developing surveillance imaginaries?

Participation is increasingly commonplace. But what sort of participation works best to promote practices geared to digital democracy, the common good and human flourishing? Earlier language offered us privacy and data protection. How far do these still speak to today's surveillance world and in what ways might it be necessary to go beyond them?

5
Total Transparency

The era of the early internet was full of dizzy dreams about the world-changing potential of global communication and the breathtaking possibilities of creating a 'world brain' of readily available information. Few commented, at first, on the unrealized surveillance dimensions of the internet, although two decades in, jaded jeremiads became much more common, especially focused on the transparency of billions to the gaze of a group of global corporations and agencies. Few technological developments – atomic bombs excepted – have unmitigated negative consequences for humanity. So how to discern a dystopian from a utopian situation is an ongoing challenge.

Historical philosopher Michel Foucault had a keen sense of, and a disdain for, utopia: 'It was the dream of a transparent society, visible and legible in each of its parts, the dream of there no longer existing any zones of darkness, zones established by the privileges of royal power or the prerogatives of some corporation, zones of disorder.'[1] Here he deplores Jean-Jacques Rousseau's democratic dream that once everything was in the open, as it were, there would be equality and freedom. Foucault contrasted this with Jeremy Bentham's equally utopian scheme of the all-seeing place, the panopticon, with its opposite outcome of perfect control, through self-discipline. In each case, transparency was seen as the cure of social ills, the panacea for human problems. In one, public opinion would play its part. In the other, a sort of social engineering would ensure the smooth working of society. Utopian transparency takes different forms.

Any discussion of surveillance culture also has to confront the issue of transparency. Twentieth-century critiques of surveillance often complained about the secretiveness of surveillance, on the one hand, and its capacity to bring out into the open matters that were properly private, on the other. They also lamented the lack of transparency on the part of those doing surveillance. But the culture of surveillance, in which the ambiguity is augmented, not only allows for more transparency, but also judges it, either as an inevitable if regrettable product of our engagement with new media, or as, once more, good in itself.

How to get a handle on transparency today? It raises questions of how people relate to each other in everyday life, what they are prepared to divulge or show to others and what anyone may know about them if they so wish. But it also concerns how far there should be *expectations* of transparency. Is it acceptable that any photo taken of me can appear without my knowing on Facebook or Instagram and be identified as my likeness by facial recognition technology? I recently saw a photo – that I didn't know existed – in the *Washington Post* of myself sitting behind Canadian Prime Minister Justin Trudeau in a town-hall meeting. But I have also seen photos from Facebook in which I was tagged, completely without my knowledge.

Enter Eggers. *The Circle* is a 2013 novel by Dave Eggers about technologically enabled transparency.[2] If Orwell's *Nineteen Eighty-Four* offered us the concepts – 'Big Brother is watching you!' – with which to assess twentieth-century state surveillance, *The Circle* is an apt candidate for evaluating twenty-first century surveillance culture. It concerns a Silicon Valley company with a lush campus and laidback lifestyle that is completely enamoured of transparency, from its symbolically glass-clad buildings to its 24/7 participatory monitoring and exposure of all that goes on. Forget Big Brother; 'Everything That Happens Must Be Known' is one of its soothingly reassuring slogans – until you ask, why or by whom?

Novels play an important role in shaping a common cultural understanding of social phenomena and indeed in fuelling our social imaginaries. Among a number of others, Orwell's *Nineteen Eighty-Four* has done sterling service in informing surveillance imaginaries for many decades. But this is an invitation to turn to a contemporary novel for fresh insights. While it is difficult to squeeze into one book an overview of surveillance culture, informed by contemporary social sciences, a novel offers a different view. It is complete in itself but – in this case – intended to throw into sharp relief some key features of the new surveillance condition, including its imaginaries and practices.

If such an imaginative novel or film does its work well, its audience has the task of deciding what is really going on and, in this case, where the truth about transparency lies. As Gary Marx reminds us, 'Stories along with images and music are one component of the culture of surveillance that so infuses our minds and everyday life.'[3] *The Circle* is offered as one such story; *Black Mirror*, a TV series taken up by Netflix, offers some parallel insights. Readers will think of other popular cultural offerings, too. So the point of this chapter is to bring into focus some of the contradictions and conundrums that have been explored in earlier chapters and to permit readers to work out where they stand and how they participate in the culture of surveillance.

'My God,' Mae murmurs at the start of *The Circle*, 'this is heaven'; 491 pages later, the reader should be ready to say if she is correct. The experiences of Mae Holland, the Circle's newest employee, lead us through the book. Her growing enthusiasm for being perpetually present, constantly on display and her rationalizing of each surveillance practice as necessary and beneficial is telling. She keeps the lid on her unease. The novel portrays in playful, funny and always satirical ways what it is like to be permanently available, always performing. But there are also shadows cast by her inability to switch off, unplug from the grid and by the fact that all data are retained indefinitely and may return to haunt her.

The Circle concerns the culture of surveillance. While readers are invited to judge whether the Circle is utopian or dystopian, one makes parallel checklists throughout because the answers are not offered on a plate. It is science fiction, sort of, but it is so close to our world that it feels as if the future has arrived. The fact that it takes place in Silicon Valley underscores that sense. Utopian and dystopian literature is meant to help us to see the world differently, to recognize ourselves in the plot and to empathize with the characters that most match our perspectives, our practices. At the same time, it is a dynamic process – we pursue a plot, after all – and we may find ourselves uncomfortably, or surreptitiously, siding with someone we at first thought we disapproved of or doubted.

After sketching the storyline, and discussing some aspects of Eggers' work, this chapter reviews key themes: one, the rise of social surveillance and its merging with state, corporate and workplace surveillance and how this shapes imaginaries and practices; two, the ambiguities and contradictions of visibility in everyday life; three, the corporate ownership of 'private' spheres, and the associated emerging imaginaries and practices; and four, the coded construction of the novel itself as a vehicle for dystopian critique, a segue to ethical and political analysis.

The Circle

Mae has found what she is looking for at the Circle. She has arrived, after having desperately wanted to participate in this, the world's leading internet company. She thinks that working for this company – which resembles, and is, Facebook, Yahoo, Google (often voted the world's best company to work for)[4] and other internet companies rolled into one – is the greatest opportunity she can imagine. The messiness and uncertainty of life seem to be a thing of the past. She wallows in the Circle, sometimes gushes. It contrasts profoundly with the drab and routine job she had with a utility company, which seemed to suck out her soul. She has found her dream.

At the Circle, Mae is part of the future, in a bright, green environment with a relaxed ambience, in buildings where everyone can see what is happening and where many social events and even overnight accommodation for late workers are freely available. Because Mae believes the Circle is heaven she successively shuts out other thoughts, including doubts sown by her ex-boyfriend Mercer, whose troubled comments she finds increasingly annoying – especially when they question her utopia. When challenged by colleagues who demand to know why she is not participating more fully, she deliberately suppresses her initial responses that suggest she has a life of her own and acknowledges her failure to give herself fully.

Mae soon meets two of the 'three wise men', co-founders and directors of the Circle, but for Eggers their epiphany is questionable. As one of them, Bailey, launches the 'SeeChange' cameras, Steve Jobs style, to an enthralled audience of thousands, he intones, 'we will become all-seeing, all-knowing'. Do we sense that the biblical serpent speaks here? Not merely because if we heed it we might inadvertently expose our nakedness – that happens later – but because it is actually a 'knowing' and a 'seeing' shrivelled down to data. That is the star guiding these wise men, which is why the Circle's quantified selves seem so content and why Big Data has the aura of the Holy Grail.

Mercer creates some tension over against Mae's acceptance of the Circle, by inserting some nagging doubts. He urges that she try to assess the spirit of these new times before being sucked into the vortex of 'sharing' everything. He tries to remain off the grid ...

> Mercer: Mae, I've never felt more that there is some cult taking over the world.
> Mae: You're so paranoid.
> Mercer: I think you think that sitting at your desk, frowning and smiling, somehow makes you think you're actually living some fascinating life. You comment on things, and that substitutes for doing them.

But Mae only fleetingly feels doubts about the Circle. So much pleasure, warmth and performance reward pulsates here that there is no going back. The brightness of the buildings, the sense of inclusion; why would one hesitate, hold back?

Enabled by the digital, sci-fi and real life merge in *The Circle*. When Steven Spielberg made *Minority Report* – another strongly surveillance-themed story – for its 2002 release, he carefully researched emerging technologies and built them ingeniously into the plot. His Pre-Crime Department seemed to come spookily to life in the Department of Homeland Security, founded in the same year to secure the US after 9/11. Eggers, too, must have done some tech homework. *The Circle* sounds like sci-fi but many of its referents are already available off the shelf – which may distract or distress those in the tech field. Above all there are the ways that personal data spell power and profit in a world saturated in social media. The future is already here.

Take the tiny, cheap 'SeeChange' cameras that may be deposited unobtrusively in any location, to send back constant feed through the internet. This is indeed occurring today and small webcams appear – if that is the right word for something you might not notice – everywhere. Take – real world, now – 'Dropcam' for instance – cheap, easy-to-install cameras that capture crime, views and intimate moments at a rate that vastly exceeds YouTube's 100 hours per minute upload rate. These devices are uploaded at 1,000 hours per minute. Their price and ease of use make for rapid proliferation.[5]

Not only are movements tracked and traced using phones, in this smart-city style campus the everyday environment is increasingly surveillant. Many devices and apps in *The Circle* speak to this, including the 'TruYou' system that features a one-stop ID for every purpose. Vehicles have also become logjects[6] – objects that record and log their own use and frequently also transmit those data elsewhere. Cars with GPS, internet connections, data recorders and high-definition cameras are becoming standard.[7] And when in the real world you lose things, people or pets, you already have choices of ways to find them again, such as the tiny Bluetooth 'Tile' app that can be stuck or attached to almost anything for easy short-range retrieval or, beyond range, crowd-sourced back to its owner or family member.[8]

That Eggers wants his readers to see this as a surveillance novel is clear from his dependence on pithy Orwellesque slogans such as 'Secrets Are Lies', 'Sharing Is Caring' and 'Privacy Is Theft'. In *The Circle*, these ideas are warnings but come attractively gift-wrapped; 'Sharing Is Caring', for instance, appears to be a virtuous, desirable condition. It chimes with Mark Zuckerberg's remarks: 'If people share more, the world will become more open and connected. And a world that's more open and connected is a better world.'⁹ 'All that happens must be known' sounds like a nugget of wisdom, a quote from some sacred text, perhaps, that gives a cosmic context for increasingly transparent lives. In *Nineteen Eighty-Four*, Big Brother's slogans jar and grate against the lives that Winston and Julia wish to lead, whereas in *The Circle* they seem so natural, so acceptable, so virtuous that Mae has but brief moments of uncertainty before allowing herself to sink into their comfortable common sense.

Why does Mae permit herself to become so fully absorbed in the Circle? For one thing, it is gently but strongly demanded from her. She is supposed to post 'zings' all the time, and about everything, including the quiet, solitary hour paddling her kayak in the bay. Details are fed into her gamified 'participation rank', which in turn, after her initial hesitation, impels her to keep zinging with the best of them – or to be the best of them.¹⁰ Despite the odd 'blasphemous flash', a deeply embarrassing sex scene featuring her parents, and the annoying warnings about tech addiction and totalitarian tendencies from former boyfriend Mercer, Mae manages to maintain her commitment to the Circle's transparency policy. Eggers' message is as subtle as headlines: Mae is us.

In the end, she's a true believer. In an exchange with Kalden, she affirms:

> 'I think everything and every*one* should be seen. And to be seen, we need to be watched. The two go hand in hand.'
> 'But who wants to be watched all the time?'
> 'I do. I *want* to be seen. I want proof I existed.'¹¹

Of course, Mae is young, idealistic and, like many others in Silicon Valley, a visionary who believes she is contributing to a better world. The Circle's vision becomes Mae's mission but, as portrayed by Eggers, her experience almost resembles absorption into a cult. So is Mae really us? That is the question the rest of the chapter pursues.

Social surveillance revisited

No reader of *The Circle* can fail to recognize that social media are one of its key themes. Everyone is constantly connected through multiple platforms, 'zinging' each other and sending 'smiles' and 'frowns' to indicate approval or disapproval. Eggers acknowledges the reality of the urge to maintain the flow of messages, along with the desire to be seen and to be affirmed by others. At the same time, he cannot but insert some literary cautions, not only about the possible risks of being embarrassingly exposed to family, friends and authority figures but also about having one's freedom compromised by the flow of personal information through channels unseen and unknown to the individual.

How can the dynamics of the social life of today's internet and especially the phenomenon of social media best be understood? When so many are immersed in the daily round of sharing, posting, emailing, following, tweeting and updating their status it is hard to detach yourself for long enough to get a sense of what this world means. How did it come into being and how does it differ from earlier forms? How is it structured and what are its basic values and norms? We can engage usefully in historical and sociological studies, but a film or a novel are other good ways to hold up a mirror so that we can catch ourselves at work, at play in our burgeoning digital domain.

Ethnographic studies offer much by way of parallel analysis where the author is positioned as an anthropologist getting to grips with a little-known culture. One of the best is Christena Nippert-Eng's *Islands of Privacy*. This connects nicely with Mae's subjective experiences of negotiating surveillance. Nippert-Eng's fine-grained study covers aspects of the offline world as well, but what she says about digital communication is very telling, especially in the light of *The Circle*. Her understanding of 'privacy' as 'the amount of control people want over their communication'[12] is appropriate for today's conditions in which privacy is persistently mutating.

For many, the idea of privacy connects our lives as members of social units with our lives as 'unique individuated' selves.[13]

Indeed, the idea of 'islands' of privacy in a sea of the public world gives way today, Nippert-Eng suggests, to constantly negotiated boundaries. This is where the 'work', the practice, happens, of trying to maintain some sense of privacy or to limit who may impinge upon it and under what circumstances. Spam filters and special email addresses may help make such boundary work lighter, but the real issue for people interviewed by Nippert-Eng was keeping personal information safe, rather than just keeping things to oneself. Such insights help to frame the issues now experienced in social media.

Mae quickly catches on to the fact that others are constantly checking on her, as she in different ways checks on others. This parallels Marwick's work on 'social surveillance',[14] that is, how users of Twitter, Facebook, Instagram, WhatsApp and other platforms check to see what others are up to. It may be dubbed innocently as 'looking', but also as 'creeping' or 'stalking', and whatever it is called it may have panoptic-like effects. Watching and being watched are taken for granted in such spaces and may also be discussed as 'lateral' or 'participatory'[15] surveillance.

Marwick concludes: 'Social media has a dual nature whereby information is both consumed and produced, which creates a symmetrical mode of surveillance in which watchers expect, and desire, to be watched themselves.... In the absence of face-to-face cues, people will extrapolate identity and relational material from any available digital information.'[16] The watching is two-way, however. She notes that an expectation of surveillance among users is an 'intrinsic aspect of the medium'. As well, she adds, this can also create anxiety and conflict.[17] The latter are far from absent in *The Circle*. Mae's relationships with bosses, friends and her parents are destabilized more than once by personal information flows.

Marwick also observes that social surveillance differs from more conventional kinds; power is involved in every social relationship, surveillance is between individuals, rather than being weighted towards organizations, and it is also reciprocal, with both parties being watcher and watched. But, she says, the effects are to domesticate surveillance practices more generally. The primary concern of social surveillance is other users – especially parents or bosses – rather than surveillance by government or corporations. Given this, the experience of 'context collapse' is highly significant, seen in the increasingly blurred boundaries between work and home, school and private life or friends and family.[18]

Thus Marwick finds that although hierarchy is apparently flattened through the use of common categories – such as Facebook friends – the hierarchies reappear within local relationships, showing how power is still present. Indeed, the very practices of social surveillance are geared to a quest for power, such as compensating for perceived weakness by obtaining knowledge or as a way of trying to regain lost control in romantic relationships. Importantly, Marwick argues that people use social media in order to be seen – to show they exist, as Mae puts it. In the quest of status or attention, people perform deliberately to an unseen audience. As Marwick crisply comments, 'Social media has a dual nature in which information is both consumed and produced, which creates a symmetrical model of surveillance in which watchers expect and desire to be watched.'[19]

As for the panoptic effects to which Marwick alludes, she shows that while surveillance in general acts to manage, control or influence populations, social surveillance produces self-management and direction. The surveillance gaze is in this case internalized, thus modifying the practices of involved users. In terms of Foucault's work, this surveillance occurs at the micro-level, capillary scale, 'at work in the mundane day-to-day activities that make up human life'.[20] Thus self-discipline and impression management are at the core of social surveillance, something that is eminently clear in Mae's experiences at the Circle.

The same is true of the *Black Mirror* series, especially the 'Nosedive' episode in season three (2016). Charlie Brooker, its writer, clearly has social media in mind for his searing satire. Validation-seeking users now discover that they themselves are involved in the rating and ranking game – anyone can contribute their assessment of the other, with repercussions extending far beyond 'likes'. Rather like the Circle, all interactions are now in one ubiquitous platform that allows anyone to rate and rank anyone else on a five-point scale. The results, transmitted to corporations and government, determine who may do what. The protagonist, Lacie Pound, tries jealously to boost her ranking, only to fail, spectacularly and terrifyingly. As in the Circle, social approval is power. Crowd-sourced review systems, like Yelp, become the judgement of the world.

In what follows we look more closely at two aspects of *The Circle* – transparency and visibility – to suggest sociologically what is going on and to show how these concepts are a tremendous help in getting to grips with contemporary surveillance. By transparency I mean how contemporary surveillance exposes in unprecedented ways the details of our lives to large organizations and also, through social media, to each other. This is a major theme of *The Circle* and is a development that naysayers such as Mercer find deeply troubling. By visibility I refer to the experience of being transparent to others, and how people may contest but also be content, comply with or even covet transparency. Mae allows herself to become increasingly visible; her earlier denials give way to desire.

Transparency and visibility

> They would find each other, soon enough, in a world where everyone could know each other truly and wholly, without secrets and without shame, and without the need for permission to see or to know, without the selfish hoarding of life – any corner of it, any moment of it. All of that would be, so soon, replaced by a new and glorious openness, a world of perpetual light.[21]

These words appear on the last page of *The Circle*. One of the capitalized slogans, dispersed like Orwellian codes throughout *The Circle*, is All That Happens Must Be Known. Invisibly inscribed in the very architecture of the corporate campus but also hammered home to Mae by her colleagues, total transparency is the goal and, for some, the challenge. After only a week at *The Circle*, Mae is obliged to realize that what she thinks of as extracurricular is viewed by the Circle as intrinsic to work. Gina informs her: 'We actually see your profile, and the activity on it, as integral to your participation here.'[22]

Gina helps Mae set up her three screens on her desk. There is one for her Customer Experience work, one for her contact with the team. This includes CircleSearch, which allows her to see where anyone is at any given moment, with an app that documents the history of each person's movements during the day. A third screen is for her social and Zing feeds, which connect her immediately with the other 10,041 people at the Circle, but divided into Inner and Outer Circle contacts. By the end of the novel she has no fewer than seven screens at her work station. All work-time activity is recorded, but is this also true of her leisure?

Mae is a kayaker, but one day, after her innocent paddle out into the bay, she discovers that this, too, should have been reported. Initially she baulks at this. Paddling through water glinting with the warm light of the setting sun is a personal pleasure, she thinks at first. After enduring an uncomfortable interview with her immediate superior, she finds out that it is not only against company policy but – a dimension that had not previously struck her – against her best interests as a human being both to seek solitude and *not* to share everything. Such sharing is vital if the overall company goal of total transparency is to be realized.

Mae is eager to merge with the Circle's philosophy of total transparency, but in many scenes, such as this event, that process includes friction, if not abrasion. She sometimes struggles to keep up with the pace and pressures of participation, feels intense shame at missing a co-worker's party, and experiences data overload, especially when she is the ongoing object of observation and measurement. But the high-pressure metrics act as an urgent incentive to achieve rather than a warning that all is not well at the Circle. And even what she does outside of worktime now has to be shared.

Eggers signals his own unease with this through the coded nickname given to Mae for her Zings: MaeDay. As Margaret Atwood wryly observes, although Mae is told, erroneously, that the homonym 'MayDay' is a national holiday, it is in fact a distress signal, not to mention a Stalinesque holiday satirized in *Nineteen Eighty-Four*.[23] What thrills Mae as she grows to accept that all that happens must be known also comes with a small print authorial health warning. Eggers has penned a morality play for the social media era. Conformity may have unpleasant consequences.

Transparency is thus a key concept that connects *The Circle* with social analyses of surveillance. Of course, in the latter, the term may refer to the very positive demand that those who gather and process data be clear and open about what they are doing, why and with what desired outcomes. We *ask* or demand of organizations and governments that they be transparent. In the twenty-first century this becomes more urgent, because the organizations that monitor and profile our lives have made our activities, friendships, connections, preferences, beliefs and habits more transparent – *to them* – than ever. Our research team gave our cumulative work on major current trends of surveillance the title of *Transparent Lives*, in order to foreground this feature of surveillance today.[24]

Sometimes, transparency has been seen as a good thing and, of course, in an ideal world, as with nothing to hide and thus nothing to fear, it might appear as a legitimate good. Back in the 1990s, David Brin argued for it.[25] He suggested that a way to overcome imbalances of information access is to create situations of 'reciprocal transparency' – sharing information with others if they do the same in return. The electronic village. Then we could no longer hide our dark sides; deception would be harder. Transparency would undermine surveillance.[26] In principle, this sounds plausible.

And this, as other researchers have shown, is still part of the Silicon Valley – young white male pioneer – dream; transparency along with openness.[27] Alice Marwick says, 'The tech scene idealizes openness, transparency, and creativity but these ideals are realized as participation in entrepreneurialism, capitalism, work-life integration, heavy social media use and the inculcation of large audiences.' Thus engineers and programmers guide social media development after their image. 'Status is crucial but it must be the right kind of status.'[28]

Would this radical transparency work? The most prominent problem with this idea is that while smart Silicon Valley entrepreneurs may imagine that the rest of the world resembles them – young, white, male and well-off – the differences are in fact considerable. The main differences have to do with power and access, which in most cases of everyday surveillance such as credit ratings, job applicant pre-screening, police checks or airport security are very unevenly distributed. If ordinary citizens, consumers or employees were to ask for reciprocal full transparency from police officers or security agents, marketers or managers, the chances of receiving it would be pretty slim.

What is needed to contain and curtail total transparency, argue others, is the protection of legal measures to prohibit certain kinds of surveillance and to impose penalties on those whose watching transgresses acceptable transparency. Brin wrote as someone who shared the Silicon Valley dream that more technological affordances could create a world of freedom – before it became clear that corporations as well as government departments do surveillance and before social media allowed millions of others to join them in *social* surveillance. Brin wrote before 9/11 and its surveillance aftermath and before Snowden and the shocking revelation that new technologies were already being permitted – yes, encouraged and facilitated – to make visible to security agencies more details of everyday life in ways that go far beyond what most had imagined.

Interestingly, Dave Eggers responded to Edward Snowden's disclosures about the National Security Agency in 2013, the year that *The Circle* appeared. As he wrote:

> Think back to all the messages you have ever sent. All the phone calls and searches you've made. Could any of them be misinterpreted? Could any of them be used to damage you by someone like the next McCarthy, the next Nixon, the next Ashcroft [former US Attorney General, under George W. Bush]? This is the most pernicious and soul-shattering aspect of where we are right now. No one knows for sure what is being collected, recorded, analysed and stored – or how all this will be used in the future.[29]

Clearly, this was a Kafkaesque moment for Eggers but his purpose was clear. He wanted to rouse writers and journalists and remind them of their crucial role in speaking out. It was easily understood by Wajahat Ali, an American lawyer and playwright who said of the outrage about Snowden's revelations – 'welcome to our world'. American Muslims had gotten used to being thought of as potential suspects for more than a decade: 'We've had to assume that all our phone calls, emails, social media and text messages are being monitored in some way.' For Ali, as for Eggers, the message is starkly clear – resist, resist, resist! Their ally in this would be law, and the pressing need for assurances of privacy and the protection of data.

There is, however, a crucial aspect of contemporary transparency that we have not yet discussed fully: namely, that the process of our lives being laid bare for many unknown others to see is not one that simply happens to us. Crucially, users participate in the process, both knowingly and unknowingly, willingly and unwillingly. After all, many social media users rate and rank each other through likes, as Mae does through zings, but consumers also rate and rank others through Airbnb, Uber or a host of other systems – that are not yet officially reduced to one mega-platform, but that share data in ways to which ordinary users are not privy.

To focus on transparency alone, however, is to miss some of Eggers' message. True, 'Everything That Happens Must Be Known' seems like a recipe for a potentially fearful omniscience, but Mae does not see it that way. She negotiates this new world like a novice; she wants to be part of it and is determined to overcome whatever fleeting doubts or even lingering hesitations she might have. By the end of the novel, she speaks as an insider, an ambassador, a believer. She is living the Circle, 24/7. To grasp how this happens, we must hear how she experiences the multi-screened life of constant audience awareness.

As we noted earlier in this book, there has been a steady switch from the employment identities of the twentieth century, focusing on 'discipline', to the consumer identities of the twenty-first, characterized by 'performance', that is transparent to all. So it comes as no surprise that this is reinforced by social media, to the extent that very little space remains, if any, in Goffman's 'backstage' of life. Where can we really be ourselves? 'What happens to us if we must be "on" all the time?' asks Margaret Atwood. 'Then we're in the twenty-four-hour glare of the supervised prison. To live entirely in public is a form of solitary confinement.'[30]

Mae is an earnest wannabe who divulges more and more over time, with less and less apprehension. Though Mae occasionally has 'impure' thoughts about whether to keep to herself instead of hopping into the Circle, as employees are expected to do – with feeling! – she strives to post more. In doing so, she 'feels a profound sense of accomplishment and possibility'.[31] The desire to achieve is fuelled by the constant expectations of online platforms of every sort. It is not hard to guess that Eggers is implicitly endorsing 'impurity' – and while some of his references are slyly subtle, others are strident. He wants the satire to strike home.

At the same time, Mae is a slow learner in some respects. When she goes out for that solitary kayaking evening in the bay, she finds that the rental agent is no longer there, so she removes the craft without permission. Later, she has to make a public presentation back at the Circle and she confesses her lapse. One of her bosses, Bailey, asks if she thought she was protected, 'enabled by some, what, some cloak of invisibility?'[32] As the conversation continues, she is shamed into saying that not only should she not have taken the kayak out, but she should have ensured that everything she saw was recorded. Because 'Sharing Is Caring'.

Visibility – especially social visibility – is, as we have seen, important as a sociological category. It is a site of strategy where we try to choose how we present ourselves and contest how we are seen, in our effort to shape and manage the process. It is essential for a politics of recognition, to obtain fair treatment for differences. Being visible or invisible involves moral as well as practical skills but in itself does not signify oppression or liberation.[33]

Focusing on negotiated visibility means thinking not only about protection – such as privacy – but also about skills to do with our responsibilities to ourselves and each other. Not withdrawal, but our movements in many directions.[34] This is how we organize social relations through visibility arrangements. Invisibility questions which data should be collected. One could say that it is part of a critical ethics of care,[35] a practice of liberative potential towards human flourishing.

Big Data surveillance

'Wise man' Bailey knows nothing but data; using data, everyone will become all-seeing, all-knowing. This pretended omniscience is in fact tightly circumscribed, as Eggers demonstrates repeatedly. Even 'sentiment analysis' cannot plumb emotions and neural scans cannot capture thought. The attempts to do so are limited by the algorithms, which have only pragmatic purposes. This, of course, makes some real-world reliance on data dangerous because it often gives the impression that data can do much more than the results demonstrate.

Mae finds out the hard way that data do not tell all. Her friend Annie, who helped land her the Circle job, falls ill and is in a coma. To her chagrin, Mae cannot communicate with her. Language is not in Annie's gift at that moment and Mae finds herself frustrated. What could have been sympathy rises as irritation; data alone will not do what Mae now expects. Data dependence, Eggers seems to say, may miss some crucial clues, rendering it not only inadequate for some circumstances but perhaps an altogether misleading approach to the enterprise of life.

Today's inflated talk of Big Data builds on this. It is clear that those who enthuse about its capacities believe there is an analytic future in sucking up all the data available and keeping it forever, just in case. Big Data surveillance involves 'increasingly automated forms of data mining, sorting and analysis ... finding patterns, trends, correlations'.[36] More and more, those with access to databases will create a new digital divide, something also hinted at in *The Circle*. Population-level intelligence gathering becomes central to security regimes. Track first, target later – which reverses all earlier modes of surveillance practice. All data are potentially relevant. As Mark Andrejevic puts it succinctly, if sarcastically, 'We're not collecting data about you because you're a suspect but because you can help us identify who the real suspects are.'[37] With Big Data there is no anonymity; all too often, interest slides seamlessly from causes to correlations.

What we discover about the culture of surveillance in a Big Data era, however, is that what is known about us is also provided by us, and the primary system for so doing is social media. So what is shared may, as in Mae's case, bring personal desire and gratification. At the same time, recall the ambiguity of what was discussed in relation to Kirstie Ball's work on exposure. The concept draws attention to the ways in which a combination of media cultures and psychotherapy imperatives may encourage subjects to believe that they ought to divulge things about themselves. As she says, 'the giving of data satisfies individual anxieties, or may represent patriotic or participative values to the individual'. Also, 'the pleasures of performative display override the scrutinies that come hand-in-hand with self-revelation'.[38]

And as Gary Marx asks, 'Where is the notion that personal exposure and the capturing of ever more private aspects of the self is desirable, normal and harmless, located?' His reply is that 'soft surveillance' from the consumer realm, which is a less intrusive means of personal data collection, makes the giving of body data less controversial when couched in particular languages and a particular media and cultural climate.[39] At the same time, such exposure is actively sought by the Circle and all mega-corporations that aspire to the same goals.

Mae's understanding about why she should expose her life to others comes from the expectations of her employers, in relation to rewards and satisfactions of a consumer kind and also because of the 'therapeutic' impulse of being accepted by her colleagues and workmates. Of course, this also means that each employee's utility is measured according to their contribution to company profits and they are also in competition with all other co-workers, indeed, everyone in a given team.[40]

Unsurprisingly, this connects with Zuboff's Google-based analysis of surveillance capitalism dependent on Big Data.[41] If for the purpose of analysis data are treated as if there were no embodied person generating them, then why reconnect the two in the human resources or marketing departments? Here again is Zuboff's 'formal indifference', seen in the new business model, towards both employees and consumers or users. There may be employer expectations that workers will check in 24/7, but it is not reciprocated by any kind of care for the same workers. In

2014, for example, a Gallup poll showed that around a third of US employers expected workers to keep in touch by email in non-work time.[42]

Jodi Dean mentions the well-worn phrase, 'if you have nothing to hide, you have nothing to fear', suggesting it resonates with the notion that if it is not public then it has been withheld.[43] As Ball says, 'some individuals explicitly perceive themselves as surveillance targets, required to reveal more about themselves in order to avoid further scrutiny or to promote their own "truths"'. And Dean again: 'Technoculture materialises the belief that the key to democracy can be found in uncovering secrets.'

Is *The Circle* utopia or dystopia?

The Circle is what one might call a utopian-dystopian novel. Is it one or the other, or both? One of the three wise men, Bailey, sounds like Mark Zuckerberg, complete with a hoodie, who is a total believer in total transparency. Bailey also sounds suspiciously like Jeremy Bentham, who created the famous panopticon prison design, when he says: 'We can cure any disease, end hunger, everything, because we won't be dragged down by all our weaknesses, our petty secrets, our hoarding of information and knowledge. We will finally reach our full potential.' Bentham himself said of his plan, 'Morals reformed – health preserved – industry invigorated – instruction diffused – public burthens lightened – Economy seated, as it were, upon a rock – the Gordian Knot of the poor-law not cut, but untied – all by a simple idea in Architecture!'[44]

Long before *The Circle* appeared, Bauman once mused: 'This seems to be a dystopia made to the measure of liquid modernity – one fit to replace the fears recorded in Orwellian and Huxleyan-style nightmares.'[45] But his phrasing fits *The Circle* perfectly. What he had in mind was the disintegration of the social, the melting of 'bonds which interlock individual choices and collective projects and actions'[46] due to the changing relationship between space and time. New technologies enable not only speed but also acceleration, which in turn makes mobility a basic feature of life. Everything is short term, until further notice, disposable, now including social relationships. Bauman sounded perhaps more pessimistic than in his earlier phase of enthusiasm for 'socialism, the active utopia'. But Bauman still quotes the Apostle Paul: 'hope that is seen is not hope; for who hopes for what he sees?'[47]

In contrast, Margaret Atwood, in reviewing *The Circle*, avers, 'Some will call The Circle a "dystopia", but ... we are in the green and pleasant land of a satirical utopia for our times, where recycling and organics abound, people keep saying how much they like each other, and the brave new world of virtual sharing and caring breeds monsters.'[48] Her take, then, is that *The Circle* is not so much a dystopia as a 'satirical utopia'. Of course, much dystopian writing is satirical as well, so the fact that *The Circle* oozes with satire does not decide the case. Atwood's status not only as an astute literary critic but also as the acclaimed author of several bestselling dystopian novels[49] should maybe give me pause if I differ. My best hope is that readers make up their own minds – based hopefully on reading the novel, not merely my summary notes on it.

The Circle is a novel with a strong storyline about everyday life in the digital age. You do not have to be a student of surveillance to realize this – subtlety is not Eggers' strong suit here, deliberately so, as I see it. Indeed, not only does the Silicon Valley mega-corporation aim at total transparency, which creates the taut tension throughout the book, but its author takes pains to reference several other surveillance dystopias, from Zamyatin's *We* to Huxley's *Brave New World* as well as Orwell's *Nineteen Eighty-Four*. Eggers reveals Mae's own rootedness – if that is the right word – in consumer culture because she is employed in 'Customer Experience'.

Eggers' descriptions are dramatic and sometimes distressing. I believe that Eggers' own view is that *The Circle* is dystopic. Dystopia, as I understand it, is an undesirable but avoidable future, often described in fictional terms. In the realm of surveillance, the most famous in the West is Orwell's *Nineteen Eighty-Four* but many others also exist as both novels and films. They draw attention to the negative logic of present trends, warn about where things are heading and about what could happen if a change of direction does not occur.

To count as dystopian they must also contain clues about ways out and alternatives. Margaret Atwood would say that I miss the point: *The Circle* is a satirical utopia. True, the founders of the Circle see it as a place of light and love, and even Eggers' description locates all poverty, disease and degradation *outside* the Circle's campus. And although Mae's own life finally merges with the Circle, Eggers more than hints that this was both undesirable and avoidable.

Surely this novel is dystopian in the sense used by Bauman when he describes life in *Liquid Modernity* and in *Liquid Surveillance*.[50] In the former book, Bauman saw the 'end of the Panopticon' as 'the end of the era of mutual engagement'.[51] Now the settled majority, he says, is ruled by a nomadic and extraterritorial elite with its light and fluid – even pleasant, I might add – practices of power. Any tight or solid network of social bonds must be dissolved by the disposable and the fluid. That is why he perceives another era taking shape than that of Orwell or Huxley.

The Circle still has an edge over the irritated, grumpy critique; it tells a story, draws you in, helps you to recognize what is going on, assess unfolding plot and locate yourself in relation to one character or another. Of course, Eggers himself is not immersed in Silicon Valley. Is he, as Mercer said of Mae, also commenting from outside, rather than living the world he describes? People working in Northern California may well be dubious about his description and may object that he doesn't understand them. But does one have to be part of the situation to describe it accurately? Is it not enough to wade into the edge of the ocean to get the feel for its waves and tides, its currents and its cold?

The dark side of hope

Margaret Atwood states: 'The critical dystopia is the dark side of hope, and hopes for a way out; anti-utopia attributes the darkness to the utopia itself, and tells us the exits are ambushed.'[52] Those grand twentieth-century dystopias from Zamyatin, Huxley or Orwell, Ursula Le Guin or Margaret Atwood dump the reader right into a world where it does seem that the exits are ambushed. The cold darkness presses in, oppressively. But Eggers signals only the trail that ends in tyranny. Much of today's everyday reality is there, albeit in compressed scenes and vivid metaphor. He is nervous lest we miss the message. He asks that we pull back the wool, open our eyes, do differently.

Can one go beyond this, to a more critical utopian vision that explores alternatives to current social, political, economic and cultural arrangements such that they might catalyse social transformation? Snowden might be said to attempt such a shift, with reminders about the original values of the internet. As a thoughtful technical expert, he believes in the potential for democratic development and human flourishing in the internet, responsibly opened up. Snowden says less, however, about how the world of internet surveillance is a product of and expresses neatly a neoliberal political economy and a culture of consumer surveillance, with all that entails.

It is all too clear to many that current political-economic arrangements spell poverty for the global majority, and produce alienation, repression, competition, conflict, friable relationships and separations for all, rich and poor alike. And today's surveillance undoubtedly contributes to and facilitates this world. And in the way surveillance develops today, suspicion supplants trust, categorization produces cumulative disadvantage and people are treated according to their characterizations as disembodied, abstract data. Is there really an exit? What does Eggers say?

Does Eggers' novel suggest a way out, or does he too succumb to a paralysing anti-utopianism rather than a hopeful dystopianism? *The Circle* may be unsubtle in some ways but it is never trivial or superficial. Eggers' aim is to show us how surveillance society arrived rather than to propose a way out. In a sense, recognizing how people – you and I – comply, how common it is to go with the flows, may be the first step to more critical and cautious involvement in the digital world. His point is that the world that Mae is so enamoured with – and in the end won over by – appears utopian but is in fact dystopian. By indicating how it may appear attractive to Mae but by heavy-handedly labouring the downsides his satire becomes sarcasm. He wants the reader to wake up but, appropriately for a novelist, he does not prescribe what she should do when she does.

There is a moment, however fleeting, when it seems that the dominant culture of the Circle is threatened by a lurking fifth columnist. Kalden, with whom Mae has secret trysts and with whom she shared her confession that 'everything and everyone should be seen', appears to be less than convinced: 'But who wants to be watched all the time?' When it turns out that Kalden is none other than Ty Gospodinov, one of the three wise men, the extent of the reversal becomes clear. The new convert rhapsodizes to a corporate senior who is having serious second thoughts. He eventually tries to enlist her as a co-conspiratorial ally in undermining what he now fears is the totalitarian Circle. Mae feigns agreement and things start to unravel ...

The utopian-dystopian viewpoint thus stimulates awareness of our current choices, whether just in the world of social media involvement or more generally in relation to surveillance in a post-9/11, post-Snowden world. To set the tension as Eggers does raises the question of whether things have to be thus. To show, ironically, that the apparent 'heaven' is, in its least attractive aspects, closer to hell – understood as the full realization of the consequences of everyday choices – is Eggers' contribution. The narrative has to be unsubtle at times in order to make this more subtle point. If Eggers' *The Circle* is a dystopia, as I suggest, do we need more than dystopian views of 'surveillance society' in which the utopia turns out to be anything but?

Perhaps there is also a need for a robust utopianism to indicate some alternatives. Not an imaginary society, some impractical proposals or an escapist fantasy so much as a description of some real alternatives to the present. Something which might fuel desire for something different, something better, which goes beyond variations in the content, form or function of utopias.[53] I have in mind Eric Stoddart's haunting question about whether we can go beyond 'surveillance of' others to consider the possibilities of 'surveillance *for* others'.[54] Or Julie Cohen's proposal that we appropriate

Amartya Sen's concept of 'human flourishing' for the world of surveillance and privacy.

'Human flourishing requires not only physical well-being but also psychological and social well-being, including the capacity for cultural and political participation,' claims Cohen.[55] How should surveillance be considered in relation to the common good?[56] Eggers, like these theorists, goes far beyond an approach that merely minimizes harms towards a more careful interpretive approach that considers people in their real daily practices. The imaginaries and practices of surveillance culture do not have to remain the same, Eggers hints, heavily. The final chapter explores some of these plausible futures of alternative possibilities.

6
Hidden Hope

The culture of surveillance, seen through the lens of the imaginaries and practices of mundane, everyday life, troubles more common visions of surveillance today. The mention of surveillance often summons images of spooks and spies, of video cameras recording what goes on in the street or perhaps the personal profiles held by corporate or government bodies in some data centre. This book urges that we look beyond such images to consider people's everyday experiences of surveillance, how they think about them and act on what they know. And this includes a variety of responses, from accepting and even adopting surveillance practices to assessing and sometimes opposing surveillance at any scale.

As we have seen, today's is a much more complex cultural landscape than a them-and-us binary, where 'they' watch 'us', intrude on our privacy, violate our rights. These things happen, of course, and vigilance about them is paramount in ever more intensively surveillant situations. But they sometimes happen because ordinary citizens have acquiesced in the use of new technologies or because social media users are turning the tools of surveillance on each other. Not that security agency overreach is the fault of complacent citizens or that social surveillance is somehow equivalent to police surveillance. Rather, to engage with surveillance culture is to ask about hearts and minds, everyday attitudes and actions, as well as to analyse technologies, profits or policies.

These tensions inform the debate in this final chapter, about what sorts of imaginaries and practices might develop, and which ones might be fostered in the future. The paths taken in the book bring together the worlds of surveillance capitalism and surveillance culture, showing how they grow symbiotically. I stress the ways that, in the twenty-first century conditions of digital modernity, there is a need to go beyond the Orwellian frame of *Nineteen Eighty-Four* and find suitable depictions of surveillance that capture today's realities. From the many possible options I chose to focus on *The Circle*, just because it captures so clearly and cleverly today's social and cultural realities.[1]

The Circle is also a fine foil for *Nineteen Eighty-Four* because, like the latter, it touches on the deeper questions raised by the enlargement of surveillance. No single novel has had a fraction of the impact in the West that Orwell's has enjoyed, but equally, no other contemporary novel than that by Eggers that I have encountered encapsulates so sympathetically yet in such scorching satire the themes that I have endeavoured to expose and explain in this book. If I knew a film that did a better job, for instance, I might have used that. Beyond this, *The Circle* also offers some memorable characters who may be used to typify different elements of surveillance culture.

As well, within its fictional format, *The Circle* addresses simultaneously the questions of surveillance culture and surveillance capitalism. On the one hand there is the deftly described experience of Mae's 'going transparent', with her initial uncertainty, emotional turmoil and eventual embrace. She would lead the way, become a celebrity employee. Her creative kayaking, unreported and, she thought, off-camera, was behaviour that could be rectified, levelled to the norm. Which brings us to the other hand – the way that the Silicon Valley corporation demands and delights in transparency because it makes the machine work more smoothly, operationalizing and accelerating all processes.[2] The Circle seeks the standardized style, disliking the different, the foreign, the Other.

To recap. The three central chapters in Part II of the book examine performance and compliance, the normalization of surveillance and how selves are formed in surveillance culture. Chapter 5, on *The Circle*, shows how the same sorts of themes are treated in a novel. No single social or cultural analysis could hope to catch so engagingly the spirit of surveillance culture, or to display so convincingly its downsides and dilemmas. In a sense, while social-cultural analysis attempts to diagnose today's world of surveillance saturation, smartphone and social media use, a novel like *The Circle* diagnoses us. If 'diagnosis' sounds critical – suggesting there is something not quite right about this world – this is not a mistake. Some aspects of the emerging surveillance culture are less welcome than others.

This chapter responds to the diagnosis, to the assessment of today's social-cultural condition. Earlier, I affirmed Jonathan Finn's assertion that, having grasped that 'surveillance is no longer the purview of police, the state and corporations but that it is a constitutive element of life ...' then this 'requires a self-reflexive look at our own willingness and desire to watch, record and display our lives and the lives of others'.[3] So this chapter suggests two key areas for focus that could be construed technically as ethics and politics but that, in keeping with the book's central theme, lean towards imaginaries and practices.

Under the heading of 'recognition and responsibility', I suggest that the real issue lying behind other important questions such as visibility and exposure is that of persons; how they are recognized and how they take responsibility. Following from this, under 'rights and regulations', I propose that power be understood as something within reach rather than simply over against ordinary people. And that a notion of 'good gazing' relating to fairness could underlie approaches to those rights and regulations.

'There is a crack in everything,' growls Leonard Cohen, 'that's how the light gets in.'[4] The 'cracks' producing surveillance culture are evident in this book, but where might one hope for light to break through? The hidden hope advertised in the chapter title draws the book to a close or, better, to an opening. The hidden hope refers in part to what the previous sections show – that while some forms of analysis produce a sense that nothing can be done about massive global forces, in fact, human agency is never restricted to the codes of the dominant culture. The quest for alternatives or even for outright resistance is not futile. But the hidden hope is also a humble reminder that hope's fulfilment is never fully understood or experienced by those seeking it. We cannot know in advance how things will work out, but it is possible to articulate more clearly and strive towards some desirable features of the hoped-for world.

The Circle and surveillance culture

The Circle holds up a mirror in which we see ourselves. Maybe you are like Mae, increasingly at home and at ease with the wise men, having been initiated into the importance of being always on, always available, always open to the world. If so, you have become accustomed to the metrics-and-performance-driven world of work or you have fallen prey to the seductive sirens of social media. In either case, performance is the purpose. In Mae's story we recognize others we know or know about. They, with Mae, represent the *dominant* elements of surveillance culture, those most closely aligned with the techno-political-economic status quo of surveillance capitalism, which live by the nothing-to-hide-nothing-to-fear mantra and are okay with checking the profiles of strangers.

Or perhaps you identify with Mae's ex, Mercer, for his nagging doubts about transparency and being 'always on'. And, of course, in her kayak, don't forget that Mae herself once relaxed into a comfortable switching off for a while. Is Eggers hinting that such sporadic disengagement would help to keep being online in perspective? Absolutely, as I see it! Mercer had no intention of succumbing to the belief that life online exhausts the meaning of life itself. There is so much more than onlife! Mercer could be seen as representing a *residual* element in surveillance culture. He is a Luddite in the historical sense of someone who has a reasoned and ethical scepticism about new technologies. After all, he drives a truck, listens to the radio. His attempt to escape was prompted not by technophobia but by Mae's turning a fugitive-finding program on him.

A third possibility is that you feel like the shadowy figure, Kalden, with whom Mae has an uncertain romantic attachment. She shares freely with him but does not know clearly where she stands with him. Kalden, revealed as Ty Gospodinov, one of the Circle's founders, has apparently seen the light, recognized the totalitarian tendencies of his own creation and is ready to dismantle what he has made before more harm is done. Kalden is an *emergent* element in surveillance culture. Despite his association with the dominant culture, his increasingly radical questioning leads not merely to seeking alternatives but to outright opposition, from within.

Throughout the book, I have stressed how surveillance culture may be seen as a shadow of mainstream surveillance strategies, now, arguably, understood as surveillance capitalism. Such mainstream activities include controlling crime, managing cities, securitizing transport and communication systems – all of which are, in Michel de Certeau's sense, 'strategies' of power. In his stimulating analysis, turning to everyday life is to find 'tactics' of power that contrast with and sometimes contest the dominant codes of control and efficiency. From trying to understand what some of those tactics might be, through exploring imaginaries and practices, we discover new kinds of creativity as people identify and pursue meanings that are important to them. Some may be normalizing and complacent. Others offer fresh ways of seeing and being, in digital environments.

Of course, tactical activities may be found, on occasion, *within* the sphere of strategies. Think of Kalden. Or they may be mixed, or just negatively disposed towards the internet, as in the case of Mercer. Or apparently innocent and healthy tactics, such as switching off for a while, could be squeezed by pressures – even pleasures – of conformity, which of course was what happened with Mae. The sorts of tactics that we discuss in what follows are informed by situations and initiatives described and explored in the rest of this book, coloured by the kinds of priorities that seem appropriate for confronting pressing questions such as security agency overreach or corporate obsessions with valorizing personal data.

If this book is to encourage a stepping back to yield a wider range of vision, three issues should be borne in mind. The first is the need to notice the wider contexts of small-scale experiences of surveillance. Giving them names, such as the Internet of Things, Smart Cities, or Wearables, for example, even if these are promotional labels, indicates what sorts of processes prompt the micro-level experiences of, for example, being asked by an employer to wear a tracking device. How might these experiences undermine trust, generate disadvantage for some, or simply be an instance of treating others only in terms of disembodied, abstract data?

Secondly, how may emerging surveillance imaginaries and practices relate to actual ethical and political responses that could be shared responsibilities? After all, what may at first feel like personal troubles often turn out to be public issues.[5] Is there room for alliances or coalitions with others of like mind and purpose? How can online connections be used for this activity? While today's surveillance sorts people into social categories, it provides no means for those finding themselves in the same categories to join forces in a democratic way to propose alternatives to current developments.

Thirdly, it is worth recalling a point made repeatedly here, that the attitudes and actions of users make a difference. One of the indirect ways in which the Snowden revelations became relevant to internet users was through demonstrating how profoundly security agencies as well as internet companies depend on data gleaned from social media and other internet use. User-generated surveillance, in the sense of everyday online activities yielding constant data streams, is critical to the successful operation of numerous platforms and systems, from GCHQ – the UK partner of the NSA – to Amazon or Uber. Surveillance imaginaries and practices affect how well the systems that construct subjects as commodities or suspects actually work. The elements for surveillance imaginaries and practices described here are personal and local as well as having globalized corporate and governmental scope.

Recognition and responsibility

In this section I push the argument about visibility a little further. Having noted how important visibility is within surveillance culture, I now want to accent an aspect of visibility often referred to as recognition. Mae wanted to be seen online as a feature of her very existence. She wanted recognition as having a distinct identity, something she shares with millions of internet and social media users. What I wish to tease out of this are some possibilities for what I call good gazing, in which an ethics of care linked with human flourishing informs surveillance imaginaries.

While I often refer to those engaging with the internet and social media as users, this could be thought of as a way of ignoring the many other dimensions of their lives, despite my actual desire to do justice to their humanity. In discussing the use of data analysis, earlier in the book, I acknowledged that the critical issue is the assumptions made about human beings as persons, and how their identities and relationships are affected by Big Data practices.[6] The same applies to surveillance imaginaries of those commonly using social media and the internet. Personhood is crucially important and needs to be asserted and struggled for at every level. Visibility and recognition are one aspect of this.

Another way of saying this relates to what Nicholas Mirzoeff calls 'looking'.[7] His superb history *The Right to Look* focuses on large-scale cultural modes of visuality from the plantation to the colony and to the military-industrial complex, but he begins with the 'right to look' at a personal level, 'with the look into someone else's eyes to express friendship, solidarity or love'. It must be a mutual look, too, says Mirzoeff, and it implies something much larger: 'It means requiring the recognition of the other in order to have a place from which to claim rights and to determine what is right.'[8] What I have to say follows a parallel trajectory, from the personal to the political in an unbroken line.

The desire for visibility is a vital component, conveniently choreographed by new media consumerism, but it is sometimes tempered by anxieties from a different source, national security strategies and their paradoxical insecurities. Wishing to be seen in Instagram photos or Facebook posts may simultaneously be linked with fear of potential consequences of exposure. Imaginaries and practices relating to exposure betray a complex array of emotions and activities. But which of them feed into positive responses to issues of recognition, relationships and responsibility?

Recall that in chapter 4 the issue was aired of how the presentation of online selves is imagined. As we saw, some security experts think in terms of 'narcissism', a self-absorbed approach to self-presentation where the unknown online audience has to be presented with a persona that will be more or less artificial. Narcissism is not usually used in a complimentary fashion, however. That it may be present in some cases is not a good reason for using it in a blanket fashion. Kate Hawkins suggests that something like Foucault's 'confession' is closer to the mark than 'narcissism'.[9] In this view, online subjects are not merely subjects *of* powers that draw confessions from us, but also subjects *of* confession, seeing themselves as knowledgeable, thinking subjects. The former is disempowering, the latter, empowering. In this sense, says Hawkins, online confession could be seen as a search for accuracy of representation or of truth in determining how you are made visible.

When Goffman wrote in the mid-twentieth century, he thought that self-presentation performances could sometimes be relaxed, for example after a job interview. But online life does not really allow such relaxation. Maintaining the persona is constant hard work. At the same time, internet companies' use of multiple sources of data means that their sense – and probably with them, security agencies' sense – of who people are is the one that counts behind the scenes, as it were.[10] What internet users think of as their mode of visibility, their self-presentation, works on different criteria from the corporate and state systems, which make them visible for other purposes. Internet users are much more likely to present themselves to known than unknown others.

Visibility is an all too real aspect of daily life, which demands constant negotiation.[11] It is definitely relational, in that seeing and being seen are each involved. Moreover, our *ways* of seeing are socially crafted and varied. Without being seen in some way, we cannot be recognized or identified. Online, as in offline life, with some effort, people can be relatively invisible, at least in relation to other ordinary users, almost to the point of disappearance. Others, however, notably social media celebrities, become supervisible.[12] Building on this, Eric Stoddart speaks of negotiating visibility by invoking a notion of 'in/visibility'.[13]

For Stoddart, in/visibility is active, perhaps performative, in that it is able to evaluate the conditions of being seen or not, as well as the resources on which people draw to make themselves more and less visible for specific strategic[14] purposes. In relation to social media in particular, this negotiating skill can inform attitudes to large internet companies as well as what to disclose, or not. Given that data are both in the foreground – phones, tablets – and the background – financial information, traffic monitoring – of daily life, how one interacts with data has to be considered at every level. Under what conditions, consciously or unconsciously, do people give access to their data?[15]

As *The Circle* or *Black Mirror* reflect daily realities, in satire or caricature, further questions arise of how new online media affect relationships at the most basic level. Negotiating visibility occurs in contexts where being drawn together with others or pushed apart are constantly in flux. For Roger Silverstone, a key issue of all contemporary media is their capacity to bring people together and simultaneously to keep them apart.[16] Proximity, not distance, he argues, is required for properly moral responses. Of course, there does also have to be some separation of self and other, as Emmanuel Levinas insists, to provide a context for respect and responsibility. Levinas stresses that subjects are brought into being, at a profound level, by responsibility for the other. The 'face', for him, is crucial.[17]

Paradoxically, perhaps, the ethics of the 'face' offers hope for reconsidering today's surveillance practices. For Levinas, the face of the other calls us to a basic human responsibility for the welfare, the flourishing, of the other. But while it is true that technologies of data processing distance one person from another and may contribute to forgetting that responsibility, one has to wonder whether literal proximity is required for humanity to be asserted. The face is a reminder that seeing surveillantly, whether done by organizations or just curious individuals, depends on a data image or online persona, not the presence of the flesh-and-blood person. Are there really no ways for maintaining responsibility for the other at a distance, using internet technologies?

Some, such as Bauman, say modernity has created social spaces with no moral proximity. Craig Calhoun, for example, traces how relationality is affected by modern conditions, especially those dependent on information technologies.[18] If primary relations are face-to-face and secondary ones are mediated, for example through bureaucracy, then the third and fourth levels take this further. There may be no co-presence in tertiary relationships – say, an email to the bank about an error on a statement – and not even any direct contact at all in quaternary ones. These latter are largely the product of surveillance, in which, for example, a sociotechnical system such as WhatsApp, prompted by someone sending a text message, also analyses the data thus generated. Thus a further communication is created from the original text, of which the original author is unaware and with consequences for her that she can probably not even guess.

Some implications of this are discussed dramatically in Sherry Turkle's critical social-psychological analysis *Alone Together*. The second half of the book is about young people on the internet,[19] which for many users is not merely compelling but compulsive (Turkle is also a psychotherapist, which helps explain some use of language). Their digital absorption is scarcely comprehended by older adults, particularly when teens might find a phone call threatening in its real-time immediacy, as the live performance requires unedited spontaneity. Other users, according to Turkle, may be thought of by these same young people as resources to be used or problems to be managed, which sounds, to me, ominously like the approach of surveillance capitalism. It denies that the other, above all else, should be seen as a person to be cared about.

Of course, one could carp about Turkle's rather psychologized approach or the limited range of respondents in her study. But she is not attempting to investigate the political economy of the internet or to provide some representative sample of internet users. Two factors make her work worthy of serious attention. One is that she has been examining human–computer relations for decades, starting with a very optimistic account of the computer as a 'second self'.[20] Turkle's conclusions are much more measured today. The other factor, linked with the first, is that her work hits unavoidably an ethical note. She asks whether a line is being crossed, not so much in people's relations with 'technology' but fundamentally in how people see each other.

This, I believe, is why recognition is an important category. Negotiating visibility is indeed what dealing with surveillance is about. But seeking visibility is not the end of the story. Persons wish to be recognized for a sense of who they are and the value accorded to them. Charles Taylor, who initiated current debates over recognition, sees recognition as related to identity, a sense of what is human.[21] And identity develops through interaction with others; it is not something generated individually. It also relates to dignity, a vital plank on which democracy rests.

It may sound like an impossible goal in a world of surveillance capitalism, and even an almost unattainable aspiration for surveillance culture, but if surveillance imaginaries had at their heart a sense that such recognition is desirable, then this would contribute to some very different kinds of surveillance. Indeed, this sort of surveillance could be construed as good gazing, something that reaffirms the human rather than reducing humanness to data images. To see the other not as a competitor or a component of one's own ladder to success, but as someone to be cared about, even to take responsibility for, would contribute to human flourishing rather than the shrinking of humanity. Needless to say, this speaks to practices as well as to imaginaries.

Rights and regulations

The benefits of recognition spill over from surveillance imaginaries to practices. Our identities are shaped in part by recognition, but that recognition, in turn, is an essential dimension of democracy, where being recognized on equal terms with others is a constant goal. Just as *The Circle*'s Mae finds herself trying out a new identity as she accepts and models transparency, so also she propels herself into a role of leadership in democratic development. As the three wise men declare their desire to promote democracy by making every Circle member a voter, Mae caps it with a further step: make voting compulsory. Pure, direct democracy! Quickly, they arrange a beta version and try the first test: 'Should we have more veggie options at lunch?'

For Circle leaders, full knowledge and participation could be assured through democracy, or 'demoxie' in their words. For Bailey, knowledge, and 'equal access to all human experience', are basic human rights. Everyone has access; everyone has a say. The reader might be thrown for a moment – where is the satire? Pressures for equal inclusion on the basis of race, gender and sexuality are contemporary political priorities. And attempts at exploiting the political possibilities of social media sound suspiciously like what is already occurring in European and Brazilian populist groups that use 'liquid feedback' to obtain direct comment on government policy.[22]

The satire is in Mae's naive dreams of the outcome of the Circle's 'completion'. It 'would bring peace, and it would bring unity, and all that messiness of humanity until now, all those uncertainties that accompanied the world before the Circle, would be only a memory'. It is the persistent messiness of humanity and those nagging uncertainties to which most Circlers seem oblivious. While equal access and equal say may be good goals, they are neither uncontroversial nor easy to implement. As well, other aspects of technological innovation in the political process, such as voter surveillance that appears to undermine some vital aspects of democracy, could clash with liquid feedback.[23]

So what sorts of surveillance practices might actually support democratic development in quest of human flourishing and the common good? Is there some hopeful realism that both sees the ongoing potential of human agency and also admits that messiness and uncertainty are an unavoidable part of the human condition? Several questions are considered, briefly, that offer ways to develop fresh surveillance practices. We start with the question of agency, before commenting on data justice and fairness, context and care with data, and lastly, digital citizenship.

Acting against the dominant code

Raymond Williams notes that agency is never limited by the dominant code. In all but the most extreme cases, alternatives are possible. It is all too easy to imagine that, given the power of states and corporations, no action is possible. But if, as I have proposed throughout, knowledge of feedback loops can be encouraged, then it becomes easier to see how the activities of everyday internet users – and others engaged with new technologies – can be shown to make a difference.

These are the local tactics that engage with the global strategies of large-scale organizations. The latter are geared to control, efficiency and profit, the former with the meanings, for them, of their interaction with everything from street cameras to online gaming. In everyday life, people interpret their uses of technology in the light of their imaginaries, out of which practices grow. Even in the case of one of the largest entities, Facebook, the corporation does not have everything its way. We have seen that its users may object to new developments such that the behemoth has to back down.

To assume that resignation is the dominant mood or the only available option is to accept a lopsided view of subjects and of power. Such negative and defeatist views are fed by notions of internet users merely as 'subjects *to* power', as Balibar and Isin and Ruppert put it,[24] in the thrall of global corporations supported by government, and not also, simultaneously, as 'subjects *of* power'. Fed by images of Big Brother as a feature of global security agencies and internet corporations, it is easy for surveillance imaginaries to be dominated by the sense of remote, out-of-control organizations. After all, they are hugely powerful and often resist moves to make their activities more open or accountable.

Of course, citizens may well participate in their own submission by accepting terms of service without reading them or going along with security theatre at the airport. But even within those situations, opportunities for questioning, negotiating and even subversion may open up. Such participation offers chances for making rights claims that can contribute to the overall shaping of the internet or for contributing to the mitigation of unnecessary security procedures. Small but significant acts that could stimulate shared practices.

It is true that the challenges are tremendous; we do not downplay them here. Surveillance is opaque to those with no technical background; few know how it works; surveillance is invisible because it is usually digital – increasingly miniature or hidden cameras or the use of plastic cards with barcodes and other sensors are the tip of the iceberg – and algorithmic; and surveillance is often covert or inadequately publicized, especially in relation to policing or national security. At the same time, because personhood is played down and life-chances and opportunities are directly or even indirectly affected, matters such as these should be a matter of public scrutiny and participation, attuned to data justice and fairness.

Data justice and fairness

Social sorting is a feature of all surveillance and represents a key social and political challenge that should prompt appropriate practices. Interestingly, Charles Taylor's work speaks to this via what he calls the politics of recognition. Resources ought to be justly distributed, in this view, and recognition is a way to ensure that this happens, over against opaque criteria such as the marketers' 'lifetime value' of consumers. Others have tweaked Taylor's position: Nancy Fraser, who says that distribution and recognition cannot be reduced to each other, and Axel Honneth, who insists that recognition is enough to ensure that matters of distribution can be dealt with justly.[25] When a key aspect of large-scale surveillance is social sorting, with all too real consequences materially and in terms of life-chances for those involved, the significance of recognition becomes very evident.

Having stressed that the culture of surveillance affects everyone, its politics, too, is an everyday affair, in shopping, social media use, how to handle others' data and our own in the workplace and myriad other sites. If surveillance is embedded within, brought about by and generates cultural imaginaries and practices, then it is plainly important to see surveillance within the frames of reference of ordinary people; the insider, not just the outsider view. So the big questions have to do not only with algorithms and encryption – where technical expertise as well as sound wisdom are required – but with a more general 'data justice'[26] and with the everyday means of making a difference, of exercising agency. For instance, Helen Kennedy and Giles Moss imagine 'conditions in which data mining is not just used as a way to know publics, but can become a means for publics to know themselves'.[27]

As noted earlier, Helen Kennedy and her colleagues found, in studying user responses in the UK, Norway and Spain, that a key question is 'fairness'.[28] Rather than rely on quantitative studies of opinions on using social media, they chose a different method. They asked social media users in focus groups what they thought about data mining, based on their internet use. It turned out that their varying viewpoints on data-mining practices had in common an expressed concern about fairness. Kennedy et al. found that the context is crucial[29] and that fairness was salient in relation to more general concerns with well-being and social justice. By not framing the focus groups in terms of surveillance or privacy, the researchers were able to let the users offer their own responses in their own words.

If we are to understand the issues for surveillance practice in relation to fairness, then it is appropriate to conceive these issues in terms of 'data justice'. Using loyalty cards or engaging with social media, or even walking freely along city streets watched by video cameras, means that data pertaining to our everyday lives are available to others. And those organizations analyse the data in ways that affect our opportunities for better or for worse. In the world of service provision in American cities, practices such as red-lining are seen as a means of reproducing social inequalities. It occurs when services are denied or made inaccessible to certain areas based on the racial make-up of those areas. How much more so those automated surveillance practices that affect others across a whole range of life-chances and choices? This is even further accented when the very nature of capitalism is undergoing change as it depends increasingly heavily on the manipulation of data.

Several commentators and analysts note that, following Snowden, there has been a resurgence of political activism in the digital realm.[30] In Canada, for instance, OpenMedia. ca has become a leading commentator and activist group in relation to the internet. A number of sophisticated technical forms of political activism and resistance involve encryption, more secure networks or other specialized responses to data-driven surveillance. But these tasks are often outsourced to expert groups. Unfortunately, such experts often expect users to protect themselves using tools provided by developers.

To address this apparent divide, Lina Dencik, along with others,[31] suggests that security engineers and others learn more of the language of collective action, rather than merely individual assistance, to try to expand the scope of potential action. Encouraging users to understand the outlook of technical experts would also help the situation. Beyond the potential for opposition to unwarranted and unwanted surveillance, however, is a further issue of how internet users might themselves benefit from data mining, rather than it merely being a tool used by powerful corporations.

Context and care with data

Wider concerns with personal data, expressed in terms of fairness and data justice, are the context within which all everyday data issues arise. Data are highly valued by corporations as well as by government departments. While a key problem is that fully living persons may be reduced to their data doubles by marketers or security agents, the other side of the coin is seen when less care than necessary is given to personal data. These data are not merely significant because they spell profit for companies or profiles for police. Their real significance, however limited or inconsequential they may appear, is that they refer to persons. The care with which someone is treated in face-to-face presence should be extended when handling personal data, in whatever context. Of course, such radically countercultural surveillance practices have to be worked out practically in varying contexts, but the person-oriented starting point is of the essence.

Contexts are crucial. Surveillance practices require sensitivity to the situation in question. Nissenbaum's insights on 'contextual integrity' are fruitful and widely cited in this field, informing and prompting a number of studies that try to engage more directly with how issues of personal information handling are understood by ordinary users of the internet.[32] For Nissenbaum, context cannot safely be ignored. People disclose information in specific contexts and expect that it will be used appropriately in that context. To ignore this is to violate their rights, she argues. Not limiting herself to the circulation of personal data on the internet, Nissenbaum also discusses this in relation to loyalty cards used in consumer surveillance, to public and private video cameras, and the use of biometrics such as fingerprints and facial recognition.

Indeed, Nissenbaum's initial studies of contextual integrity appeared just as social media were taking off, which meant that her proposals were available to be applied in that area, too.[33] Her work, in other words, is highly pertinent to surveillance culture. She provides evidence of how surveillance imaginaries are nuanced and how different norms of practices circulate within each area.

Because the internet is so important today, it is essential that emerging practices be seen for what they are. Not only are issues of surveillance intelligence-gathering and analysis primarily *about* the internet, arguments relating to them are frequently conducted *on* and *through* the internet. Most of what is discussed as the culture of surveillance relates to the internet in some way, not only national security surveillance but also social media, the internet of things, and the ways that our devices and environments are increasingly inter-linked and, of course, self-recording and sharing data. This again prompts questions of how people communicate online and what differences are made to their everyday practices by so doing.

Digital citizenship

Daily life involves a whole bundle of roles that have to be performed and negotiated constantly. Some of them refer to close relationships of domestic and familial kinds, some to relationships with friends, workmates, team members and neighbours, and yet others to those that connect us with institutions and authorities, whether banks or bars, churches or charities, city councils or national governments. Each set of relationships is now, at least partially, mediated digitally, and that digital mediation, as should now be quite clear, is by definition surveillant. Although surveillance is not their exclusive concern, Engin Isin and Evelyn Ruppert's *Being Digital Citizens* helps explain why the politics of surveillance takes on some new and different characteristics today.

The idea of 'digital citizens' is not limited to some famous or notorious activists such as Edward Snowden, Julian Assange or Chelsea Manning. Digital citizens appear wherever the internet is the medium through which things are done. While legal or technical documents often describe internet users as 'data subjects', this suggests they are simply created or at least controlled by the data. On the other hand, some activists put the shoe on the other foot, describing users as 'sovereign subjects', in other words, people capable of more but who are constrained by the internet. Isin and Ruppert remark that, while digital citizens are in some ways compliant, they may also contest what is happening by claiming their rights.

The central issue is that, while 'subjects' is a good word, it has to be thought of in two ways at the same time. People are both 'subjects *to* power' in that our lives are profoundly affected in positive and negative ways by data and the internet, and 'subjects *of* power' in that they may demonstrate subversive as well as submissive behaviours in online life. Digital citizens come into being, in part, as data politics begins to form in recognizable ways, generating 'worlds, subjects and rights'.[34] Our very relationship as citizens with states is now mediated by the internet and by data, and as we make rights claims about those data, we do so prompted and provoked into governing ourselves and others through such claims.

After all, these authors hint, we are not talking about mere 'dead data' as if data do nothing. It is those data that actually help to generate certain kinds of everyday realities such as whether or not we are eligible for some government benefit or, as we have been discussing, who gets detained in airport security. As well, debates about data are all too often a bit like shooting stars. Seen momentarily, as bright, newsworthy flashes of light, they create controversies about security breaches that leave personal data vulnerable to misuse, or about corporations like Google claiming that they can predict flu outbreaks better than centres for disease control. Then they fade in the firmament and we wait for the next to flare. But in fact these issues are ongoing and may form patterns – of data politics.

Regrettably, data politics is often reduced to an individual level rather than being seen as something much broader. The recommended self-protection by encryption or even by taping over one's computer camera lens is symptomatic of this 'atomism' that deflects attention from the possibility of concerted, collective activities and practices that could be crucial aspects of data politics. Digital citizens, in this view, engage in data politics especially when they make claims to rights. These may be fairly familiar claims, as in demanding that established civil liberties or human rights be maintained or developed in relation to the internet and data. Or they may be rights claims that are only just coming into view, starting with a fuzzy focus and then turning clearer, about how and with whom to share data, for example.

Finding ways forward

Under contemporary conditions of rapidly augmented government and corporate surveillance practices, the politics of surveillance, as an aspect of data politics, becomes a vital activity. In a critical vein, Colin Bennett's fine work on privacy advocates is a good example, based on the idea that controlling information about ourselves is a fundamental right.[35] He interviewed many players globally in the advocacy enterprise so his work gives a good all-round sense of the issues, although it would be interesting to see what has changed since Snowden. He comments on the practices of various players and comments on how the different agencies work together – or not!

If surveillance is embedded within, brought about by and generative of cultural practices, then it is important to see surveillance within the frames of reference of ordinary people. In line with our overall theme, this is not just the operator perspective, but the user perspective – the insider, not just the outsider, view. So who questions surveillance today and why? Internet users, travellers, workers, citizens and consumers raise questions about privacy and surveillance. It is likely that many more, who may not even consider those categories, do discern some relevant questions about fairness. So the question is, what sorts of emerging practices speak appropriately – even if not yet adequately – to the questions now confronting us? Responses will vary depending on age, gender, context and other factors, but there are green shoots worth nurturing.[36]

Among the most interesting developments are those of today's post-Snowden context, in which many players have appeared, some forming new alliances, such as with journalists and activists for freedom of the press. Debates about national security intelligence and its reliance on Big Data prompt new practices, ones that are taking place over a much broader terrain than was visible in recent years. Coalitions form around commitments to a free and open internet, which also make extensive use of the same media and platforms available online, evidencing a fresh phase of citizenship that seems to recognize the risks of being 'subjects *to* power' while simultaneously embracing new opportunities as 'subjects *of* power'. Several approaches to being 'subjects *of* power' are taken.

One is to seek fixes for the perceived problems. Much in the new world of surveillance is a product, direct or indirect, partial or complete, explicit or implicit, of new technologies. Plenty of fixes are available that would at least mitigate the worst difficulties. Often known as privacy-enhancing technologies, or PETs, these use encryption or other devices to increase the security of the systems in question, so that they are less data leaky. A more subtle and systematic approach is to try to foster a climate for socially responsible technology, to find ways of designing in features that reduce the risks of surveillance to those affected. Either way, one limit of these kinds of approaches is that they may be seen merely as technical fixes or as economically viable solutions.

Another approach is to address the issues by way of regulation. To use privacy or data protection law and fair information practices – FIPs – to limit the use of certain kinds of data and to ensure that important things like informed consent are introduced or that data are used only for the purposes for which they were collected and are destroyed within a certain period. Of course, the very notion of consent has become problematic in a Big Data era. Also, the collection of data is one thing. Crucially, its analysis for specific purposes is another.

If FIPs were indeed taken seriously by organizations processing personal data, many difficulties could in principle be overcome. But unfortunately it is relatively easy for organizations to pay lip service to 'privacy' while pursuing policies that – legally – discriminate negatively or simply profit from personal data as if they had no connection with those from whom it was extracted. Yet regulation and law still hold promise for long-term limits to egregious or inappropriate surveillance – which includes the modes of analysis of the data and not only the kinds or amounts of data garnered.[37] At the same time, 'privacy', defined broadly, includes the very issues of fairness and of social values such as the importance of relationships and democratic participation.[38]

A third approach is to mobilize in quest of more careful treatment of personal data, whether in consumer groups, such as CASPIAN (Consumers against Supermarket Privacy Invasion and Numbering) in the US, or anti-identification campaigns, such as the NO2ID initiative against the proposal for a UK ID card in 2010, or civil liberties organizations, particularly those concerned with border and security issues, such as the International Civil Liberties Monitoring Group in Canada. Plenty of such groups exist, though they tend to be inadequate to the task before them. They may also have self-imposed limits due to their focus on specific, short-term issues or circumscribed sectors. Still, 'privacy advocacy', or the claims to rights in data politics, or the expansion of user-level surveillance practices, are on the increase.[39] Struggling for rights, especially relating to freedom, is a profoundly worthwhile surveillance practice.

A fourth approach raises questions about contemporary surveillance in a more radical way. This book approaches the familiar world of contemporary living, with its everyday reliance on technical mediation, using the internet and connecting though social media, with a key aim: to make the familiar unfamiliar. To discern surveillance imaginaries and practices. To show how, in some important ways, everyday life shadows the global world of surveillance capitalism. And to ask how appropriate this is as a way of seeking human flourishing and the common good. The defamiliarizing process obliges one to see things differently and consider how things might be done differently, too.

Too often, surveillance substitutes 'customer relationship management' for knowing your customers, or attending to the immigration data screen rather than asking to hear the story of the asylum seeker. And the surveillance culture may easily substitute a coded text for actually speaking with someone, or continuing to be online 24/7 for taking breaks to play – holding no phone – with your children, smell the roses or feel the wind in your hair.

There is also a massive imbalance of access to information that could be beneficial to those to whom it refers, but from whom it is hidden through arcane algorithms or sheer proprietary secrecy. The 'control society' is all about 'managing', not about responsibility, except among those who tend to be most vulnerable,[40] who are expected to handle their own fate. Encouraging access, and open data, is another way forward. These outlooks and actions are constantly expanding and making themselves more and more indispensable to the way that today's society works.[41]

Modern bureaucracy denies the morally pregnant effects of human actions; ethics is 'not its department'. How much more this applies to today's surveillance capitalism whose practices are in so many ways cut off from ethical considerations. Bauman suggests that 'ethical tranquillizers' are in use such as short-cut solutions and fixes – 'technology fetishism' – that morally deskill actors and give them the sense that they have no responsibilities.

Yet the issues raised by contemporary surveillance are manifold and profound. They need an ethical seriousness, not technical fixes. And such ethics would start, for example with putting care before control, and of placing the person in a position superior to the data image. Is it too much to hope that emerging surveillance imaginaries and practices might ignite a counter-movement, from below and in everyday contexts of home and workplace?

Claiming digital rights already happens in regard to expression, access, privacy, openness and innovation. These are emerging practices that are already visible in digital modernity. The results of these new struggles are by no means clear, but what does become clearer every day is that they are necessary. If the gains made in earlier centuries and decades towards greater political participation, the growth of freedom, *human* security and the reduction of inequalities are not to be lost in an era of consumerist and self-absorbed pseudo-priorities and of Big Data fetishism, then the nurturing of new imaginaries and practices appropriate to a digital modernity is an urgent and eminently worthwhile task.

The emergence of the culture of surveillance, of watching as a way of life, is both something that may be readily observed, but also, by definition, something to which constructive contributions are being made. They will be truly constructive if the emerging surveillance imaginaries and practices connect with the large canvas of the common good, human flourishing and the care of the other. This, of course, is easy to say, but it is a risky path to take. Actually to put human flourishing first or to care properly for the other is to put yourself out there, make yourself vulnerable, to make a sacrifice and to let go.

A passion for the possible

This chapter does not close, it opens. Mine is not to prescribe but to propose some open questions about where surveillance culture is heading and how some emerging trends might channel it in some fresh ways.[42] I have pointed to ways that contemporary cultural developments may foster human flourishing[43] and the kinds of fairness that are sought by some over against tendencies towards a colder and more calculating surveillance capitalism. This accords with the notion of utopia-as-method.[44] Here, beyond fictional accounts of idealized worlds, sociology works not only as a critical account of current cultural directions but also as a means of proposing and promoting alternative futures that embody holistic, reflexive and democratic imaginaries and practices.

The Circle offers some sobering scenes about a possible future, foreclosed by internet giants. It is dystopia dressed as utopia. But there is a role for utopia too, not as a means of escape, but as a method for seeking alternatives. A means of getting back on track and avoiding distracting detours. So what aspects of surveillance culture's emergent imaginaries should be nurtured? What actual examples are available of alternative imaginaries that might inform our own?

You can ponder such questions on your own, but how much more constructive – not to mention convivial – to discuss them with others, in the pub, with friends and family, within your religious community or your book club (start with *The Circle!*). Of course this is not for a moment an exercise pitting some 'new' and wholesome approach over an 'old' and deleterious one. After all, as Torin Monahan observes, the tensions between care and control will continue in the surveillance world.[45] The point is to bring these issues to the surface, be mindful of them and to raise them as social issues, not just personal troubles.

The challenge is to see the culture of surveillance for what it is, a development beyond the surveillance state and surveillance society, which nonetheless is imbued with the all too familiar features of each. To take surveillance culture seriously means several things. For a start, while keeping a focus on how surveillance works, how it operates in a surveillance capitalist context, driven by Big Data, it is also vital to keep an eye on the ways that surveillance is experienced. The future cannot be read from political economy any more than from the latest techno-gadgets and gizmos. How surveillance is experienced varies tremendously and those variations make a difference. And ultimately, the struggle is for the deep wells of culture, the ways people think, the direction their hearts take them and what is done in the routines of everyday life.

This is true on a spectrum from those who may enjoy the experience of surveillance, who find it entertaining or who can play with it, through those who are cautious and compliant, to others who are the most vulnerable, for whom it is anything but entertaining. Each dimension needs to be understood and each has its own imaginaries and practices associated with it, that help to determine how far we are able to see ourselves only as subjects *to* surveillance power or also as 'subjects *of* power' in this context.

But understanding surveillance culture also means recognizing ways in which people not only experience but also engage with surveillance themselves. This too has two dimensions, in that surveillance may be done both on others and on ourselves. In what ways these are appropriate, and contribute to human flourishing, are matters that urgently need to be worked out. If in the twentieth century our understanding of surveillance could so profoundly be affected by fictional literature – Orwell's *Nineteen Eighty-Four* – then in the twenty-first it would be worth allowing all such work to hold up a mirror so that we may recognize our own world for what it is today. Even a Black Mirror.

Recognizing our world for what it is is a vital step. Realizing that things do not have to continue as they are at present is the second. The doctrine of technological inevitability is false because doing technology is a human endeavour and is socially shaped. Those who insinuate that technology is an unstoppable juggernaut usually have an interest in preventing resistance or denying the role of human agency. 'Common good' and 'human flourishing' alternatives are worth working for; another world is possible.

If the work of novels and of movies mirrors effectively the culture of surveillance, then we shall also be in a better position to evaluate and assess our own roles within this emerging world, as well as what our fears and hopes for it might be. As I have more than hinted, however new and committed to change the culture of surveillance turns out to be, and however unfamiliar the issues it must face, the ways of wisdom for imagining and acting within it are likely to be familiar, even ancient. They just await realistic, sensitive and practical retrieval.

Notes

Introduction

1   G. Orwell, *Nineteen Eighty-Four* (London: Penguin, 1948), p. 5.

2   The term 'surveillance culture' has appeared before, but it has yet to be treated as a broad phenomenon in its own right and theorized as a development distinct from others such as 'surveillance state' and 'surveillance society'. For instance, William Staples used 'surveillance culture' in a book title, exploring 'postmodern' developments in our everyday interactions with surveillance. 'Surveillance culture' also appears in John McGrath's subtitle to *Loving Big Brother*, a study that points to some of the performative dimensions of surveillance. Or think of Jonathan Finn's insights, with regard to camera surveillance in particular. For him, with the proliferation of public space cameras, surveillance has become a 'way of seeing, a way of being'. Each provides a good springboard into 'surveillance culture'. W. Staples, *The Culture of Surveillance* (New York: St Martin's Press, 1997); J. McGrath, *Loving Big Brother: Surveillance Culture and Performance Space* (London: Routledge, 2004); J. Finn, 'Seeing surveillantly: surveillance as social practice', in A. Doyle, R. Lippert and D. Lyon, eds, *Eyes Everywhere: The Global Growth of Camera Surveillance* (London: Routledge, 2012).

3   See e.g. P. Marks, *Imagining Surveillance: Eutopian and Dystopian Literature and Film* (Edinburgh: Edinburgh

University Press, 2015); G. T. Marx, *Windows into the Soul: Surveillance and Society in an Age of High Technology* (Chicago: University of Chicago Press, 2016).

4 Marks, *Imagining Surveillance*, p. 161.

5 See e.g. T. Monahan, 'Regulating belonging: surveillance, inequality and the cultural production of abjection', *Journal of Cultural Economy* 10.2 (2017): 199.

6 Marx, *Windows into the Soul*, p. 173.

7 As argued later, this point is made by Michel de Certeau and elaborated by authors such as Andrew Feenberg in *Questioning Technology* (London: Routledge, 1999), pp. 131–47. My own use of the term 'users' does not imply a depersonalized approach to those engaged with smartphones, social media or the internet. Without doubt, the word 'users' is sometimes used reductively by technology corporations. But it also is hard to replace, simply, in English.

8 Dave Eggers, *The Circle* (Toronto: Knopf Canada, 2013).

9 See D. Lyon, *Surveillance after Snowden* (Cambridge: Polity, 2015).

10 R. Williams, *Culture and Society: 1780–1950* (London: Chatto & Windus, 1958).

11 R. Williams, *Marxism and Literature* (Oxford: Oxford University Press, 1977). While I use Williams's terminology, this does not necessarily indicate agreement with the *way* he used these terms. In any case, his notions of culture are used in this book to indicate not the culture of a society at large, but a culture whose elements are visible transnationally.

12 C. Kuner, *Transborder Data Flow Regulation and Data Privacy Law* (Oxford: Oxford University Press, 2014); V. Mosco, *To the Cloud: Big Data in a Turbulent World* (London: Routledge, 2014).

13 There are many discussions of the role of social media in the Arab Spring. Among them are G. Wolfsfeld, E. Segev and T. Sheafer, 'Social media and the Arab Spring: politics comes first', *International Journal of Press/Politics* 18.2 (2013): 115–37; H. Brown, E. Guskin and A. Mitchell 'The role of social media in the Arab uprisings', Pew Research Centre, 28 November 2012, at http://www.journalism.org/2012/11/28/role-social-media-arab-uprisings/.

14 See e.g. P. S. N. Lee, C. Y. K. So and L. Leung, 'Social media and Umbrella Movement: insurgent public sphere in formation', *Chinese Journal of Communication* 8.4 (2015): 356–75.

15 On this, see J. Meyrowitz, *No Sense of Place: The Impact of*

Social Media on Social Behaviour (Oxford: Oxford University Press, 1986).

16 'Discipline' is a central concept in the analysis of modernity, meaning the processes of training people to obey rules or follow codes. It was vital for developing modern military and bureaucracy organizations.

17 The ideas of Byung-Chul Han are significant here. He writes of performance culture in *The Burnout Society* (Stanford: Stanford University Press, 2015). For him, 'performance' is replacing the old disciplinary society analysed by Michel Foucault and others.

18 Zygmunt Bauman grapples with this in one of his very last books, *Strangers at Our Door* (Cambridge: Polity, 2016), pp. 56–60.

19 K. Ball, A. Canhoto, E. Daniel, S. Dibb, M. Meadows and K. Spiller, *The Private Security State? Surveillance, Consumer Data and the War on Terror* (Copenhagen: Copenhagen Business School Press, 2015).

20 The Five Eyes refers to the partnered foreign intelligence-gathering agencies of Australia, Canada, New Zealand, the United Kingdom and the United States.

21 Here I echo the classic work of K. Pike, *Language in Relation to a Unified Theory of the Structure of Human Behavior* (The Hague: De Gruyter Mouton, 1967; originally published by the Summer Institute of Linguistics, 1954).

22 C. Bennett, K. Haggerty, D. Lyon and V. Steeves, eds, *Transparent Lives: Surveillance in Canada*, New Transparency Project (Edmonton: Athabasca University Press, 2014); K. Haggerty and R. Ericson, 'The surveillant assemblage', *British Journal of Sociology* 51.4 (2000): 605–22; D. Lyon, *Surveillance Studies: An Overview* (Cambridge: Polity, 2007).

23 An excellent history of creditworthiness is provided by Josh Lauer, *Creditworthy: A History of Consumer Surveillance and Financial Identity in America* (New York: Columbia University Press, 2017).

24 See Lyon, *Surveillance after Snowden*.

25 S. Zuboff, 'Big Other: surveillance capitalism and the prospects of an information civilization', *Journal of Information Technology* 30 (2015): 75–89, at https://papers.ssrn.com/sol3/papers.cfm?abstract_id=2594754.

26 D. Garland, *The Culture of Control: Crime and Social Order in Contemporary Society* (Chicago: University of Chicago Press, 2001).

27   D. Lyon, *Surveillance after September 11* (Cambridge: Polity, 2003).

28   G. Wolf, 'The data-driven life', *New York Times Magazine,* 28 April 2010, at http://www.nytimes.com/2010/05/02/magazine/02self-measurement-t.html?mcubz=3.

29   K. Crawford, J. Lingel and T. Karppi, 'Our metrics, ourselves: one hundred years of self-tracking from the weight scale to the wrist wearable device', *European Journal of Cultural Studies* 18.4–5 (2015): 479–96.

30   J. van Dijck, *The Culture of Connectivity: A Critical History of Social Media* (New York: Oxford University Press, 2013); J. van Dijck, 'Datafication, dataism and dataveillance: Big Data between scientific paradigm and ideology', *Surveillance & Society* 12.2 (2014): 197–208, at http://ojs.library.queensu.ca/index.php/surveillance-and-society/article/view/datafication/datafic/. Such secular beliefs are part of what I call 'surveillance imaginaries'. See chapter 1.

31   S. Ledbetter, 'America's top fears 2015', blog, 13 October 2015, at https://blogs.chapman.edu/wilkinson/2015/10/13/americas-top-fears-2015/.

32   L. Rainie and M. Madden, 'Americans' privacy strategies post Snowden', Pew Research Center, 16 March 2015, at http://www.pewinternet.org/2015/03/16/americans-privacy-strategies-post-snowden/.

33   Z. Bauman and D. Lyon, *Liquid Surveillance: A Conversation* (Cambridge: Polity, 2013).

34   D. Lyon, ed., *Surveillance as Social Sorting: Privacy, Risk and Digital Discrimination* (London: Routledge, 2003); D. Lyon, 'Everyday surveillance: personal data and social classification', *Information, Communication and Society* 5.1 (2002).

35   J. Ball, 'Angry Birds and "leaky" phone apps targeted by the NSA and GCHQ for user data', *The Guardian,* 27 January 2014, at https://www.theguardian.com/world/2014/jan/27/nsa-gchq-smartphone-app-angry-birds-personal-data.

36   Metadata refers to those fragments of data about the time and place of communications or web searches, who was connected with whom and for how long. Security agencies try to define them in ways that distinguish them from 'personal' data but they are highly revealing in practice. Indeed, in some ways, more may be learned from metadata than, for example, the actual content of an email or text.

37   J. Lacan, 'The mirror-phase as formative of the function of the I', *New Left Review* 51 (1968): 63–77.

38   G. Sewell and B. Wilkinson, '"Someone to watch over me": surveillance, discipline and the just-in-time labour process', *Sociology* 26.2 (1992): 271–89.

39   K. Murnane, 'iRobot clarifies its position on how Roomba-created maps of people's homes will be used', *Forbes*, 1 August 2017, at   https://www.forbes.com/sites/kevinmurnane/2017/08/01/irobot-clarifies-their-position-on-how-roomba-created-maps-of-peoples-homes-will-be-used/#7ee973eb7d81/.

40   L. Floridi, ed., *The Onlife Manifesto: Being Human in a Hyperconnected Era* (Dordrecht: Springer, 2015).

41   E. Goffman, *The Presentation of Self in Everyday Life* (New York: Anchor, 1959).

42   *The Circle* (2017), feature film directed by James Ponsoldt and starring Emma Watson and Tom Hanks.

43   This idea is a conclusion of Eric Stoddart's work; see *Theological Perspectives on a Surveillance Society: Watching and Being Watched* (Farnham: Ashgate, 2011).

1   Crucibles of Culture

1   Bauman and Lyon, *Liquid Surveillance*.

2   M. Madden and A. Smith, 'Reputation management and social media: introduction', Pew Research Center, 26 May 2010, at http://www.pewinternet.org/2010/05/26/introduction-4/.

3   L. Sweeney, 'Simple demographics often identify people uniquely', Data Privacy Working Paper 3, Carnegie-Mellon University, 2000, at https://dataprivacylab.org/projects/identifiability/paper1.pdf.

4   See e.g. Z. Bauman, *Liquid Modernity* (Cambridge: Polity, 2000); Bauman and Lyon, *Liquid Surveillance*.

5   See D. Lyon, 'The border is everywhere: ID cards, surveillance and the Other', in E. Zureik and M. Salter, eds, *Global Surveillance and Policing* (London: Routledge, 2005).

6   See D. Trottier, *Identity Problems in the Facebook Era* (London: Routledge, 2014).

7   'Data: getting to know you', *The Economist*, 11 September 2014,   at   http://www.economist.com/news/special-report/21615871-everything-people-do-online-avidly-followed-advertisers-and-third-party.

8   G. Deleuze, 'Postscript on the societies of control', *October* 59 (1992): 3–7.

9   Haggerty and Ericson, 'The surveillant assemblage'.

10   W. Staples, *Everyday Surveillance: Vigilance and Visibility in Postmodern Life* (Lanham: Rowman & Littlefield, 2014), p. 9.

11   J. Kantor and D. Streitfeld, 'Inside Amazon: wrestling big ideas in a bruising workplace', *New York Times*, 15 August 2015, at https://www.nytimes.com/2015/08/16/technology/inside-amazon-wrestling-big-ideas-in-a-bruising-workplace.html?_r=0.

12   S. Turkle, *Alone Together: Why We Expect More from Technology and Less from Each Other* (New York: Basic Books, 2012).

13   Bauman, *Strangers at Our Door*, p. 110.

14   N. Anand and R. L. Daft, 'What is the right organization design?', *Organizational Dynamics* 36.4 (2007): 329–44.

15   See e.g. R. Kitchin, *The Data Revolution: Big Data, Open Data, Data Infrastructures, and Their Consequences* (London: Sage, 2014).

16   D. Bigo, 'Security, a field left fallow', in M. Dillon and A. W. Neal, eds, *Foucault on Politics, Security and War* (London: Palgrave Macmillan, 2011), p. 109.

17   L. Wacquant, *Punishing the Poor: The Neoliberal Government of Social Insecurity* (Durham, NC: Duke University Press, 2009).

18   See P. Virno, *A Grammar of the Multitude: For an Analysis of Contemporary Forms of Life*, trans. I. Bertoletti, J. Cascaito and A. Casson (Cambridge, MA: MIT Press, 2004).

19   McGrath, *Loving Big Brother*.

20   R. Hall, T. Monahan and J. Reeves, 'Surveillance and performance', *Surveillance & Society* 14.2 (2016): 154–67.

21   Bauman, *Strangers at Our Door*.

22   This, too, is a tactic of Bauman; see K. Tester, 'Reflections on reading Bauman', *Cultural Politics* 13.3 (2017).

23   D. Smith, *The Everyday World as Problematic: A Feminist Sociology* (Boston: Northwestern University Press, 1987).

24   The terms are de Certeau's.

25   J. Cohen, *Configuring the Networked Self: Law, Code and Play in Everyday Practice* (New Haven: Yale University Press, 2012).

26   N. K. Hayles, *How We Became Posthuman: Virtual Bodies in Cybernetics, Literature, and Informatics* (Chicago: University of Chicago Press, 1999).

27   E. Zureik, L. Harling Stalker, E. Smith, D. Lyon and Y. E. Chan, eds, *Surveillance, Privacy and the Globalization of Personal Information* (Kingston: McGill-Queen's University Press, 2010).

28   See e.g. Bauman and Lyon, *Liquid Surveillance*.

29 See the fuller argument at D. Lyon, 'The emerging surveillance culture', in M. Christiansen and A. Jannsen, eds, *Media, Surveillance and Identity: Social Perspectives* (Oxford: Peter Lang, 2014).

30 Lyon, *Surveillance after September 11*.

31 D. Murakami Wood and W. Webster, 'Living in surveillance societies: the normalisation of surveillance in Europe and the threat of Britain's bad example', *Journal of Contemporary European Research* 5.2 (2009): 259–73.

32 A. Albrechtslund, 'Online social networking as participatory surveillance', *First Monday* 13.3 (2008).

33 D. Trottier, *Social Media as Surveillance: Rethinking Visibility in a Converging World* (London: Ashgate, 2012), p. 2.

34 L. Pinto and S. Nemorin, 'Who's the boss? The elf on the shelf and the normalization of surveillance', *Our Schools, Our Selves* 25.2 (2014): 13–15, at https://www.policyalternatives. ca/publications/commentary/whos-boss.

35 The ambiguities of surveillance often appear in poignant form in domestic contexts. While the elf on the shelf may be a fairly obvious case of how socialization-for-surveillance occurs, some forms of domestic surveillance, such as cameras over cribs, may well be instances of surveillance-as-care.

36 C. Taylor, *Modern Social Imaginaries* (Durham, NC: Duke University Press, 2004), updated and extended in C. Taylor, *A Secular Age* (Cambridge, MA: Harvard University Press, 2007). Richard Ericson also made constructive use of Taylor's analysis in *Crime in an Insecure World* (Cambridge: Polity, 2007), pp. 3–4, 29–30.

37 M. McCahill and R. Finn, *Surveillance, Capital and Resistance* (London: Routledge, 2014), p. 4.

38 T. Monahan, 'Surveillance as cultural practice', *Sociological Quarterly*, 52 (2011): 495–508.

39 K. Vanhemert, 'Weird tee-shirts designed to confuse Facebook's auto-tagging', *Wired*, 10 February 2013, at https://www.wired. com/2013/10/thwart-facebooks-creepy-auto-tagging-with-these-bizarre-t-shirts/#slideid-253281.

40 d. boyd, 'Making sense of privacy and publicity', paper presented at SXSW conference, 13 March 2010; version at http://www.danah.org/papers/talks/2010/SXSW2010.html/.

41 M. de Certeau, *The Practice of Everyday Life* (Berkeley: University of California Press, 1984), pp. xvii–xx.

42 An excellent discussion of these matters may be found in J. B. Thompson, 'Shifting boundaries of public and private life', *Theory, Culture & Society* 28.4 (2011): 49–70.

43 J. Anderson and L. Rainie, 'Digital life in 2025', Pew Research Centre, 11 March 2014, at http://www.pewinternet. org/2014/03/11/digital-life-in-2025/.

44 See e.g. Trottier, *Social Media as Surveillance*.

45 Taylor, *A Secular Age*, p. 179.

46 Taylor, *A Secular Age*, pp. 207–11.

47 C. Calhoun, 'Nationalism and ethnicity', *Annual Review of Sociology* 19 (1993): 211–39.

48 See G. Marx, *Undercover: Police Surveillance in America* (Berkeley: University of California Press, 1989); Lyon, *Surveillance Studies*, p. 185.

49 Monahan, 'Surveillance as cultural practice', 501.

50 Finn, 'Seeing surveillantly'.

51 Finn, 'Seeing surveillantly', p. 69. Finn also quotes Lev Manovich's proposal that digital imagery is fundamentally different from photochemical imagery in material and technical form but remarkably similar in practice. Highly advanced digital technologies are often used in ways that mimic earlier, non-digital, media. Using a digital camera for 'traditional' photography, such as taking portraits of loved ones or documenting birthday parties, vacations or other important life events, is a case in point. Finn's other telling examples of surveillant seeing are from advertising, television and online cellphone footage.

52 The protests in Kingston, Ontario, took place in 2010. See the documentary film *Until the Cows Come Home* (2014), at http://www.prisonfarmfilm.org/.

53 'Palestinians shoot back with video cameras', *Time*, at http://content.time.com/time/video/player/0,32068,77026694001_1981400,00.html.

54 The series ran from 2011 to 2016.

55 de Certeau, *The Practice of Everyday Life*.

56 P. Bourdieu, *Outline of a Theory of Practice* (Cambridge: Cambridge University Press, 1977).

57 Monahan, 'Surveillance as cultural practice'.

58 de Certeau, *The Practice of Everyday Life*, p. xiv.

59 J. Gilliom, *Overseers of the Poor: Surveillance, Resistance and the Limits of Privacy* (Chicago: University of Chicago Press, 2001).

60 Milton Santos refers to this process as 'counter-rationality'. See L. Melgaço, 'Security and surveillance in times of globalization: an appraisal of Milton Santos' theory', *International Journal of E-Planning Research* 2.4 (2013): 1–12.

61 M. Andrejevic, 'The work of watching one another: lateral

surveillance, risk and governance', *Surveillance & Society* 2.4 (2005): 494.

62 Trottier, *Social Media as Surveillance*, ch. 1.

63 Trottier, *Social Media as Surveillance*, pp. 155–8.

64 Albrechtslund, 'Online social networking as participatory surveillance'.

65 This is discussed further in chapter 3.

66 J. Rule, *Private Lives and Public Surveillance* (London: Allen Lane, 1973).

67 There is, of course, a growing number of treatments of surveillance that analyse differing experiences in terms of class, gender and race. To mention but three: Wacquant, *Punishing the Poor*, on class; E. Van der Meulen and R. Heynen, eds, *Expanding the Gaze* (Toronto: University of Toronto Press, 2016), on gender; and S. Browne, *Dark Matters* (Durham, NC: Duke University Press, 2015), on race.

68 Zureik et al., *Surveillance, Privacy and the Globalization of Personal Information*.

69 W. Benjamin, 'Theses on the philosophy of history', in W. Benjamin, *Illuminations*, ed. H. Arendt (Boston: Houghton Mifflin Harcourt, 1968).

2 From Convenience to Compliance

1 A. Schwarzschild, 'My (short) life as an airport security guard', *The Guardian*, 29 June 2017, at https://www.theguardian.com/world/2017/jun/29/my-short-life-as-an-airport-security-guard.

2 A. Saulnier, 'Surveillance studies and the surveilled subject', PhD dissertation, Queen's University, Kingston, Ontario, 2016, p. 44.

3 T. Akseer, 'Understanding the impact of surveillance and security measures on Canadian Muslim men', PhD dissertation, Queen's University, Kingston, Ontario, 2016.

4 J. Lacan, *Écrits* (New York: W. W. Norton, 2006).

5 Akseer, 'Understanding the impact of surveillance'.

6 N. Klein, *Shock Doctrine: The Rise of Disaster Capitalism* (New York: Metropolitan Books, 2007).

7 S. Mêstrović, *Anthony Giddens: The Last Modernist* (London: Routledge, 1998), p. 78. The 'affective turn' in the humanities has echoes in the social sciences.

8 See the discussion in M. Gray, 'Urban surveillance and panopticism: will we recognize the facial recognition society?',

Surveillance & Society 1.3 (2003), at http://ojs.library.queensu.ca/index.php/surveillance-and-society/article/view/3343/3305/.

9 See R. Meyer, 'Everything we know about Facebook's secret mood manipulation experiment', *The Atlantic*, 28 June 2014, at https://www.theatlantic.com/technology/archive/2014/06/everything-we-know-about-facebooks-secret-mood-manipulation-experiment/373648/; V. Goel, 'As data overflows online, researchers grapple with ethics', *New York Times*, 13 August 2013, at https://www.nytimes.com/2014/08/13/technology/the-boon-of-online-data-puts-social-science-in-a-quandary.html?_r=0/.

10 V. Steeves, 'Reclaiming the social value of privacy', in I. Kerr, V. Steeves and C. Lucock, eds, *Lessons from the Identity Trail* (Oxford: Oxford University Press, 2009), at http://www.idtrail.org/files/ID%20Trail%20Book/9780195372472_kerr_11.pdf.

11 A. Hochschild, *The Managed Heart: Commercialization of Human Feeling* (Berkeley: University of California Press, 2003), p. 212n; cited in L. Stark, 'The emotional context of information privacy', *Information Society* 32.1 (2016): pp. 14–27.

12 G. Smith, *Opening the Black Box: The Work of Watching* (London: Routledge, 2015).

13 Cohen, *Configuring the Networked Self*.

14 I. Altman, 'Privacy regulation: culturally universal or culturally specific?', *Journal of Social Issues* 33.3 (1977): 66–84. Christena Nippert-Eng uses the term 'boundary management' in *Islands of Privacy* (Chicago: University of Chicago Press, 2010).

15 V. Steeves and P. Regan, 'Young people online and the social value of privacy', *Journal of Information, Communication, Ethics and Society* 12.4 (2014): 298–313.

16 K. Bolan, 'Ottawa team zooms in on passengers at airports coast to coast', *Ottawa Citizen*, 2 October 2006.

17 J. Sharkey, 'Whole-body scans pass first airport tests', *New York Times*, 6 April 2009.

18 J. Tibbetts, 'Airport officials make plans to conduct virtual strip searches', *Ottawa Citizen*, 6 May 2009.

19 Saulnier, 'Surveillance studies and the surveilled subject'.

20 R. Hall, *The Transparent Traveler: Performance and Culture of Airport Security* (Durham, NC: Duke University Press, 2015).

21 M. Foucault, *'Society Must Be Defended': Lectures at the Collège de France, 1975–1976* (New York: Picador, 2003), p. 245.

22 Hall, *The Transparent Traveler*, p. 3.

23 J. Penney, 'Chilling effects: online surveillance and Wikipedia use', *Berkeley Technology Law Journal* 31.1 (2016): 119–82.

24 Penney, 'Chilling effects'.

25 D. Solove, 'A taxonomy of privacy', *University of Pennsylvania Law Review* 154.3 (2006).

26 PEN International, *Global Chilling: The Impact of Mass Surveillance on International Writers*, PEN American Center, 5 January 2015, p. 4, at https://www.pen.org/sites/default/files/globalchilling_2015.pdf.

27 PEN International, *Global Chilling*, pp. 8–9.

28 L. Rainie, 'The state of privacy in post-Snowden America', Pew Research Center, 21 September 2016, at http://www.pewresearch.org/fact-tank/2016/09/21/the-state-of-privacy-in-america/.

29 Akseer, 'Understanding the impact of surveillance', p. 118.

30 Akseer, Understanding the impact of surveillance', p. 114.

31 Daniel Solove considers the usefulness of the Kafka imagery for today's surveillance in R. J. Rosen, 'Why should we even care if the government is collecting our data?', *The Atlantic*, 11 June 2013, at https://www.theatlantic.com/technology/archive/2013/06/why-should-we-even-care-if-the-government-is-collecting-our-data/276732/.

32 See S. Dingman, 'Watchdog slams Ashley Madison over privacy failures', *Globe and Mail*, 23 August 2016, at https://www.theglobeandmail.com/report-on-business/company-behind-ashley-madison-agrees-to-improve-security-after-massive-hack/article31508144/.

33 J. Ellenberg, 'What's even creepier than Target guessing that you're pregnant?', *Slate*, 9 June 2014, at http://www.slate.com/blogs/how_not_to_be_wrong/2014/06/09/big_data_what_s_even_creepier_than_target_guessing_that_you_re_pregnant.html/.

34 H. Tomlinson and R. Evans, 'Tesco stocks up on inside knowledge of shoppers' lives', *The Guardian*, 20 September 2005.

35 See e.g. S. Burnett, 'Tesco revamps loyalty program', Customer Insight Group, 20 September 2010, at http://www.customerinsightgroup.com/loyaltyblog/loyal-customers-in-britain-the-tesco-story/.

36 C. Duhigg, 'What does your credit card company know about you?', *New York Times*, 12 May 2009.

37 Sami Coll's original research was 'Consommation sous surveillance: l'exemple des cartes de fidélité', Faculté des sciences économiques et sociales, Université de Genève, 2010.

38 M. Foucault, *A History of Sexuality*, vol. 1: *An Introduction* (New York: Vintage, 1978), p. 178.

39 See a popular report, 'Foodflex from Safeway', 6 March 2008, at https://www.popsugar.com/fitness/FoodFlex-from-Safeway-1096899/.

40 See Coll, 'Consommation sous surveillance'.

41 A technical word for such possibilities is 'affordances'. That is, those things that users may do with their artefacts and the material limits of the technology in question. You may be able to use your smartphone figuratively to get from one place to another, but only a bicycle or other vehicle can truly transport you. On the other hand, too loose a use of this term may imply that technology's limits are *only* material. They may also be corporate, as when a service is simply shut down.

42 P. Ganapati, 'Eye spy: filmmaker plans to install camera in his eye socket', *Wired*, 4 December 2008.

43 See 'About the project', at http://eyeborgproject.tv/.

44 See P. J. Watson, 'Houston police chief wants surveillance cameras in private homes', Information Liberation, 16 February 2006, at www.informationliberation.com/?id=6506/. This idea parallels the suggestion made by Stephen Graham in the UK context that by the 1990s it seemed that CCTV cameras were becoming the 'fifth utility'.

45 S. Rosenbloom, 'I spy; doesn't everyone?', *New York Times*, 7 September 2006.

46 Personal information from Lucas Melgaço, a Brazilian professor at Vrije Universiteit Brussel.

47 K. Zetter, 'To tag or not to tag', *Wired*, 5 September 2008, at www.wired.com/politics/security/news/2005/08/68271/.

48 Romans 13:4 (*The Message: The Bible in Contemporary Language*). The preceding words state: 'Duly constituted authorities are only a threat if you're trying to get by with something.'

49 As I have noted elsewhere, there are of course authoritarian states that depend heavily on surveillance. The point is that corporate, consumer surveillance is perhaps more subtle and effective as a means of establishing a form of rule – governmentality – through surveillance.

50 The background for this and following remarks on Canada come from a 2016 Environics public opinion survey, reported in T. Coulson, 'How a frightening world shapes Canadians' values', *Globe and Mail*, 27 December 2016, at http://www.theglobeandmail.com/opinion/how-a-frightening-world-shapes-canadians-values/article 33424279/.

51 O. Gandy, *Coming to Terms with Chance: Engaging Rational Discrimination and Cumulative Disadvantage* (London: Ashgate, 2009).

52 See Lyon, *Surveillance after September 11*.

53 J. Bronskill, 'Ottawa compensates and apologizes to three Canadians tortured in Syria', *Toronto Star*, 17 March 2017, at https://www.thestar.com/news/canada/2017/03/17/ottawa-compensates-and-apologizes-to-three-canadians-tortured-in-syria.html.

3 From Novelty to Normalization

1 See D. Muoio, 'Nest could be working on a smart crib that can tell you why your baby is crying', *Business Insider*, 30 June 2016, at http://www.businessinsider.com/google-patents-smart-crib-2016-6/.

2 T. Leaver, 'Intimate surveillance: normalizing parental monitoring and mediation of infants online', *Social Media + Society* (April–June 2017): 1–10, at http://journals.sagepub.com/doi/full/10.1177/2056305117707192.

3 See A. Smith, 'US smartphone use in 2015', Pew Research Center, 1 April 2015, at http://www.pewinternet.org/2015/04/01/us-smartphone-use-in-2015/.

4 M. Dodge and R. Kitchin, *Code/Space* (Cambridge, MA: MIT Press, 2011), p. 58.

5 K. Sears, 'Alexa and the dawn of so-what surveillance', *Seattle Weekly*, 29 March 2017, at http://www.seattleweekly.com/news/alexa-and-the-dawn-of-so-what-surveillance/.

6 S. Degli Esposti, 'When Big Data meets dataveillance', *Surveillance & Society* 12.2 (2014): 209–25, at 222.

7 A. Ellerbrok, 'Playful biometrics: controversial technology through the lens of play', *Sociological Quarterly* 52 (2011): 528–47.

8 J. Huizinga, *Homo Ludens: A Study of the Play-Element in Culture* (Kettering, OH: Angelico Press, 2016; originally published 1938). Thanks to Pablo Esteban Rodriguez for this reminder.

9 D. Lyon, *Identifying Citizens: ID Cards as Surveillance* (Cambridge: Polity, 2009).

10 Ellerbrok, 'Playful biometrics', 533.

11 See S. Perez, 'Facebook Moments launches in the EU & Canada without facial recognition', TechCrunch, 10 May 2016, at

https://techcrunch.com/2016/05/10/facebook-moments-launches-in-the-eu-canada-without-facial-recognition/.

12 See the discussion in the Electronic Privacy Information Center report that also mentions the Canadian Internet Policy and Public Interest Clinic complaint about Facebook at https://epic.org/privacy/facebook/EPIC_FB_FR_FTC_Complaint_06_10_11.pdf

13 Ellerbrok, 'Playful biometrics', 542. She describes this as 'enacting subjectivities of categorical dominance'.

14 This is discussed by C. Campbell, 'The desire for the new: its nature and social location as presented in theories of fashion and modern consumerism', in R. Silverstone and E. Hirsch, eds, *Consuming Technologies: Media and Information in Domestic Spaces* (New York: Routledge, 1992), pp. 48–66.

15 A. Huxley, *Music at Night & Other Essays* (London: Chatto & Windus, 1931).

16 C. McGoogan, 'Elon Musk: Tesla's Autopilot is twice as good as humans', *Telegraph*, 25 April 2016, at http://www.telegraph.co.uk/technology/2016/04/25/elon-musk-teslas-autopilot-makes-accidents-50pc-less-likely/.

17 M. Andrejevic and M. Burdon, 'Defining the sensor society', *Television & New Media* 16.1 (2015): 19–36.

18 D. Glancy, 'Privacy in autonomous vehicles', *Santa Clara Law Review* 52.4 (2012), at http://digitalcommons.law.scu.edu/cgi/viewcontent.cgi?article=2728&context=lawreview.

19 R. Neate, 'Uber faces FTC complaint over plan to track customers' locations and contacts', *The Guardian*, 22 June 2015, at https://www.theguardian.com/technology/2015/jun/22/uber-ftc-privacy-customer-location-contacts.

20 J. Jones, 'How Steve Jobs made the world more beautiful', *The Guardian*, 6 October 2011, at https://www.theguardian.com/technology/2011/oct/06/steve-jobs-world-more-beautiful/.

21 D. Lupton, *Digital Sociology* (London: Routledge, 2015), p. 166.

22 H. Shaw, D. A. Ellis, L. R. Kendrick, F. Zeigler and R. Wiseman, 'Predicting smartphone operating system from personality and individual differences', *Cyberpsychology, Behaviour and Social Networking* 19.12 (2016): 727–32.

23 Pew Research Center, 'Millennials: Confident. Connected. Open to change', 24 February 2010, at http://www.pewsocialtrends.org/2010/02/24/millennials-confident-connected-open-to-change/.

24 J. W. Woodard, 'Critical notes on the culture lag concept', *Social Forces* 12.3 (1934): 388–98; W. F. Ogburn, 'Cultural lag as theory', *Sociology & Social Research* 41.3 (1957).

25 Smith, 'US smartphone use in 2015', p. 1.

26 N. Thrift, *Knowing Capitalism* (London: Sage, 2005).

27 Surveillance capitalism is a term coined by Shoshana Zuboff; see Zuboff, 'Big Other'.

28 Milton Santos, the Brazilian geographer, argues that some new technologies become 'territorial prostheses' such that it becomes harder to distinguish 'nature' from 'technology'.

29 M. Weiser, cited in L. Hallnäs and J. Redström, 'From use to presence: on the expressions and aesthetics of everyday computational things', *ACM Transactions on Computer-Human Interaction* 9.2 (2002): 106–24, at http://dl.acm.org/citation.cfm?id=513665&CFID=976170369&CFTOKEN=84714787.

30 A. Borgmann, *Holding onto Reality: The Nature of Information at the Turn of the Millennium* (Chicago: University of Chicago Press, 1995).

31 See e.g. S. Mattern, 'A city is not a computer', *Places*, February 2017, at https://placesjournal.org/article/a-city-is-not-a-computer/?gclid=EAIaIQobChMI7Oecs7KT1QIVklt-Ch1vZAMPEAAYAiAAEgLRNfD_BwE/.

32 R. Arbes and C. Bethea, 'Songdo, South Korea: city of the future?', *The Atlantic*, 27 September 2014, at http://www.theatlantic.com/international/archive/2014/09/songdo-south-korea-the-city-of-the-future/380849/.

33 Such sensors are also discussed in many other locations, of course; see e.g. A. M. Kenner, 'Securing the elderly body', *Surveillance & Society* 5.3 (2008), at https://pdfs.semanticscholar.org/814b/2e87380f29d9ae4612a62aff67fab5244d07.pdf.

34 P. L. O'Connell, 'Korea's high-tech utopia, where everything is observed', *New York Times*, 5 October 2005, at http://www.nytimes.com/2005/10/05/technology/techspecial/koreas-hightech-utopia-where-everything-is-observed.html?mcubz=3.

35 Arbes and Bethea, 'Songdo, South Korea: city of the future?'.

36 N. K. Hayles, 'RFID: Human agency and meaning in information-intensive environments', *Theory, Culture and Society* 26.2–3 (2009): 47–72.

37 Mattern, 'A city is not a computer'.

38 See 'NEDAP: Santander, a role model for smart cities', Nedap Mobility Solutions, 2017, at http://www.nedapmobility.com/on-street-parking/cases/nedap-santander-a-role-model-for-smart-cities/.

39 R. Kitchin, 'The real-time city? Big data and smart urbanism', *GeoJournal* 79 (2014): 1–14.

40 S. Richardson and D. Mackinnon, *Left to Their Own Devices?*

Privacy Implications of Wearable Technology in Canadian Workplaces (Kingston, Ontario: Surveillance Studies Centre, Queen's University, 2017).

41 Richardson and Mackinnon, *Left to Their Own Devices?* p. 7.

42 D. Lupton, 'Personal data practices in the age of lively data', in J. Daniels, K. Gregory and T. McMillan Cottom, eds, *Digital Sociologies* (Bristol: Policy Press, 2016).

43 Andrejevic and Burdon, 'Defining the sensor society'.

44 F. Pasquale, *The Black Box Society* (Cambridge, MA: Harvard University Press, 2015), p. 14.

45 J. Angwin, J. Larson, S. Mattu and L. Kirchner, 'Machine bias: there's software used across the country to predict future criminals. And it's biased against blacks', ProPublica, 23 May 2016, at https://www.propublica.org/article/machine-bias-risk-assessments-in-criminal-sentencing/.

46 J. Cheney-Lippold, *We Are Data: Algorithms and the Making of Our Digital Selves* (New York: New York University Press, 2017).

47 A. Rouvroy and B. Stiegler, 'The digital regime of truth: from the algorithmic governmentality to a new rule of law', *La Deleuziana: Online Journal of Philosophy* 3 (2016): 6–27, at 9, at http://www.ladeleuziana.org/wp-content/uploads/2016/12/Rouvroy-Stiegler_eng.pdf.

48 P. Bourdieu, *Distinction: A Social Critique of the Judgement of Taste* (Cambridge, MA: Harvard University Press, 1984).

49 R. Burrows and N. Gane, 'Geodemographics, software and class', *Sociology* 40.5 (2006): 793–812.

50 This point was made in Lyon, *Surveillance after September 11.*

51 Z. Bauman, *Community: Seeking Security in an Insecure World* (Cambridge: Polity, 2000).

52 See Lyon, *Surveillance as Social Sorting.*

53 J. Turow and N. Draper, 'Advertising's new surveillance ecosystem', in K. Ball, K. Haggerty and D. Lyon, eds, *The Routledge Handbook of Surveillance Studies* (London: Routledge, 2012). See also J. Turow, *The Aisles Have Eyes: How Retailers Track Your Shopping, Strip Your Privacy and Define Your Power* (New Haven: Yale University Press, 2017).

54 D. Murakami Wood, ed., *A Report on the Surveillance Society: For the Information Commissioner by the Surveillance Studies Network* (Wilmslow, UK: Office of the Information Commissioner, 2006).

55 See, for example, A. Rosenblat, T. Kneese and d. boyd, 'Networked employment discrimination', Data & Society

Working Paper, 8 October 2014, at https://www.dataso-
ciety.net/pubs/fow/EmploymentDiscrimination.pdf. A similar
picture emerges in the South African context; see S. Singh,
'Social sorting as "social transformation": credit scoring and
the reproduction of populations as risks in South Africa',
Security Dialogue 46.4 (2015): 365–83.

56 See N. Pleace, 'Workless people and surveillant mashups:
social policy and data-sharing in the UK', *Information,
Communication and Society* 10.6 (2007): 943–60.

57 P. Lewis, 'Surveillance cameras in Birmingham track
Muslims' every move', *The Guardian*, 4 June 2010, at
www.guardian.co.uk/uk/2010/jun/04/surveillance-cameras-
birmingham-muslims/.

58 See Gandy, *Coming to Terms with Chance*.

59 A. Albrechtslund and P. Lauritsen, 'Spaces of everyday surveillance: unfolding an analytical concept of participation',
Geoforum 49 (2013): 310–16.

60 J. Cohen, 'The surveillance-innovation complex: the irony of
the participatory turn', in D. Barney, G. Coleman, C. Ross,
J. Sterne and T. Tembeck, eds, *The Participatory Condition*
(Minneapolis: University of Minnesota Press, 2016).

4   From Online to Onlife

1 A. Calhoun, 'I can find out so much about you', Salon, 19
January 2011, at http://www.salon.com/2011/01/19/what_i_
can_find_online/.

2 See A. Marwick, *Status Update: Celebrity, Publicity and
Branding in the Social Media Age* (New Haven: Yale University
Press, 2013).

3 McGrath, *Loving Big Brother*.

4 H. Koskela, 'Webcams, TV shows and mobile phones: empowering exhibitionism', *Surveillance & Society* 2.2–3 (2004):
199–215.

5 A. Albrechtslund and L. Dubbeld, 'The plays and arts of
surveillance: understanding surveillance as entertainment',
Surveillance & Society 3.2–3 (2005): 216–21.

6 Albrechtslund, 'Online social networking as participatory
surveillance'.

7 Cohen, 'The surveillance-innovation complex'.

8 Haggerty and Ericson, 'The surveillant assemblage', esp. pp.
608–9.

9 Zygmunt Bauman's analysis of liquid modernity resonates strongly with that of Haggerty and Ericson. See Z. Bauman and D. Lyon (2013) *Liquid Surveillance*.

10 Haggerty and Ericson, 'The surveillant assemblage', p. 610.

11 M. Poster, *The Mode of Information: Post-structuralism and Social Contexts* (Chicago: University of Chicago Press, 1990), p. 93.

12 G. Deleuze and F. Guattari, *Anti-Oedipus: Capitalism and Schizophrenia* (Minneapolis: University of Minnesota Press, 1983), p. 26.

13 B. Harcourt, *Exposed: Desire and Disobedience in the Digital Age* (Cambridge, MA: Harvard University Press, 2015).

14 Deleuze and Guattari, cited by Harcourt, *Exposed*, p. 51.

15 Harcourt, *Exposed*, p. 52.

16 See e.g. C. Epstein, 'Surveillance, privacy and the making of the modern subject: habeas what kind of corpus?', *Body & Society* 22.2 (2016): 28–57; and C. Epstein, 'Theorizing agency in Hobbes's wake: the rational actor, the self, or the speaking subject', *International Organization* 76 (2013): 287–316.

17 A. Hochschild, *The Outsourced Self: Intimate Life in Market Times* (New York: Metropolitan Books, 2012).

18 R. Sennett, *The Fall of Public Man* (New York: Knopf, 1977).

19 This is also an important theme in C. Taylor, *The Sources of the Self* (Cambridge, MA: Harvard University Press, 1989).

20 McGrath, *Loving Big Brother*.

21 Meyrowitz, *No Sense of Place*.

22 Goffman, *The Presentation of Self in Everyday Life*.

23 M. McLuhan, *Understanding Media: The Extensions of Man* (Toronto: McGraw-Hill, 1964).

24 These treatments of Meyrowitz et al. may suggest that the 'effects' of 'technology' appear in a somewhat mechanical and deterministic manner, which is not my purpose here. It is worth rehearsing what the key writers argue before proposing what I believe is a more nuanced mode of analysis.

25 J. Meyrowitz, 'We liked to watch: television as progenitor of the surveillance society', *Annals of the American Academy of Political and Social Science* 625.1 (2009): 32–48.

26 R. J. Magill, *Sincerity* (New York: W. W. Norton, 2013).

27 Z. Bauman and K. Tester, *Conversations with Zygmunt Bauman* (Cambridge: Polity, 2001).

28 Bauman and Lyon, *Liquid Surveillance*.

29 For Zygmunt Bauman this means a condition where social

forms (structures limiting individual choice, institutions guarding routines, and patterns of acceptable conduct) do not keep their shape for long, melting faster than they are cast: *Liquid Times* (Cambridge: Polity, 2007), p. 1.

30   The distinction between the few watching the many, as in conventional surveillance, and the many watching the few, as in TV audiences watching personalities and celebrities, was captured by the terms 'panoptic' versus 'synoptic' by Thomas Mathiesen; see 'The viewer society: Foucault's panopticon revisited', *Theoretical Criminology*, 1.2 (1997). See also D. Lyon, '9/11, synopticon and scopophilia: watching and being watched', in K. Haggerty and R. Ericson, eds, *The New Politics of Surveillance and Visibility* (Toronto: University of Toronto Press, 1997).

31   J. Lynch, 'Applying for citizenship? US citizenship and immigration wants to be your "friend"', Electronic Frontier Foundation, 12 October 2010, at https://www.eff.org/deeplinks/2010/10/applying-citizenship-u-s-citizenship-and. See also e.g. K. Ball and L. Snider, eds, *The Surveillance-Industrial Complex* (London: Routledge, 2012).

32   Facebook privacy policy, see www.facebook.com/policy.php/.

33   Office of the Privacy Commissioner of Canada, 'Privacy Commissioner completes Facebook review', news release, 22 September 2010, at https://www.priv.gc.ca/en/opc-news/news-and-announcements/2010/nr-c_100922/.

34   J. Cheng, 'Govt relies on Facebook "narcissism" to spot fake marriages, fraud', Ars Technica, 13 October 2010, at http://arstechnica.com/tech-policy/news/2010/10/govt-takes-advantage-of-facebook-narcissism-to-check-on-users.ars/.

35   See e.g. 'Google Analytics versus Facebook conversion tracking', at https://support.yotpo.com/en/article/google-analytics-versus-facebook-conversion-tracking.

36   A. Giddens, *The Nation-State and Violence*, vol. 2 of *A Contemporary Critique of Historical Materialism* (Cambridge: Polity, 1985).

37   Penney, 'Chilling effects'.

38   Rule, *Private Lives, Public Surveillance*; J. Rule, *Privacy in Peril* (New York: Oxford University Press, 2007), p. 163.

39   M. Stone, 'Silicon Valley CEOs just want a little privacy', *Slate*, 18 May 2015, at http://www.slate.com/blogs/business_insider/2015/05/18/tech_billionaires_and_privacy_why_facebook_s_mark_zuckerberg_is_spending.html/.

40   A. Marwick, 'The public domain: social surveillance in everyday life', *Surveillance & Society* 9.4 (2012): 378–93.

41   d. boyd, 'Networked privacy', *Surveillance & Society* 10.3–4 (2012): 348–50.

42   V. Steeves, 'Swimming in the fishbowl: young people, identity, and surveillance in networked spaces', in I. van der Ploeg and J. Pridmore, eds, *Digitizing Identities* (London: Routledge, 2016), pp. 125–39.

43   Steeves, 'Swimming in the fishbowl', p. 131.

44   Marwick, 'The public domain', p. 379.

45   A. Marwick and d. boyd, 'I tweet honestly, I tweet passionately: Twitter users, context collapse, and the imagined audience', *New Media & Society* 13.1 (2011): 114–33.

46   Marwick, 'The public domain', p. 390.

47   V. Steeves and J. Bailey, 'Living in the mirror: understanding young women's experiences with online social networking', in E. van der Meulen and R. Heynen, eds, *Expanding the Gaze: Gender and the Politics of Surveillance* (Toronto: University of Toronto Press, 2016).

48   'Social media surveillance in Canada, the US and the UK' (July 2012) was a survey commissioned by the Surveillance Studies Centre at Queen's University, Kingston, Ontario, and constructed by the Vision Critical (Canada) division of the polling company Angus Reid Global.

49   Trottier, *Social Media as Surveillance*.

50   Trottier, *Social Media as Surveillance*, p. 53, citing de Certeau, *The Practice of Everyday Life*.

51   See C. Fuchs, *Social Media: A Critical Introduction* (London: Sage, 2017); M. Andrejevic, *Infoglut: How Too Much Information Is Changing the Way We Think and Know* (London: Routledge, 2013).

52   See e.g. M. J. Kwok Choon, 'La déconnexion temporaire à Facebook: entre le FOMO et l'intériorisation douce du contrôle social', *tic et société* 10.1 (2016): 1–19.

53   Like many contemporary neologisms, this ugly one has a high cringe factor.

54   R. Burrows, 'Living with the h-index? Metric assemblages in the contemporary academy', *Sociological Review* 60.2 (2012): 355–72. See also M. Berg and B. Seeber, *The Slow Professor: Challenging the Culture of Speed in the Academy* (Toronto: University of Toronto Press, 2016).

55   J. Whitson, 'Gaming the quantified self', *Surveillance & Society* 11.1–2 (2013): 163–76, at http://ojs.library.queensu.ca/index.php/surveillance-and-society/article/view/gaming/0.

56   See J. R. Whitson and B. Simon, eds, 'Surveillance, games and play', special issue, *Surveillance & Society* 12.3 (2014), at http://

ojs.library.queensu.ca/index.php/surveillance-and-society/issue/view/games/.

57 Whitson is referring to the idea of 'care of the self' from Michel Foucault's work in *The History of Sexuality*.

58 Some employers encourage the use of wearable devices for increasing productivity; see Richardson and Mackinnon, *Left to Their Own Devices?*

59 Whitson cites the work of M. Pantzar and E. Shove, 'Metering everyday life', draft, 2005, at http://www.lancaster.ac.uk/staff/shove/choreography/meteringdraft.pdf/.

60 A. Dizic, 'Can gaming at work make you more productive', Capital, 8 July 2016, at http://www.bbc.com/capital/story/20160707-can-gaming-at-work-make-you-more-productive/.

61 H. Koskela and L. Mäkinen, 'Ludic encounters: understanding surveillance through game metaphors', *Information, Communication and Society* 19.11 (2016): 1523–38.

62 Koskela and Mäkinen, 'Ludic encounters', p. 1535.

63 Cohen, 'The surveillance-innovation complex', pp. 4–5.

64 Of course, the self is never shaped in some kind of autonomous way. It is a product of complex social and environmental interactions. See e.g. Taylor, *Sources of the Self*, and, in relation to surveillance, Lyon, *Identifying Citizens*.

65 Cohen, 'The surveillance-innovation complex', p. 5.

66 McGrath, *Loving Big Brother*, p. vii.

67 K. Tester, 'Review of McGrath's *Loving Big Brother*', *Media, Culture & Society* 27.6 (2005): 961–3.

68 d. boyd, *It's Complicated: The Social Lives of Networked Teens* (New Haven: Yale University Press, 2015).

69 Cheng, 'Govt relies on Facebook "narcissism"'.

70 C. Lasch, *The Culture of Narcissism: American Life in an Age of Diminishing Expectations* (New York: W. W. Norton, 1979).

71 K. Ball, 'Exposure: exploring the subject of surveillance', *Information, Communication and Society* 12.5 (2009): 639–57.

72 Ball, 'Exposure', p. 641.

73 G. T. Marx, 'Soft surveillance: the growth of mandatory volunteerism in collecting personal information – "Hey buddy can you spare a DNA"', in T. Monahan, ed., *Surveillance and Security: Technological Politics and Power in Everyday Life* (London: Routledge, 2007).

74 F. Furedi, *Therapy Culture: Cultivating Vulnerability in an Uncertain Age* (London: Routledge, 2004).

75 J. Dean, 'Publicity's secret', *Political Theory* 29.5 (2001): 624–50.

76 J. Dean, *Publicity's Secret: How Technoculture Capitalizes on Democracy* (Ithaca: Cornell University Press, 2002).

77 Hochschild, *The Outsourced Self*, p. 11.
78 Andrejevic, *Infoglut*, p. 50.
79 See H. Wilks, 'I outsourced my social media presence to a virtual assistant for 24 hours', *Motherboard*, 30 May 2016, at https://motherboard.vice.com/en_us/article/i-let-a-robot-take-over-my-social-media-for-48-hours/.
80 K. Raynes-Goldie, 'Aliases, creeping and wall-cleaning: understanding privacy in the age of Facebook', *First Monday* 15.1–4 (2010).
81 H. Nissenbaum, 'Privacy as contextual integrity', *Washington Law Review* 79.1 (2004): 119–58; H. Nissenbaum, 'A contextual approach to privacy online', *Daedalus* 140.4 (2011): 32–48.
82 H. Nissenbaum, *Privacy in Context: Technology, Policy and the Integrity of Social Life* (Stanford: Stanford University Press, 2009).
83 H. Kennedy, D. Elgesem and C. Miguel, 'On fairness: user perspectives on social media data mining', *Convergence* (2015): 1–19.
84 Kennedy, Elgesem and Miguel, 'On fairness', 16.

5 Total Transparency

1 M. Foucault, *Power/Knowledge* (New York: Pantheon, 1980), p. 152.
2 There is also a feature film of *The Circle*, but while Tom Hanks puts on a good performance as Bailey, overall the film does not fulfil its potential to offer some serious and engaging critique of Big Data surveillance and online life.
3 Marx, *Windows in the Soul*, p. 173.
4 '100 best companies to work for, 2017', *Fortune*, at http://fortune.com/best-companies/.
5 Q. Hardy, 'Webcams see all (tortoise, watch your back)', *New York Times*, 7 January 2014, at http://www.nytimes.com/2014/01/08/technology/webcams-see-all-tortoise-watch-your-back.html?nl=todaysheadlines&emc=edit_th_20140108&_r=0/.
6 Dodge and Kitchin, *Code/Space*, discuss 'logjects', see chapter 3.
7 J. Trop, 'The next data privacy battle may be waged inside your car', *New York Times*, 10 January 2014, at https://www.nytimes.com/2014/01/11/business/the-next-privacy-battle-may-be-waged-inside-your-car.html?mcubz=3.

8   J. O'Grady, 'Bluetooth "Tile" allows you to find lost keys, bikes, dogs, anything really', ZDNet, 21 June 2013, at http://www.zdnet.com/article/bluetooth-tile-allows-you-to-find-lost-keys-bikes-dogs-anything-really/.

9   M. Zuckerberg, 'From Facebook, answering privacy concerns with new settings', *Washington Post*, 24 May 2010, at http://www.washingtonpost.com/wp-dyn/content/article/2010/05/23/AR2010052303828.html?tid=a_inl/.

10 This practice of scoring and ranking others is also the theme of the disturbing *Black Mirror* series by Charlie Brooker, that began on UK Channel 4 in 2011 and is now on Netflix.

11 Eggers, *The Circle*, p. 485.

12 Reference to writers who see 'control over communication' as a key way of understanding privacy.

13 Nippert-Eng, *Islands of Privacy*, p. 6.

14 Marwick, 'The public domain'.

15 Andrejevic, 'The work of watching one another'; Albrechtslund, 'Online social networking as participatory surveillance'.

16 Marwick, *Status Update*, p. 220.

17 Marwick, *Status Update*, p. 222.

18 Marwick and boyd, 'I tweet honestly, I tweet passionately'.

19 Marwick, 'The public domain', 380.

20 Marwick, 'The public domain', 382.

21 Eggers, *The Circle*, p. 491.

22 Eggers, *The Circle*, p. 95.

23 M. Atwood, 'When privacy is theft', *New York Review of Books*, 21 November 2013, at http://www.nybooks.com/articles/archives/2013/nov/21/eggers-circle-when-privacy-is-theft/.

24 Bennett, Haggerty, Lyon and Steeves, *Transparent Lives*.

25 D. Brin, *The Transparent Society: Will Technology Force Us to Choose between Privacy and Freedom?* (Cambridge, MA: Perseus, 1998).

26 V. Meyer-Schönberger, *Delete: The Virtue of Forgetting in the Digital Age* (Princeton: Princeton University Press, 2009).

27 Marwick, *Status Update*, p. 27.

28 Marwick, *Status Update*, pp. 110–11.

29 D. Eggers, 'US writers must take a stand on NSA surveillance', *The Guardian*, 19 December 2013, at http://www.theguardian.com/books/2013/dec/19/dave-eggers-us-writers-take-stand-nsa-surveillance/.

30 Atwood, 'When privacy is theft'.

31 See B. Morais, 'Sharing is caring', *New Yorker*, 30 October 2013.

32 Eggers, *The Circle*, p. 296.

33 A. Brighenti, 'Democracy and its visibilities', in K. Haggerty

and M. Samatas, eds, *Surveillance and Democracy* (London: Routledge, 2007), p. 240.

34   Cf. Cohen, *Configuring the Networked Self*.

35   Stoddart, *Theological Perspectives on a Surveillance Society*, p. 158.

36   Andrejevic, *Infoglut*, p. 34. Of course, Big Data is more than this, as Andrejevic discusses in his book. It is also discussed in D. Lyon, 'Surveillance, Snowden and Big Data: capacities, consequences, critique', *Big Data & Society* 1.1 (2014). I also insist that while Big Data is often described in terms of Volume, Velocity, Variety and so on, the 'missing V' is vulnerability; see 'The missing V of Big Data', in P. Albanese and L. Tepperman, eds, *Reading Sociology*, 3rd edn (Oxford: Oxford University Press, 2017).

37   Andrejevic, *Infoglut*, p. 38.

38   Ball, 'Exposure', 641.

39   Marx, 'Soft surveillance'.

40   Z. Bauman, 'Solidarity: a word in search of flesh', *Eurozine*, 8 May 2013, at http://www.eurozine.com/articles/2013-05-08-bauman-en.html/.

41   Zuboff, 'Big Other'.

42   Gallup, 'Work and workplace', at http://www.gallup.com/poll/1720/work-work-place.aspx%20/.

43   Dean, 'Publicity's secret', 641.

44   J. Bentham, *The Works* (London, 1843), vol. 4, p. 39.

45   Bauman, *Liquid Modernity*, p. 15.

46   Bauman, *Liquid Modernity*, p. 6.

47   See also D. Lyon, 'Bauman's sociology of hope', *Cultural Politics* 13.3 (2017).

48   Atwood, 'When privacy is theft'.

49   e.g. *The Handmaid's Tale* and the MaddAddam trilogy are four such.

50   Bauman and Lyon, *Liquid Surveillance*.

51   Bauman, *Liquid Modernity*, p. 11.

52   R. Levitas and L. Sargisson, 'Utopia in dark times', in R. Baccolini and T. Moylan, eds, *Dark Horizons: Science Fiction and the Dystopian Imagination* (New York: Routledge, 2003), p. 26.

53   R. Levitas, *The Concept of Utopia* (Oxford: Peter Lang, 2010), p. 8.

54   Stoddart, *Theological Perspectives on a Surveillance Society*.

55   Cohen, *Configuring the Networked Self*, p. 223.

56   N. Wolterstorff, *Journey towards Justice: Personal Encounters in the Global South* (Grand Rapids, MI: Baker Academic, 2013), p. 117.

6   Hidden Hope

1   I am aware of the criticisms that could be made of my choice of Eggers' novel *The Circle*, that, for instance, it privileges the written word and a particular kind of literature and neglects many other popular cultural modes of understanding the digital in general and surveillance in particular. YouTube videos, online games, social media, films, drama, music and many art forms each have their takes on surveillance and may be drawn upon for social-cultural understanding and critique. I have tried to refer to some of these but I acknowledge the limits of my knowledge and expertise.

2   See the related analysis by Byung-Chul Han, *The Transparency Society* (Stanford: Stanford University Press, 2015), p. 2.

3   Finn, 'Seeing surveillantly', 79.

4   L. Cohen, 'Anthem', from his album *The Future* (1992).

5   This is C. Wright Mills's classic phrase explaining the role of sociological imagination; *The Sociological Imagination* (New York: Oxford University Press, 1959), p. 8.

6   This discussion occurs in chapter 3, in regard to Sara Degli Esposti's work.

7   N. Mirzoeff, *The Right to Look: A Counterhistory of Visuality* (Durham, NC: Duke University Press, 2011).

8   Mirzoeff, *The Right to Look*, p. 1.

9   K. Hawkins, 'Browsing the performative: a search for sincerity', *Art & Education* (2012).

10 See A. Oram, 'What sociologist Erving Goffman could tell us about social networking and internet identity', Radar, 26 October 2009, at http://radar.oreilly.com/2009/10/what-sociologist-erving-goffma.html/.

11 A. Brighenti, *Visibility in Social Theory and Social Research* (London: Palgrave Macmillan, 2010).

12 A. Brighenti, 'Visibility – a category for the social sciences', *Current Sociology* 55.3 (2007): 323–42.

13 Stoddart (building on Brighenti), *Theological Perspectives on a Surveillance Society*, p. 158.

14 I use 'strategic' here in its commonsense everyday sense, not in the technical sense used by de Certeau.

15 R. Mortier, H. Haddadi, T. Henderson, D. McAuley and J. Crowcroft, 'Human–data interaction: the human face of the data-driven society', Social Science Research Network, 1 October 2014, at http://ssrn.com/abstract=2508051.

16   R. Silverstone, 'The sociology of mediation and communication', in C. Calhoun, C. Rojek and B. Turner, eds, *The Sage Handbook of Sociology* (London: Sage, 2005), p. 201.

17   E. Levinas, *Totality and Infinity* (Pittsburgh: Duquesne University Press, 1985), p. 53.

18   C. Calhoun, 'The infrastructure of modernity: indirect social relationships, information technology, and social integration', in H. Haferkamp and N. J. Smelser, eds, *Social Change and Modernity* (Berkeley: University of California Press, 1992).

19   S. Turkle, 'Part Two: Networked', in Turkle, *Alone Together*.

20   S. Turkle, *The Second Self* (Cambridge, MA: MIT Press, 1984), was followed by a rather more cautious *Life on the Screen* (New York: Simon & Schuster, 1997), before *Alone Together* first appeared in 2012.

21   C. Taylor, 'The politics of recognition', in A. Gutmann, ed., *Multiculturalism: Examining the Politics of Recognition* (Princeton: Princeton University Press, 1994), pp. 25–73.

22   See e.g. R. De Rosa, 'The Five Stars Movement in the Italian political scenario', *JeDEM* 5.2 (2013): 128–40.

23   C. J. Bennett, 'Trends in voter surveillance in Western societies: privacy intrusions and democratic implications', *Surveillance & Society* 13.3–4 (2015): 370–84.

24   E. Balibar, *Citizen Subject* (New York: Fordham, 2016); E. Isin and E. Ruppert, *Being Digital Citizens* (London: Rowman & Littlefield, 2015).

25   N. Fraser and A. Honneth, *Redistribution or Recognition: A Philosophical-Political Exchange* (London: Verso, 2003), p. 32.

26   See L. Dencik, A. Hintz and J. Cable, 'Towards data justice? The ambiguity of anti-surveillance resistance in political activism', *Big Data & Society*, 24 November 2016, at http://journals.sagepub.com/doi/full/10.1177/2053951716679678.

27   See H. Kennedy and G. Moss, 'Known or knowing publics? Social media data mining and the question of public agency', *Big Data & Society* (July–December 2015), at http://journals.sagepub.com/doi/pdf/10.1177/2053951715611145.

28   H. Kennedy, D. Elgesem and C. Miguel, 'On fairness: user perspectives on social media data mining', *Convergence* 23.3 (2015): 270–88.

29   Nissenbaum, *Privacy in Context*, p. 3.

30   Dencik, Hintz and Cable, 'Towards data justice?', 1–12.

31   Dencik, Hintz and Cable, 'Towards data justice?'; M. Aouragh, S. Gürses, J. Rocha and F. Snelting, 'Let's first get things done! On division of labour and techno-political practices of

delegation in times of crisis', *Fibreculture Journal* 26 (2015): 208–35.

32 For example, Cohen, *Configuring the Networked Self*, or S. Barocas and A. D. Selbst, 'Big Data's disparate impact', *California Law Review* 104.3 (2016): 671–732.

33 Nissenbaum, 'Privacy as contextual integrity'. The fuller treatment is in Nissenbaum, *Privacy in Context*.

34 E. Ruppert, E. Isin and D. Bigo, *Data Politics: Worlds, Subjects, Rights* (London: Routledge, forthcoming).

35 C. Bennett, *The Privacy Advocates: Resisting the Spread of Surveillance* (Cambridge, MA: MIT Press, 2008).

36 Bernard Harcourt also refers to some of these in the final three chapter of his book *Exposed*.

37 D. Broeders, E. Schrijvers, B. van der Sloot, R. van Brakel, J. de Hoog and E. Ballin, 'Big Data and security policies: towards a framework for regulating the phases of analytics and use of Big Data', *Computer Law and Security Review* 33.3 (2017): 309–23.

38 Lyon, *Surveillance after Snowden*, ch. 5.

39 See e.g. D. Wright et al., 'Questioning surveillance', *Computer Law and Security Review* 31.2 (2015): 280–92.

40 See D. Lyon, 'Big Data vulnerabilities: social sorting on steroids', in K. Veel et al., eds, *Uncertain Archives* (forthcoming).

41 Z. Bauman, *Liquid Fear* (Cambridge: Polity, 2006), p. 75.

42 The Danish philosopher Søren Kierkegaard once defined hope as 'a passion for the possible' (in *Fear and Trembling* (1863), originally written under the pseudonym of Johannes de Silentio). He did of course think of the 'possible' in an ethically responsible way.

43 A joint report of the British Academy and the Royal Society on data governance suggests that the key criterion should be 'human flourishing'; see 'Data management and use: governance in the 21st century' (2017), at https://royalsociety.org/~/media/policy/projects/data-governance/data-management-governance.pdf.

44 R. Levitas, *Utopia as Method: The Imaginary Reconstitution of Society* (London: Palgrave Macmillan, 2013).

45 Monahan, 'Surveillance as cultural practice'.

Select Bibliography

Albrechtslund, A., 'Online social networking as participatory surveillance', *First Monday* 13.3 (2008).

Albrechtslund, A. and Lauritsen, P., 'Spaces of everyday surveillance: unfolding an analytical concept of participation', *Geoforum* 49 (2013): 310–16.

Andrejevic, M., 'The work of watching one another: lateral surveillance, risk and governance', *Surveillance & Society* 2.4 (2005).

Andrejevic, M., *Infoglut*. London: Routledge, 2013.

Andrejevic, M. and Burdon, M., 'Defining the sensor society', *Television & New Media* 16.1 (2015): 19–36.

Ball, K., 'Exposure: exploring the subject of surveillance', *Information, Communication and Society* 12.5 (2009): 639–57.

Bauman, Z. and Lyon, D., *Liquid Surveillance: A Conversation*. Cambridge: Polity, 2013.

Bennett, C., Haggerty, K., Lyon, D. and Steeves, V., eds, *Transparent Lives: Surveillance in Canada*. New Transparency Project. Edmonton: Athabasca University Press, 2014.

Borgmann, A., *Holding onto Reality: The Nature of Information at the Turn of the Millennium*. Chicago: University of Chicago Press, 1995.

Bourdieu, P., *Distinction: A Social Critique of the Judgement of Taste*. Cambridge, MA: Harvard University Press, 1984.

boyd, d., 'Networked privacy', *Surveillance & Society* 10.3–4 (2012): 348–50.

boyd, d., *It's Complicated: The Social Lives of Networked Teens*. New Haven: Yale University Press, 2015.

Brighenti, A., 'Democracy and its visibilities', in K. Haggerty and M. Samatas, eds, *Surveillance and Democracy*. London: Routledge, 2007.

Brighenti, A., *Visibility in Social Theory and Social Research*. London: Palgrave Macmillan, 2010.

Cheney-Lippold, J., *We Are Data: Algorithms and the Making of Our Digital Selves*. New York: New York University Press, 2017.

Cohen, J. *Configuring the Networked Self: Law, Code and Play in Everyday Practice*. New Haven: Yale University Press, 2012.

Cohen, J., 'The surveillance-innovation complex: the irony of the participatory turn', in D. Barney, G. Coleman, C. Ross, J. Stern and T. Tembeck, eds, *The Participatory Condition*. Minneapolis: University of Minnesota Press, 2016.

Dean, J., *Publicity's Secret: How Technoculture Capitalizes on Democracy*. Ithaca: Cornell University Press, 2002.

de Certeau, M., *The Practice of Everyday Life*. Berkeley: University of California Press, 1984.

Degli Esposti, S., 'When Big Data meets dataveillance', *Surveillance & Society* 12.2 (2014): 209–25.

Dencik, L., Hintz, A. and Cable, J., 'Towards data justice? The ambiguity of anti-surveillance resistance in political activism', *Big Data & Society* (2016).

Eggers, D., *The Circle*. Toronto: Knopf Canada, 2013.

Ellerbrok, A., 'Playful biometrics: controversial technology through the lens of play', *Sociological Quarterly* 52 (2011): 528–47.

Epstein, C., 'Surveillance, privacy and the making of the modern subject: habeas what kind of corpus?', *Body & Society* 22.2 (2016): 28–57.

Feenberg, A., *Questioning Technology*. London: Routledge, 1999.

Finn, J., 'Seeing surveillantly: surveillance as social practice', in A. Doyle, R. Lippert and D. Lyon, eds, *Eyes Everywhere: The Global Growth of Camera Surveillance*. London: Routledge, 2012.

Fuchs, C., *Social Media: A Critical Introduction*. London: Sage, 2017.

Gandy, O., *Coming to Terms with Chance: Engaging Rational Discrimination and Cumulative Disadvantage*. London: Ashgate, 2010.

Haggerty, K. and Ericson, R., 'The surveillant assemblage', *British Journal of Sociology* 51.4 (2000).

Hall, R., *The Transparent Traveler: Performance and Culture of Airport Security*. Durham, NC: Duke University Press, 2015.

Hall, R., Monahan, T. and Reeves, J., 'Surveillance and Performance', *Surveillance & Society* 14.2 (2016): 154–67.

Hallnäs, L. and Redström, J., 'From use to presence: on the

expressions and aesthetics of everyday computational things', *ACM Transactions on Computer-Human Interaction* 9.2 (2002): 106–24.

Han, B.-C., *The Burnout Society*. Stanford: Stanford University Press, 2015.

Harcourt, B., *Exposed: Desire and Disobedience in the Digital Age*. Cambridge, MA: Harvard University Press, 2015.

Hayles, N. K., 'RFID: human agency and meaning in information-intensive environments', *Theory, Culture and Society* 26.2–3 (2009): 47–72.

Hochschild, A., *The Outsourced Self: Intimate Life in Market Times*. New York: Metropolitan Books, 2012.

Isin, E. and Ruppert, E., *Being Digital Citizens*. London: Rowman & Littlefield, 2015.

Kennedy, H., Elgesem, D. and Miguel, C., 'On fairness: user perspectives on social media data mining', *Convergence* (2015): 1–19.

Kitchin, R., 'The real-time city? Big Data and smart urbanism', *GeoJournal* 79 (2014): 1–14.

Koskela, H., 'Webcams, TV shows and mobile phones: empowering exhibitionism', *Surveillance & Society* 2.2–3 (2004): 199–215.

Koskela, H. and Mäkinen, L., 'Ludic encounters: understanding surveillance through game metaphors', *Information, Communication and Society* 19.11 (2016): 1523–38.

Leaver, T., 'Intimate surveillance: normalizing parental monitoring and mediation of infants online', *Social Media & Society* (April–June 2017): 1–10.

Levitas, R., *Utopia as Method: The Imaginary Reconstitution of Society*. London: Palgrave Macmillan, 2013.

Lupton, D., *Digital Sociology*. London: Routledge, 2015.

Lupton, D., 'Personal data practices in the age of lively data', in J. Daniels, K. Gregory and T. McMillan Cottom, eds, *Digital Sociologies*. Bristol: Policy Press, 2016.

Lyon, D., '9/11, synopticon and scopophilia: watching and being watched', in K. Haggerty and R. Ericson, eds, *The New Politics of Surveillance and Visibility*. Toronto: University of Toronto Press, 1997.

Lyon, D., *Surveillance Studies: An Overview*. Cambridge: Polity, 2007.

Lyon, D., 'The emerging surveillance culture', in M. Christiansen and A. Jannsen, eds, *Media, Surveillance and Identity: Social Perspectives*. Oxford: Peter Lang, 2014.

Lyon, D., 'Surveillance, Snowden and Big Data: capacities, consequences, critique', *Big Data & Society* 1.1 (2014).

Marks, P., *Imagining Surveillance: Eutopian and Dystopian Literature and Film*. Edinburgh: Edinburgh University Press, 2015.

Marwick, A., 'The public domain: social surveillance in everyday life', *Surveillance & Society* 9.4 (2012): 378–93.

Marwick, A., *Status Update: Celebrity, Publicity and Branding in the Social Media Age*. New Haven: Yale University Press, 2015.

Marwick, A. and boyd, d., 'I tweet honestly, I tweet passionately: Twitter users, context collapse, and the imagined audience', *New Media & Society* 13.1 (2011): 114–33.

Marx, G. T., 'Soft surveillance: the growth of mandatory volunteerism in collecting personal information – 'Hey buddy can you spare a DNA', in T. Monahan, ed., *Surveillance and Security: Technological Politics and Power in Everyday Life*. London: Routledge, 2007.

Marx, G. T., *Windows into the Soul: Surveillance and Society in an Age of High Technology*. Chicago: University of Chicago Press, 2016.

Mathiesen, T., 'The viewer society: Foucault's panopticon revisited', *Theoretical Criminology* 1.2 (1997).

McGrath, J., *Loving Big Brother: Surveillance Culture and Performance Space*. London: Routledge, 2004.

Meyrowitz, J., 'We liked to watch: television as progenitor of the surveillance society', *Annals of the American Academy of Political and Social Science* 625.1 (2009): 32–48.

Mirzoeff, N., *The Right to Look: A Counterhistory of Visuality*. Durham, NC: Duke University Press, 2011.

Monahan, T., 'Surveillance as cultural practice', *Sociological Quarterly* 52 (2011): 495–508.

Monahan, T., 'Regulating belonging: surveillance, inequality and the cultural production of abjection', *Journal of Cultural Economy* 10.2 (2017).

Murakami Wood, D., ed., *A Report on the Surveillance Society: For the Information Commissioner by the Surveillance Studies Network*. Wilmslow, UK: Office of the Information Commissioner, 2006.

Nippert-Eng, C., *Islands of Privacy*. Chicago: University of Chicago Press, 2010.

Nissenbaum, H., *Privacy in Context: Technology, Policy and the Integrity of Social Life*. Palo Alto: Stanford University Press, 2010.

Pasquale, F., *The Black Box Society*. Cambridge, MA: Harvard University Press, 2015.

Penney, J., 'Chilling effects: online surveillance and Wikipedia use', *Berkeley Technology Law Journal* 31.1 (2016): 119–82.

Richardson, S. and Mackinnon, D., *Left to Their Own Devices? Privacy Implications of Wearable Technology in Canadian Workplaces*. Kingston, Ontario: Surveillance Studies Centre, Queen's University, 2017.

Rouvroy, A. and Stiegler, B., 'The digital regime of truth: from the algorithmic governmentality to a new rule of law', *La Deleuziana: Online Journal of Philosophy* 3 (2016).

Singh, S., 'Social sorting as "social transformation": credit scoring and the reproduction of populations as risks in South Africa', *Security Dialogue* 46.4 (2015): 365–83

Smith, G., *Opening the Black Box: The Work of Watching*. London: Routledge, 2015.

Stark, L., 'The emotional context of information privacy', *Information Society* 32.1 (2016): 14–27.

Steeves, V., 'Reclaiming the social value of privacy', in I. Kerr, V. Steeves and C. Lucock, eds, *Lessons from the Identity Trail*. Oxford: Oxford University Press, 2009.

Steeves, V., 'Swimming in the fishbowl: young people, identity, and surveillance in networked spaces', in I. van der Ploeg and J. Pridmore, eds, *Digitizing Identities*. London: Routledge, 2016.

Steeves, V. and Bailey, J.. 'Living in the mirror: understanding young women's experiences with online social networking', in E. van der Meulen and R. Heynen, eds, *Expanding the Gaze: Gender and the Politics of Surveillance*. Toronto: University of Toronto Press, 2016.

Steeves, V. and Regan, P., 'Young people online and the social value of privacy', *Journal of Information, Communication, Ethics and Society* 12.4 (2014): 298–313.

Stoddart, E., *Theological Perspectives on a Surveillance Society: Watching and Being Watched*. Farnham: Ashgate, 2011.

Taylor, C., 'The politics of recognition', in A. Gutmann, ed., *Multiculturalism: Examining the Politics of Recognition*. Princeton: Princeton University Press, 1994.

Taylor, C., *Modern Social Imaginaries*. Durham NC: Duke University Press, 2004.

Thrift, N., *Knowing Capitalism*. London: Sage, 2005.

Trottier, D., *Social Media as Surveillance: Rethinking Visibility in a Converging World*. London: Ashgate, 2012.

Turkle, S., *Alone Together: Why We Expect More from Technology and Less from Each Other*. New York: Basic Books, 2012.

Turow, J., *The Aisles Have Eyes: How Retailers Track Your Shopping, Strip Your Privacy and Define Your Power*. New Haven: Yale University Press, 2017.

van Dijck, J., *The Culture of Connectivity: A Critical History of Social Media*. New York: Oxford University Press, 2013.

Whitson, J., 'Gaming the quantified self', *Surveillance & Society* 11.1–2 (2013): 163–76.

Whitson, J. R. and Simon, B., 'Surveillance, gaming and play', *Surveillance & Society* 12.3 (2014).

Williams, R., *Culture and Society: 1780–1950*. London: Chatto & Windus, 1958.

Williams, R., *Marxism and Literature*. Oxford: Oxford University Press, 1977.

Zuboff, S., 'Big Other: surveillance capitalism and the prospects of an information civilization', *Journal of Information Technology* 30 (2015): 75–89.

Index